Extra! Extra!

Robert P. Molander

Trafford
PUBLISHING

Order this book online at www.trafford.com/07-1562
or email orders@trafford.com

Most Trafford titles are also available at major online book retailers.

Note for Librarians: A cataloguing record for this book is available from Library
and Archives Canada at www.collectionscanada.ca/amicus/index-e.html

ISBN: 978-1-4251-3889-9

*We at Trafford believe that it is the responsibility of us all, as both individuals
and corporations, to make choices that are environmentally and socially sound.
You, in turn, are supporting this responsible conduct each time you purchase a
Trafford book, or make use of our publishing services. To find out how you are
helping, please visit www.trafford.com/responsiblepublishing.html*

*Our mission is to efficiently provide the world's finest, most comprehensive
book publishing service, enabling every author to experience success.
To find out how to publish your book, your way, and have it available
worldwide, visit us online at www.trafford.com/10510*

Trafford PUBLISHING   www.trafford.com

North America & international
toll-free: 1 888 232 4444 (USA & Canada)
phone: 250 383 6864 ♦ fax: 250 383 6804 ♦ email: info@trafford.com

The United Kingdom & Europe
phone: +44 (0)1865 487 395 ♦ local rate: 0845 230 9601
facsimile: +44 (0)1865 481 507 ♦ email: info.uk@trafford.com

10 9 8 7 6 5 4 3 2

Acknowledgments

Many persons are worthy of thanks for their expertise and time in helping to make this book both readable and factually correct. Chief among them are James (Jim) and Susan McClatchy, without whom it never would have seen the light of day. Before his untimely death, Jim often took time from his Fresno visits to get together with me, asking "How's the book coming," and offering timely tips on how it could be. After his death, Susan continued to fill that role, always with a smile.

Also worthy of thanks are journalists George Gruner, Don Slinkard, the late Tom Kirwan, and Jim Bort, who proved that editors also need editors; Mike Cole, whose pupils are fortunate to have such a teacher; Andrea Chase, who is a true computer whiz.

There are two others on my list: Gary Molander, who put the whole publishing malaise together; and Peggy, my wife, who never forgot our marriage vows, staying with me all the way.

Table of Contents

Robert P. Molander

Foreword

Although their divergent paths took C.K. and James McClatchy far from Fresno, the brothers never forgot the special place that The Fresno Bee held in their hearts. Their jointly held desire that the story of The Fresno Bee form a separate chapter is shown in these memos, written years apart:

January 23, 1984

George Gruner
John Raytis
The Fresno Bee

Dear George and John:

All too often the people who put out newspapers fail to collect the information about their newspaper that would make possible a history of the paper. In the rush of getting out a daily paper, most of us do not think in those terms. Consequently, a lot of vital information is lost.

With this in mind, my brother Jim and I would like you to come up with a written plan to collect and organize all the material that is available about your paper - - its key figures over the years, its highlights and milestones, its impact on and role in your community. This could include oral history interviews with those retired employees who could give some insight into the earlier days. It also should include all records, yours and others, that would help tell the story of the paper.

In Fresno a start has been made in the efforts of a couple of retired employees from the newsroom. If possible the material and information already collected should be incorporated into the effort.

You may be familiar with the efforts we have made in Sacramento. We had Dick Rodda conduct oral history interviews with some of our retired employees. And we had Phil Freshwater and Charlie Duncan work with Frank McCulloch in gathering other raw material for a first draft of what may eventually be a book. They have found the newspaper's own files the best starting point for this process.

C.K. McClatchy

It is not so important that your plan pin down what we will do with the material as it is to collect all the data that is within your reach. We have learned here that much of the best material is no longer available because we did not start earlier and original sources are no longer alive. That is all the more reason to get started now.

This is a new and somewhat undefined project so you may have questions. Our experience here could be helpful so please call any of us if you want to discuss the project.

Robert P. Molander

DRAFT OF STATEMENT FOR MOLANDER & GRUNER
11/26/90, CLH

CK's letter of January 23, 1984 (copy enclosed) described the purpose of our project for accumulating historical data on the Fresno Bee. Quite a lot was done in the next few years, but then events like taking the company public arose and the plan was sidetracked. Next came CK's death, with further delays.

Now I want to resume the work. The history of the Fresno Bee is colorful and different, and important for present and future staffers to know, as well as being a part of the general history of the community. But beyond that, the character and policies and philosophy of the newspaper are part of the history of the paper, elements that gave it a distinctive personality. These elements had their source in the traditions of the Sacramento Bee, which were the convictions of the men who founded that paper in 1857.

Jim McClatchy

These convictions became editorial policies - - - opposition to special privileges for the few; opposition to land monopoly and concentrations of power; concern for the welfare and well being of the ordinary person; the protection of justice for all persons; and a fierce defense of integrity in public life. I believe these elements have been part of the Fresno Bee since its founding. Of course there have been lapses and human frailties in the observance of these policies, but these elements have run through the life of the paper for a lot of years.

These qualities have been of great importance in supporting the work of Fresno Bee staffers ... these staffers have known (I believe) that the family owning the paper did in fact care a great deal about these principles and therefore the staff gave an extra degree of commitment to the paper's work. They believed in what they were doing.

These two things go hand in hand ... first the active existence and recognition of an enlightened ownership and editorial viewpoint, which in turn encourages an extra commitment from staffers in support of the paper's causes and policies.

But times change. Newspapers increasingly are managed by persons trained in a corporate atmosphere with business school standards rather than the rough and tumble of past newspaper operations. To meet the increasingly complex challenges of newspaper publishing in modern business pressure, newspaper owners have turned to people skilled in management.

Too often, because of their background these individuals have more concern with good management than they do with publishing newspapers of distinctive quality - - - not that they are indifferent to the latter quality, but rather that they have not been exposed to the intense concerns of public service expressed by newspapers like the Bee. They have been trained more for management than for leadership in editorial causes, and simply have not absorbed the values publishers used to have.

However, I think that if this new breed knows and understand the origins of our policies, and their importance to a democratic society, they would incorporate them in their work, their thinking and response to issues.

So - - - back to our project. I want to include in our accumulated data the flavor and quality of the Bee personality and traditions so that new employees will know they have something more than just a job.

This may be hard to do, but it is necessary to try. Corporate mentality is a deadly thing in a newspaper, and to the degree we can, we should educate our people - - - who must be good managers - - - to the fact they also have an old, valued tradition to preserve.

I'm not sure whether this will come from the citation of past events and the description of attitudes that accompanied the events, or whether it will come from the general aura or totality of the stories. In any event, we need a lot of raw material to work on. How to use it can be decided later.

Warts and mistakes and failings of institutions and individuals need to be known and included. A sanitized account will not be believed. I have to think that the story we can tell is strong enough, so that it

Robert P. Molander

can include the naming of weaknesses as well as strengths, and still be respected.

This brings us directly to senior management and members of my family, including myself. Included in the raw material should be whatever that explains the events and forces and personalities involved, including the succession of managers and leaders, and problems such as I had. Very important in this is the inclusion of opinions and judgments of individuals, as well as whatever was generally believed by the staff. Obviously, the style of management followed by senior executives in Sacramento had an effect on the Fresno Bee - - - both good and bad. This needs to be told by a number of people, so the understanding the new staffers get is a blend of the individual comments. There can be no official account.

There are a couple of points where the story could end. One would be with Eleanor's death and CK's taking over her office. Another would be CK's death. And another could be the recent coincidental retirement within a short time of so many key editorial leaders, who had long careers on the Fresno Bee. The latter is probably the best stopping point, for it brought in almost as a group, new executives who - - - with one exception - - - were strangers to Fresno. Comments on the effect these newest people are having on the Bee would be premature.

We need a document or a history that will explain what the Bee has been. Without something like this, these new people have a great handicap in understanding what the character of the paper has been, what it was like over the years. It is a terribly important thing to keep this alive.

Preface

Since the 1850s, the name "McClatchy" has been synonymous with newspapers. That's when The Sacramento Bee took root, becoming the forerunner of The Fresno Bee.

The Fresno Bee's start came in 1922, with Carlos McClatchy at the helm. He had convinced his father, C.K. McClatchy, that the Central San Joaquin Valley, Fresno in particular, was the right choice for a second "Bee."

Carlos McClatchy proved to be right, and The Fresno Bee was an almost instant success. But Carlos, the heir apparent to what was to become the far-flung McClatchy Company newspapers, died at age 41 and never got to realize to the full what he had started.

James McClatchy, the man who started it all, began his career in New York on Horace Greeley's Tribune. It was Greeley who reputedly initiated the advice, "Go West, young man." Whether or not that was his reason, McClatchy did go West but not necessarily to pan for gold along with the prospectors. It's been said, with tongue in cheek, that he was prospecting, not for gold, but for lead, the kind used in those days by newspaper printers in making up newsprint pages.

1

Destination Fresno

The year was 1920, and things were looking up. The war in Europe was over; the Allies had defeated Germany. Jobs were to be had in those days before the Great Depression struck. In Sacramento, The Bee, the city's major newspaper, the one that survived the challenges from many pretenders following the Civil War years, had emerged on top in the newspaper wars. The Bee was financially secure, and was looking for further conquests.

Expansion was the goal. No, not in Sacramento; that area was blanketed by The Bee. But where else? The initial important decision was that the growth would be in California, the Golden State into which James McClatchy had disembarked at San Francisco in 1849 from the schooner John Castner. He had arrived at Ellis Island in 1840 from Belfast aboard the aptly named schooner Independence. And it was in New York that he had started his trade as a printer at Horace Greeley's Tribune. It paid better, and, McClatchy rightly believed, had a much better future than his first big-city job, as a starvation-wage baker's apprentice. Then, caught up in the news of the gold finds and heeding Greeley's wise advice to him to go West, he made tracks for California. From that decision, an empire was born.

The Sacramento Bee flourished under McClatchy's watch. His successor was his son, C.K. McClatchy, and it was C.K. who was casting about in 1920 for the location for a second Bee newspaper. C.K.'s son, Carlos, now a grown man and a World War I veteran in search of his true self, was quick to second his father's decision. His dream was to be in command of his own newspaper. That dream started out with great promise, but for Carlos McClatchy, personally, it was to come to an early end. Even so, The Fresno Bee would prosper, beyond the fondest dreams of the McClatchy clan.

The studies showed there was a city in the burgeoning San Joaquin Valley – Fresno – that was promising, even though it already had two daily newspapers. It was a city with railroad connections, and a population set optimistically by the Chamber of Commerce at 70,000, "exclusive of Orientals." A more realistic figure was in the 50,000 range, with the 1920 U.S. census setting it at 44,616.

The Sacramento Bee was owned by C. K. and his brother, V.S. McClatchy, its publisher, in equal shares. The brothers, taking the cue from their father, had pumped profits back into the organization, were solvent, and ready to expand. It was pretty well decided that C.K. would keep a firm hand on the new operation, wherever it would be, particularly at the start. The search team favored a Fresno location, reasoning the city would continue its rapid growth pace, particularly with agriculture on the upswing in the valley.

The immediate opposition would be in the form of two newspapers, each owned by the brothers Chase and George Osborn. The Morning Republican claimed a circulation of 30,000, Sundays included. The afternoon Herald gave a publisher's figure of 12,000. Both figures were inflated. The McClatchys reasoned there was room in the city for a newspaper with a different point of view. In addition, it was generally acknowledged that the Osborn brothers were lacking in newspaper savvy, both on the editorial and business sides.

With Carlos unswerving in his belief that a second Bee would succeed under his leadership, the McClatchys decided the gamble would pay off. The die was cast in the spring of 1921, just four years after Carlos' marriage to Phebe Briggs, daughter of prominent physician and Mrs. William Ellery Briggs of Sacramento. Carlos made weekly trips to Fresno for a year, returning to Phebe and their child, James, in Sacramento every weekend. Phebe was not to join him in Fresno until the summer of 1922, shortly before The Fresno Bee started publica-

Robert P. Molander

tion. She preferred to remain in Sacramento, not wanting to raise their son, James, in a hotel room. Meanwhile, Carlos liked what he saw in Fresno, and made weekly reports to his father on his progress there. He decided early on that the central San Joaquin Valley could support another newspaper, particularly one that would combat the conservative views of the Herald and Republican in Fresno. He would give the readers a choice.

Carlos and W. H. James, business director of The Sacramento Bee, did the principal spadework during that first year in Fresno. Their frequent reports were glowing. They sought out leaders of the Fresno business community. Many of those local leaders, although remaining behind the scenes officially, assured their Sacramento visitors that a newspaper modeled after The Sacramento Bee would indeed be welcomed to Fresno. Several indicated that, yes, they would buy advertising space in a Fresno Bee, should it become a reality. In Sacramento, C.K. and V.S. McClatchy were well pleased with the projections from the south, but unsubstantiated promises weren't enough for them to plunge ahead. They wanted something ironclad in hand.

So Carlos enlisted the aid of Fresno real estate man George S. Smith, who was to become The Fresno Bee's second business manager. He was asked to survey Fresno businessmen, checking whether they'd put their money behind their veiled promises of support. It took Smith two weeks to give his answer, an interminably long two weeks in Carlos McClatchy's mind. They finally met. Smith had done his job well. He was told the fledgling paper would require a minimum of 400,000 inches of advertisements in hand before making the final decision. Grinning, Smith informed them he had 700,000 inches under contract, including one for 50,000 inches from Radin & Kamp, the city's leading department store. The McClatchy clan to the north had depended to a large degree on reports sent by Carlos, but wanted final, first-hand knowledge. A delegation was formed to visit this growing city in the lush San Joaquin Valley. The movers and shakers in the group squired by Carlos were his father, C.K.; W.H. James, general manager of the Sacramento Bee; H.R. (Bob) McLaughlin, Sacramento Bee city editor who would become Fresno's managing editor; and Fred B. Moore, destined to be The Fresno Bee's first city editor.

Years later, a local artist, Milt Young, filled in the details of a portion of that visit, recalling that on a pleasant afternoon in 1922, a group of important-appearing men entered the Ennis-Anderson Advertising Agency office where Young worked. Here's the way Young remembered that day: The group told Ennis-Anderson executives they wanted to talk about starting a newspaper in Fresno. Anderson told them that if Chester Rowell were still running the Republican, the McClatchys might have a tough time because when Rowell owned and operated the newspaper, it was the "People's Bible." Anderson was not impressed by the Osborn brothers.

Carlos McClatchy retorted that if Rowell were still running the Republican, the McClatchys wouldn't be considering the move to Fresno. But he wasn't worried about the Osborns, either.

Anderson then outlined what he felt the McClatchys could expect in the way of advertising revenue in Fresno and from other sections of the San Joaquin Valley. The newspaper officials liked what they heard, and took it to heart. Fresno was ready for a third newspaper, and the McClatchy's were ready to publish it. As it was proved later, the Republican and the Herald were not.

News of the quest spread throughout Fresno and its environs. The McClatchys were coming to town. Chase and George Osborn, those young, relatively inexperienced publishers of the morning Republican and the evening Herald, knew all about it. So did the smaller newspapers in the nearby valley towns.

The McClatchys were a major threat. The valley newspapers would have to do battle with a well-armed invader –one that knew how the game was played, and had proved successful at it.

Opposition in Fresno would warn that The Bee would be a "wet" newspaper. Everyone who knew anything "knew" the McClatchys opposed the prohibition laws of the day.

Carlos and, to the north, C.K. and V.S. McClatchy, were far ahead of these doubters. Surveys taken shortly after and during the extended years of Prohibition constantly showed that the majority of U.S. adults wanted Prohibition repealed, especially as far as beer and wine were concerned. It was loudly claimed the 18th Amendment had been railroaded through while the nation's young men were on the battlefronts of World War I. (In reality, the Prohibition Amendment wasn't ratified until after the war, in 1919, but many federal anti-liquor laws had been passed during the war, to conserve grain, and many states had individual prohibition packages. California did not.)

One can picture the high glee with which Carlos McClatchy passed the word to his father and uncle concerning the prospects in Fresno. All doubt was erased. The operational word was "go!" It was time to determine the specific location of a new plant. Carlos had been in contact with Sigmund (Sig) Levy, a veteran real-estate broker and a former newsman on the business side. Carlos wanted an accessible site, one that wouldn't be too close to downtown. Levy came up with four possible locations, his favorite the corner of Van Ness Avenue and Calaveras Street "out in the country." Carlos got an option to buy that lot, and as soon as he convinced the McClatchy brothers in Sacramento to go along, he took up the option and got a building permit.

Locally, any lingering doubts about this new paper were dispelled. The McClatchys were coming. This was no fly-by-night action. There would be no mere test run. It was for real. A new plant would be built. They really meant business. In February 1921, The Fresno Bee had been merely an idea. Now, it would become a reality.

2

Moving Time

Carlos plunged ahead. Nearly all of his time was being spent in Fresno. For a time he lived in the Hotel Fresno, but he wanted his family with him, so he also kept busy checking out the real-estate market. Sig Levy, now a closer friend, did some scouting for him, but Carlos found a home himself, one he thought would be fine. It was near downtown, on Clark Street. But Levy was against it. "That house is all right," he said, "but you don't want to live in that neighborhood. You should live in a better neighborhood." Then, Levy found Carlos a home he liked, out on Yosemite Avenue, in a "better neighborhood." It was just what he wanted, and he knew Phebe would be pleased, too. Their first neighbors included a judge, a future mayor, a businessman and a doctor. In addition, their pedia-trician-to-be lived across the street.

With that problem taken care of, Carlos returned full time to his budding newspaper, putting

Carlos McClatchy, founder of The Fresno Bee

all his waking moments into it. There was plenty of work remaining to be done. The first office of The Fresno Bee was opened several months in advance of publication, in rented space in the Helm Building on Fulton Street. There, three "Mc's" – McClatchy, McLaughlin and McCardle – Carlos, H.R. McLaughlin and Laura McCardle – went to work. McLaughlin had been city editor of The Sacramento Bee and would become the first managing editor of The Fresno Bee. McCardle would be its first librarian. She spent every day clipping files of the Republican, starting to work on June 15, 1922. The Bee built its morgue (editorial library) from Feb. 1922 by clipping previously stored editions of the Republican. Miss McCardle was able to build a set of files for future Bee reporters to work from, although she was vocally unhappy that they had to be maintained in shoe boxes.

In August of that year, the temporary office was moved to another on Van Ness Avenue next to the venerable Parlor Lecture Club. More staff members were added to speed up research, and to make ready for the first day of publication. Meanwhile, McClatchy and McLaughlin were getting their heads together daily on what their paper would be, what it would stand for, how it would become operational.

The structure itself, at the southwest corner of Van Ness and Calaveras, would be something to behold. Its likes had not been seen in Fresno – five stories high, of brick-concrete construction of the California Romanesque, or Northern Italian Renaissance Palazzo, style. It was a decided break from the sedate architectural styles of the '20s in Fresno. Years later, one knowledgeable observer would write admiringly, "Resembling a Florentine palazzo, with fine arches and Renaissance Revival style." That's what Carlos McClatchy wanted for his newspaper, and that's what he got.

The move into the new building, which still had not been completed, came in October, 1922. The editorial quarters weren't ready, so staffers crowded into McCardle's library, a temporary home. There were other problems. The first press would be a right-angle Scott with four units, each capable of handling eight pages. It could run "straight" and produce a 32-page paper, or "collect," doubling it's capacity to 64 pages. It was a copy of the press in use in Sacramento, one which had worked very well. The McClatchys wanted Fresno to start with the best. But it wasn't to be that easy. The press had to be built from scratch, and the Scott factory had trouble digging up the plans and blueprints it had used in designing the Sacramento press.

Those problems were overcome, and the press was installed in time for trial runs. But McClatchy's problems weren't over. New presses have bugs that must be overcome. And the building had to be completed. Cold weather was setting in. The weather cooperated, to a degree, and the press bugs were eliminated by press foreman Dave Wiley and his crew. Trial runs were held two days before the real thing, and on the following day. The staffs of all departments worked hard for the most part of the three days and nights preceding Publication Day, October 17, 1922.

Time passed swiftly, and although there were increasing doubts by some, the paper came out on schedule, and on time for delivery. Carlos McClatchy was to credit the various departmental staffs for the instant success. The first day's paper was spread over five sections and 60 pages. Included was late-breaking news from the wires of United Press. Carlos had wanted The Associated Press service, but the afternoon Herald had a lock on it. Under its contract, no other afternoon newspaper in Fresno could use AP services.

When the big day finally came it was not without incident. Jackhammers were still blasting, bricklayers were still cementing their bricks in place, carpenters were still pounding nails. But the show went on. The Fresno Bee's first issue was published with just about everything going according to plan. Editorial staffers pounded out their stories on typewriters in the smoke-filled morgue, in those halcyon days when reporters and editors chain-smoked cigarettes, pipes or cigars, or chewed tobacco. Coleman kerosene stoves gave off heat, necessary because the heating and cooling system was not installed and the windows weren't in, letting cold breezes invade the floor.

There was just one casualty. And as fate would have it, it involved Carlos McClatchy. He was in his fourth-story office, busy making decisions and changes, checking page proofs of stories, when an errant brick from above crashed through his office window and onto his desk, causing minor cuts on his face and hand from flying splinters of glass. His reaction? Not to worry, he assured his staffers. Let's get on with it.

3

World War I

Carlos McClatchy, the man who, more than anyone, transformed The Fresno Bee from vision to reality, was the son of Charles Kenney (C.K.) McClatchy, the second editor of The Sacramento Bee, and his wife, Ella K. (Kelly) McClatchy.

It was thought that Carlos would be named Charles, but his mother, Ella K., as she was called, announced she would have no more "Charlies" around the house. She named him Carlos, with the middle name from her maiden name, Kelly. This kept the C.K. initials intact, although Carlos never went by them,

"Kenney," was a priest who had befriended the family, but Ella K. wanted nothing to do with that name because "it didn't mean anything."

She won that round, but was overruled years later in the naming of the second son born to Phebe and Carlos McClatchy. Ella K. wanted him named "Charles Kelly," to carry on the Kelly name. But Carlos and Phebe decided to name the baby for his grandfather, so he became Charles Kenney. He was called Kenney during his formative years, again because of the family aversion to "Charlie," and continued to be called Kenney until he went to work for The Sacramento Bee, when he adopted his grandfather's "C.K."

Carlos McClatchy (3rd from left), a WWI veteran, in Belgium on October 27, 1918.

Carlos McClatchy was well-educated. After finishing high school in Sacramento, he attended Christian Brothers College. Then, with Ella K.'s strong backing, he enrolled at Columbia University, an institution which boasted an excellent reputation for journalism, as well as acclaim for its other academic programs.

In those years, Carlos' main interest was history, and he also proved to be a fine writer. He had a keen analytical mind, and could easily separate the main elements of a news story from its lesser parts. This was to prove invaluable when he assumed leadership of the fledgling Fresno Bee in 1922.

The McClatchy family believed the education at Columbia gave him a much broader view then he would have had if he had attended Santa Clara, which had been another option. He later would applaud the choice, saying he had Ella K. to thank for it.

From all accounts, Carlos was not a spoiled child. This especially was a tribute to his mother, who regarded him as "the apple of my eye" and who doubtless had to fight urges to give him too much of everything.

As a youth, Carlos at every opportunity pulled work shifts at The Sacramento Bee under the watchful eye of his dad. Because of this varied early training, he was well-versed in journalism when he first entered Columbia.

After his graduation from Columbia, Carlos went to work for The Bee as a reporter. At the time, preceding World War I, the IWW (Industrial Workers of the World, a socialist labor group also known derisively as "the Wobblies," and "I Won't Work"), was becoming particularly active in the Sacramento area. It was attempting to organize the area's unskilled laborers – African-Americans in general – who worked as miners, longshoremen, migrants and lumberjacks. The Sacramento Bee had no quarrel with that – in fact, favored it – but was openly against the overall movement, which had as its ultimate aim the abolition of capitalism and the institution of a Socialist economy.

Carlos was assigned to cover the IWW's organizational efforts in its target area, which included Sacramento, Oakland and San Francisco. The area seemed to be easy pickings for the IWW, because it was where migrant workers and other laborers holed up in the agricultural off-season.

Because of his ongoing coverage, Carlos got to know the leaders of the IWW camps on a personal basis. And it was through this assignment that he met his future wife, Phebe Briggs. Home for summer vacation from Vassar, Phebe was in the middle of a senior project in economics – coincidentally, a study of the IWW. The year was 1916. The assignment was a tough one, especially for a co-ed in the midst of hard-core laborers; she needed help. And as it happened, her parents knew of a bright young man who was fast becoming an expert on the IWW and its internal workings. They were introduced.

Carlos undoubtedly took an immediate liking to what he saw, and didn't hesitate to escort this bright, beautiful young woman to the different IWW camps, introducing her to their leaders and arranging interviews. She was able to complete her paper, complete with know–ledgeable first-hand descriptions that must have wowed her professor at Vassar.

She learned how the IWW had moved into the Sacramento Valley, burning haystacks and barns. She saw its members enter Sacramento with pillage in mind. All the while, she remained close to Carlos, her protector, the man who was covering the story for The Sacramento Bee.

Carlos, Phebe was to recall years after his early, untimely death, was well acquainted with those "terrible IWW creatures" on a first-name basis, to the point where he understood them and they understood him. He knew they were trying to "buy" his allegiance so he would write stories favorable to them; they discovered they couldn't. This background would later give credence to the belief that he was a man who could be trusted, one who wouldn't bend the truth in his stories.

Carlos was to keep up his battle against the IWW during his years with The Fresno Bee. He and other editors throughout the state and the nation won out when, in 1930, the IWW lost its clout as an effective labor organization, with many of its remaining members dropping out of the public eye.

Phebe returned to Sacramento in 1917, following her graduation from Vassar. She and Carlos were married that year, shortly before he entered the Army and reported to Camp Lewis in Washington.

In 1916 he had entered the Citizens Military Training Corps, a one-month summer session of Army-type training. Then in May, 1917, he volunteered for officer's training camp at the Presidio in San Francisco. He was commissioned a first lieutenant and assigned to Headquarters Company, 362nd Infantry, 91st Division, at Camp Lewis.

Carlos McClatchy survived World War I, while in company with many other soldiers who didn't. He survived trench warfare in the Argonne. And Lys-Scheldt. And Ypres-Lys. His regiment left for France in June, 1918, and his baptism of fire came at St. Mihiel that September. He was assigned as operations officer before his regiment went over the top in the Argonne Forest, one of the major battles of the war. As an officer in the thick of things, he saw many of his new-found comrades fall from German artillery and small-arms fire.

His primary task was to motorcycle back and forth between the front and rear lines, carrying orders to the front-line officers, then returning hastily for more. During that period, he won a field promotion to captain. It was signed by Gen. John Joseph (Black Jack) Pershing, commander of the American Expeditionary Forces in France.

McClatchy's front-line service wasn't to end there. It was followed by the Lys-Scheld and Ypres-Lys offensives as the war ground to a halt. He was honorably discharged after the Armistice and returned to Sacramento, where he helped to form Post No. 61, American Legion. He was elected the first post commander.

The war had been kind to him, in that he was not wounded or killed, but he never was to forget it. Like many who have been in the thick of battle, he was not one to boast about it in civilian life. It remained in his thoughts, however, and he never was able to erase it entirely.

He took some time off after the war, getting reacquainted with his bride. But he soon hurried back to his first love, the newspaper business. His father, C.K. McClatchy, named him associate editor of the Sacramento Bee. He was entering the final phase of the groundwork for taking over as the first editor of The Fresno Bee. Working closely with him would be H.R. McLaughlin, city editor of The Sacramento Bee who was to become the first managing editor of The Fresno Bee. Those were good times for Carlos McClatchy. Not only was he realizing his life's dream, to have a newspaper of his own, he was reunited with Phebe, who had spent more than a year worrying while he was at the battlefront.

C.K. McClatchy, Carlos' father and principal mentor, was a stern taskmaster, one who demanded and got the utmost from those under his command. C.K. probably set even higher standards for his son, Carlos, because at that time Carlos appeared to be the heir-apparent to the McClatchy throne. Under this regime, Carlos was to put in long, hard hours. The approach worked, because C.K. McClatchy would never have put anyone in command of a newspaper, even a favorite son, if he had not been ready. Unfortunately, Carlos McClatchy would die at an early age with his father and mother surviving.

4

A Newspaper is Born

The Fresno Bee first published on October 17, 1922. It was also the day its struggles began. Actually, the preparations for this war, for newspaper supremacy in Fresno and its environs, had already begun. It was fought on two major fronts, and was to last a decade. When it was over, The Fresno Bee was the undisputed victor and was not to be threatened seriously again.

It was not a nice war, making laughable the opening statements by the participants to the contrary. Charges and counter charges were made, mud was slung in great gobs, and commonly recognized newspaper principles were ignored.

The losers – the Fresno Morning Republican and the afternoon Fresno Herald – sank in pools of printer's ink, never to rise again.

The battlefronts were separated, but necessarily entwined. One was concerned with popular circulation enticements, some of them truly spectacular. The others were the front-line battles of this war – how to beat hell out of the competition with better stories, quicker stories, trumped-up charges, others that had actual merit, and even the theft of a former owner-editor.

The start probably was innocuous in the eyes of the reading public. The Bee mounted its challenge with its first edition. It was a nice start, loaded with news, a plethora of advertisements – 60 total pages spread over five sections. A moneymaker.

The first salvo was fired in its lead editorial on opening day. It went like this:

The Why And Wherefore
Of The Fresno Bee

"Today, The Fresno Bee is born.

It comes into the world to serve the city whose name it bears, and the San Joaquin Valley with all the news and editorial comment thereon.

That mission is fraught with responsibilities which are fully appreciated, and surrounded by difficulties which long months and heavy expenditures have been used to overcome.

The primary purpose of The Bee is to tell the news; to tell it fairly, simply and impartially; unfairly to hurt none, no matter how lowly; to favor none, no matter how powerful.

The Bee can perform that service because it serves no master.

It is the handmaiden of neither capital nor labor. Politically, it is neither Republican, Democrat nor Socialist, holding that the man and the issue are superior to the label they bear.

An American paper first and last, it carries, however, no prejudice against or favoritism for any particular race.

As a newspaper, The Bee goes to no church, not even to Sunday School.

It is neither Baptist, Methodist, Catholic, Mohammadean, Episcopalian, Jewish, Buddhist nor Holy Roller.

It is simply and solely a newspaper interested in the lay affairs of the world, leaving religion between man, his church and his God.

Editorially, the Bee has opinions, born of sincerity and formed from long experience.

These it intends to express, for a newspaper without convictions is like an automobile without an engine.

But this expression, strong and definite as it may be, will not deny the right of disagreement to which the columns of The Bee are ever open.

Robert P. Molander

The Bee comes to Fresno as no mentor to enlighten a benighted community; no self-appointed ruler to tell the San Joaquin what it should do.

Instead, it comes to Fresno, because this community and the San Joaquin have builded well, in which labor it intends to join as a willing worker, content to leave to time what part it shall play.

As the days go by, The Fresno Bee in the discharge of its duty may incur some dislike and accumulate some opposition, as will any newspaper worth the reading.

But whatever else may be said in the future, truth will compel two admissions.

The Fresno Bee prints all the news.

Editorially, it prints what it thinks, and that thinking is its own."

That statement of newspaper aims informed one and all how The Bee intended to operate, that The Bee's "thinking is its own." This was in sharp contradiction to the belief, expounded by many, including the jointly owned Republican, the morning paper; and the Herald, the afternoon paper, that The Bee would be run by executives at the McClatchy flagship newspaper, The Sacramento Bee, nearly 200 miles to the North. The Republican and the Herald responded the following day with proper decorum. The statement, run by the Republican, on its editorial page, below the fold:

"In no spirit of mere formality, the Republican welcomes the Fresno Bee to newspaper activity in this city.

"The publishers of the Bee have already, in another field, established character for straightforward and maintained journalistic policy. However they may differ on matters of incidental policy, as public issues arise, with the directors of this paper, we are confident that they will strive for the constructive good of the community and a parallel of growth of their own usefulness in it.

"The Republican will seek no more and no less than a friendly rivalry with the Bee. In a purely business way, there will be room in Central California for as many papers as there are now. In a professional way there will be room for this many papers, just so long as they all conform to high standards and evolve sincere and intelligent purposes.

"Fresno accepts the inauguration of the Fresno Bee as one more evidence of notable growth of this city industrially and financially in the last few years. Those Fresnans who are far visioned see an even greater growth in the next decade.

"It is not inappropriate for men with an outside viewpoint to take some advantage of this development. This has taken place in mercantile life and in banking, in professional and in cultural ways. Equally important to us with 'freedom of the press' is growth of the press. We should be better for this growth."

Here was another well-planned statement, this one of "welcome." Rather thinly veiled was the "men with an outside viewpoint" phrase, obviously reminding readers of the Republican that The Bee, indeed, was an adjunct to its Sacramento sister, and would remain in a subservient role to Sacramento and to C.K. McClatchy, the ruler of the clan and the father of Carlos McClatchy, editor of The Fresno Bee.

So how does one start a newspaper war? It's easy, particularly when both sides are hungering for it. It's just a question of who fires the first salvo. In this case, it was the Republican, although surreptitiously.

To start, it continued its year-old, word-of-mouth claim, believed as gospel by some in the Fresno business community, that this Sacramento based, well-heeled organization was coming to town with a solitary aim – to wipe out the opposition, and to spread its tentacles throughout the San Joaquin Valley, posing serious threats to the community papers outside Fresno, as well as those inside. Better, they said, that this interloper be labeled The Fresno Octopus.

Second, the Republican enlisted the aid of crusty publisher William Elliott Locke at the Dinuba Sentinel.

In the week before The Bee started publication, Locke declared in print that "You can wring a pint of whiskey out of every edition" of The Bee.

He referred to The Bee and its Sacramento parent, and the general belief that the McClatchys would be much happier without Prohibition than with it. (Later, the Bees came out editorially against the repeal of the Wright Act, enacted in California to assist local police in their enforcement of prohibition under the federal Volstead Act.)

Carlos McClatchy replied in the No. 2 editorial in the Bee's first edition, imprinted on a facsimile of a tombstone:

Here Lies The Fresno Bee
Kicked To Death In Its Infancy,
By Editor Locke, Whose Dread Of Drink
Became A Fear To Let Others Think!

While no threat to the verse of Ogden Nash, it nevertheless was a sign of things to come – Carlos would brook no threat to his baby, whether with tongue in cheek or in an all-out fusillade.

And as to the matter of The Bee's being well-heeled, with more money than it could decently use, it should be noted that The Republican and the Herald were owned and operated by the brothers Chase and George Osborn, sons of wealthy Gov. Chase S. Osborn of Michigan. The governor was a millionaire in his own right and, the story goes, he bought the Herald in 1915 and the Republican in 1920 so his boys would have something constructive to fill their time. They had little proper newspaper background, and were suddenly in deep water when The Bee took to the battlefield.

George, it is said, was the hard worker of the two; Chase more the man about town.

Although both sides were spending great amounts of money for ammunition, there seemed to be an undeclared truce in the matter of advertising fees. The Bee stayed on a fairly even keel financially, until a few bad years of the Great Depression. But those came after the demise of the opposition papers.

The Herald fell in 1924, and the Republican in 1932. Each was losing heavily, but couldn't lay those losses to cut-rate ads.

Rather, they came from ever-decreasing circulation, and the resulting lower rates they could charge for ad space. (But publicly, until the end, the Osborns maintained circulation had not dropped.) The Bee, conversely, saw its circulation rising continually, enabling this powerful invader to increase its advertising rates.

It was the relatively inexperienced Osborn brothers vs. Editor Carlos McClatchy, Managing Editor H.R. McLaughlin, and Business Manager

Ed S. Riggins, hired in 1926. That triumvirate did in the Republican. Their newspaper savvy was too much for the Osborns to equal.

The Herald was sold by the Osborns to a Los Angeles syndicate, which turned a quick profit by selling it to The Bee. (Did Carlos McClatchy have a hand in making the deal? Probably, but not in the open.)

The Osborns had their hands full maintaining the Republican. It is doubtful, however, that they would have sold the Herald had they known it would be picked up and shut down by the McClatchys.

Chester Rowell told an enlightening story about the Osborns and the Republican. (Rowell started the Republican as owner-editor. He sold it to the Osborns and joined the San Francisco Chronicle as an editor. It was he, in later years, who was "purloined." The Bee hired him to write a daily column, which ran for some three years.)

"I was in the lobby of the Waldorf-Astoria in New York one day," Rowell was to recall, "when Governor Osborn came up to me and asked, 'Chester, what's wrong with my boys? You don't have to tell me what's wrong with their newspaper – I read it daily.'"

The meaning to Rowell was clear. The senior Osborn owned a newspaper himself – in Sault Ste. Marie – and he easily recognized when another newspaper was in trouble – and whom to blame.

Actually, the claim that The Fresno Bee was ruled from Sacramento had more than a little merit. For one thing, editorials other than those pertaining to Fresno and the San Joaquin Valley were written in Sacramento and published regularly in the Fresno newspaper. Those written locally, on local subjects, had to get C.K. McClatchy's stamp of approval before being published in Fresno.

That policy remained in effect until the early 1990s, when the Sacramento executives decided it was time for Fresno to have its own publisher, granting it, to all practical purposes, its long-sought autonomy. It was something Carlos McClatchy long pined for but never got. But even in those fledgling days, the news columns to a large degree were the prerogative of the Fresno editors, who generally made their own decisions on the play of the news, especially the local stories. There was some second-guessing from up north, but McLaughlin, with the solid backing of Carlos McClatchy, usually made his own, uncontested decisions on the news columns in The Fresno Bee.

Robert P. Molander

It was the Herald that made the first open attack in the newspaper war. On November 8, 1922, The Bee published an announcement of its paid circulation, setting it at 17,514 daily and citing the Merchants Association of Fresno as its source. With the announcement was this quote: "The Bee is the only afternoon paper in Fresno which has invited its advertisers through the Merchants Association to check its circulation records." It appeared devastating, and its target was obvious. The only other p.m. paper in town was the Herald, which replied swiftly. The Bee's circulation figures, it charged, were puffed up, phony.

Carlos McClatchy did a little puffing up himself, and retorted quickly, backing his fiery answer with a challenge. Prove our figures are phony, he snapped in print, and The Bee would give $1,000 to the Community Chest. And if the Herald could prove The Bee's circulation was not at least 40 percent ahead of its rival, the check would be mailed posthaste. But, he stipulated, the Herald had to match the $1,000, and its check would go to the Community Chest if it were proven wrong.

Two days later, on Page 1, The Bee ran a 60-point (letters 5/6 of an inch high) black banner headline:
Where Is That $1,000 Check From The Herald?

The deck headline below said:
The Herald Squirms Out Of An Awkward Position

And below that:
The Herald has three choices:
1. Make good by depositing its check
2. Withdraw its charges
3. Remain silent, a self-convicted welcher.

In print, the quarrel ended there. There is no further mention in The Bee archives, or those of the Republican, as to whether the Community Chest, obviously relishing the prospect of getting $1,000 or $2,000, ever got a penny.

But on February 2, 1923, The Bee did admit to a large "drop" in circulation, from 17,859 in December to 15,550 in January, a drop of 2,309. Accompanying the announcement was this explanation:

"The decrease ... was due to the expiration of the '10 weeks for $1' sales promotion made by The Bee before it began publication in October. Those numbered something over 12,000. It was expected that there would be some who would discontinue. The circulation of The Bee now is a permanent one."

That was a plausible explanation, and a good example of turning a negative into a positive.

On August 23, 1923, the first airmail plane to make a cross-country flight arrived in San Francisco from New York. The flight took 28 hours. On the same day, The Fresno Bee ran a Page 1 story about the flight, datelined Washington D.C. and written by its Washington correspondent, Leo A. McClatchy.

He was a grandson of James McClatchy, founder of The Sacramento Bee, and a son of V.S. McClatchy, first publisher of The Fresno Bee. He was the Washington correspondent for the Bees and later became chief editorial writer for the San Francisco Call-Bulletin. He died in 1945 at age 52 after suffering a heart attack in his Call-Bulletin office.

His story, detailing the advent of cross-country air mail, had been a part of the mail on that plane, and was carried in a "News Rush" envelope, The Bee wrote.

In its next-day paper, the Republican claimed the story was a fraud, that The Bee's story hadn't arrived via airmail. The Osborns probably figured the time angle made it impossible. The answer came that same afternoon in The Bee, in a quote from George W. Turner, the Fresno postmaster. Turner said that, indeed, the envelope and the story had been on the plane. How the story got to Fresno that quickly wasn't explained, but it probably came via telephone dictation, commonly used in those pre-computer days on late-breaking stories.

This type of Page 1 treatment – fastest with the latest – became one of the nails in the Republican's coffin. A prime example came on March 4, 1925, the day Calvin Coolidge was inaugurated as president in Washington D.C. On that same day, The Bee ran three Page 1 photos of the inauguration, the first time same-day pictures depicting East Coast events were published in any San Joaquin Valley newspaper.

That feat of transmission, The Bee crowed, was through the "miracle of telephony." Getting the pictures in that same-day newspaper came through the planning of McClatchy and McLaughlin. That, and the willingness to spend money, resulted in the scoop.

A local story that accompanied the photos and the inauguration story from Washington explained that the pictures were taken in the East Coast city, transmitted to San Francisco over the wires of the American Telephone and Telegraph Co., and rushed to an engraving plant in San Francisco. The Newspaper Enterprise Association made the engravings of the pictures special to The Bee. Their sizes were wired to the paper, and the page forms for that day were made up by the printers in advance, with exact space left for the photo plates.

A plane chartered by The Bee picked up the plates in San Francisco and flew them to Fresno, where they were rushed by car to the plant and placed in the printer's form. Less than a half hour later, the presses were rolling, and Fresnans were treated to the first-time thrill of seeing events from the East Coast that same day in their afternoon paper.

The following day, The Bee ran another Page 1 picture, this one showing Assistant City Editor Jack Goddard picking up the Coolidge cuts from the plane. The plane had been flown by aviator Frank Sheltz and stuntman Eddie Herzog. In an accompanying story The Bee wrote that "The day of miracles is here." It also trumpeted its belief that the only way to get today's news today was through the medium of an afternoon paper. Morning papers, it charged scornfully, couldn't get the job done.

In May, 1924, the Bee won another skirmish. It took the side of labor, backing the city's mail carriers. The Republican took the other side. In a sense, it was forced to do so – that, or agree with The Bee, which had mounted the campaign.

The issue was whether the mail carriers, who worked a six-day week, should be given Saturday afternoons off without pay during the summer. The issue got as hot as the valley's summer weather, with The Bee stories quoting residents to the effect that these hard-working civil servants deserved that half day off. Bee editorials followed that line. The Republican starchly editorialized that giving them time off would hurt business.

A popular vote was sponsored by The Bee, with citizens asked to "cast ballots" in stores and the Post Office. The vote was overwhelming – 27,917 to a paltry 122, according to The Bee – in favor of the mail carriers and The Bee's stand. When the results were announced, The Bee took its final shot: "If the Republican needs Saturday afternoon delivery, then The Bee advises that, like every well-equipped newspaper, it rent a post office box." Carlos McClatchy wasn't above – in fact delighted in – chortling over a victory.

Postmaster Turner ruled the carriers be given Saturday afternoons off, from June 14th through August 31st, and The Bee picked up the support of the working man.

On September 8, 1925, The Bee mounted its heaviest attack to date. It charged, in a Page 1 story with an accompanying editorial, that the Republican was "stuffing," or inflating, its circulation figures by 3,000 to 8,000 papers a day. The Bee demanded an independent audit of both papers – itself and the Republican.

It was a monumental charge, and The Bee backed it up, after contending that its foe was printing the excess papers and dumping them in the valley desert, or burning them. It published Page 1 photographs showing stacks of Republican issues in the desert near Taft, and other stacks in a Bakersfield garage. These pictures, The Bee wrote, proved its charges. The Republican answered the following day, denying the charges in a front-page story.

It was enough to convince County Recorder I.E. Farley, at the Bee's request, to issue affidavits charging:

1. That within the past five months the Fresno Republican deliberately and knowingly stuffed its circulation falsely in two large districts.

2. That the extent of such fraud ranged from a fourth to a third of the circulation that the Republican claimed.

3. That the papers falsely carried as paid circulation were stored in various places to escape detection.

4. That a responsible department head of the Republican had given orders for their destruction and in one case applied the match that torched a pile of newspapers.

Robert P. Molander

5.   That instructions came from the Republican office to deceive investigating agents of auditing associations, and that those instructions were carried out.

The Bee estimated the fake circulation could run as high as 8,000 a day, and if so, "The Bee would lead the Republican by far in circulation." The "fakes" referred to Bakersfield and Taft.

"If it were so done over the counties covered by the two newspapers three to eight thousand fraudulent circulation would be the result," The Bee charged.

In its editorial, the Bee chuckled: "The Fresno Bee started less than three years ago, before the first issue, with 12,000 circulation while the Republican claimed 30,000.

"It jumped to 15,000 with the Republican still claiming 30,000.

"The Bee rose to 20,000 with the Republican still claiming 30,000.

"The Bee is now over 25,000 with the Republican still claiming 30,000.

"The age of miracles is past or rather never did affect the newspaper business."

One of the affidavits was signed by F.L. Allen, former Republican agent in Bakersfield who since had been hired by The Bee. As it turned out, he had been fired by the Republican months earlier, before the "stuffing" allegations were raised.

In his affidavit, Allen claimed he was forced by Republican management to accept newspapers for which he had no subscribers. Acting on orders of the paper's country circulation manager, he said, he stored the excess papers and didn't reveal their existence to auditors. He also said he wrote to his superior, asking for cuts in his daily ration of newspapers, but that these letters were ignored.

Others told similar stories in their affidavits. Republican agent Edwin F. Schultz of Taft testified to burning excess papers. And two newsboys with Republican routes in Bakersfield told in their affidavits how 100 to 150 surplus papers were sent to Bakersfield each day, and that with not enough subscribers to buy them, the papers were either burned or stacked high in Allen's garage.

The capper was an affidavit by Schultz, who testified that he dumped about 1,500 copies of the Republican in the desert out from Taft. When they were seen by Homer Coffman, the Republican's country circulation manager, Schultz testified, Coffman ruled that the desert was not a safe hiding place, so they were hauled back to Taft and burned in Schultz's back yard, with Coffman striking the match.

In its expected next-day Page 1 denial, the Republican countered that the charges were made with malice and were ridiculous. Every newspaper, it explained, winds up with daily circulation surpluses. It contended it made every effort to check on surpluses and, when found, to eliminate them. Signed by George A. Osborn Jr., the denial contended the books of the circulation department were open for "the examination of any responsible organization, upon request."

The Republican also published the statement of Coffman, who alleged malcontents such as Allen were responsible for the charges, which he categorically denied.

The Bee wouldn't accept that. Obviously anticipating such a denial, its Page 1 editorial had concluded: "Six specific affidavits charging fraud, increased to eight today, should stir the Republican to demand that the local merchants who pay for the advertising and the public which reads the papers be given the truth.

"Will the Republican do it?"

It didn't. In fact, it never mentioned the matter in print again. Neither did The Bee.

It appears mind-boggling to drop a big story while still in hot pursuit, as The Bee did in this case. But McClatchy and McLaughlin apparently believed they had got as much mileage out of it as they could, and let the matter drop. As for the Republican, it probably was more than happy to let it die.

The first head-to-head confrontation of major proportions came on April 16, 1924, a short time after the county Grand Jury issued its annual report. The Bee had been critical of county government, and chose the occasion to bring its beliefs out in the open.

During its deliberations, the jury had hired, at a $4,000 fee, one W.D. Hamman, a public accountant who was described officially as an expert. He turned in a voluminous report, and probably thought his duties were ended. But the Grand Jury chose, on the advice of District Attorney George R. Lovejoy, not to release the entire report. (It was Lovejoy's duty to advise the jury on legal matters.) The Bee pushed the matter, but was told by Frank Davis, the jury foreman, that the jury had used Hamman's report "for what it was needed," and would not divulge the report itself.

McClatchy and McLaughlin approached Hamman, pressed him for a copy of his findings, and got it. No mention was made of whether he was paid by the newspaper. Hamman' report was dynamite – severely critical of the county's operation. It gave McClatchy and McLaughlin the ammunition they needed to press their claim.

On April 16th, more than half the front page of the Bee was devoted to the "expose." The top headline, a four-column, 42-point black italic, read, Startling Charges Made In Fresno County Affairs By Grand Jury Expert Hamman. The second headline went, Survey Scores Lax Business Methods And Waste Of Money.

And the third, Bee Starts Exclusive Publication Of Findings of Accountant Who Recommends Many Changes In County Government System To Reduce Taxes.

Accompanying the main story was a sidebar giving the "salient points" of Hamman's report, another quoting Lovejoy as saying Hamman's report was replete with errors, and a third advising anyone who threatened the Bee with libel for publishing the report that "The Bee office is at Van Ness and Calaveras and the courts are open all day."

Predictably, the Republican on the following day editorialized that Hamman's report was a "grossly inadequate attack on county." The editorial said, "An alleged expert accountant was making half-baked, inaccurate and badly opinionated suggestions about county affairs which the grand jury could not approve."

And on Page 1 of that same edition the Republican ran the headline,

DISCARDED REPORT ON COUNTY MADE PUBLIC BY HAMMAN.

The Republican rejected the report, contending it had been disregarded by the Grand Jury during its year of investigation. The newspaper said, as had Lovejoy, that the report was "filled with innumerable asserted inaccuracies." And, the Republican charged, "The Bee was trying to make an issue out of something which had no merit."

It should be noted in this case that The Bee gave Lovejoy his chance to present the other side of the story. This was not generally the practice during this decade of newspaper bickering and battling. Lovejoy's quotes:

"This report was submitted to the grand jury long before they adjourned. They held a general meeting and committee meetings and went into every assertion and obtained legal advice (from Lovejoy) on all questions of law involved.

"After thoroughly investigating and analyzing the report they found that it consisted of erroneous legal opinions promulgated by a man not skilled in the law and that most of these assertions were erroneous statements of fact. The final report of the grand jury shows that by not adopting any of Hamman's recommendations, his report was repudiated thereby."

The Bee stuck to its guns, pointing out that Hamman had performed similar services for several other counties and was widely recognized as an expert in his field. The Bee published large slices of the lengthy report daily through May 1st, a total of 14 days, exclusive of Sundays. It included several newspaper pages filled with hard-to-read "constructive criticism." The Bee mercifully cut the report for length, but unfortunately did not otherwise edit it. Its major premises and recommendations:

—   County officials failed to file inventories.
—   The budget system was an obstacle to lower tax rates.
—   Supervisors used loose methods in purchasing.
—   County officials used county cars for private outings.
—   Justice courts were costing the county $30,000 a year.
—   The county was losing money by not collecting franchise receipts.
—   The operation of the County Hospital was lax.
—   County revenues were purposely underestimated, and nearly $500,000 more than was needed to meet budget appropriations was raised through taxes.
—   Half a million dollars in Liberty Bonds was counted as cash and (the bonds) should have been sold to reduce the tax rate.
—   A scientific budget should be recommended to force a reduction in taxes.
—   The purchasing agent and the supervisors were illegally buying items that cost more than $500 (each), in violation of the

provision that such items be submitted to bid. (Here, Hamman noted, "Let the supervisors and the purchasing agent follow the law.")

— Regarding the failure to file inventories: "Never before in some dozen other counties audited have I found such flagrant dereliction of duty of officials in filing inventories"

— Forty-one county cars and 62 trucks were illegally hired out.

— Some officials and employees had not filed performance bonds.

In its opening statement, The Bee, in a serious vein, declared, "No man or woman should fail to read every line of Hamman's report as it will be published day by day exclusively by The Bee."

One must wonder how many average readers waded through the resulting acres of type, much of it legalese, or how many more would have done so had it been boiled down and rewritten.

The matter of libel came about because of a statement by county Supervisor W.A. Collins that such a suit might be filed. Asked by a Bee reporter (not identified) whether the Board of Supervisors would file suit, Collins replied, "No, but somebody undoubtedly will because it is filled with libelous matter."

That was all McClatchy needed. His answer to this "maybe" libel action was headlined on Page I, "Will They Sue Bee For Libel? Editor Has A Few Comments." The text:

"The taxpayers of Fresno County paid over $4,000 for the expert's report which The Bee is publishing. If the publication of such a report made officially to a Grand jury is libelous then The Bee learns of a new theory of libel, a theory so strange that under it the taxpayers can be prevented from learning the facts of their own business.

"It will be interesting to know just which county official will go to court to fasten upon the taxpayers here a system under which their paid servants can prevent them from receiving official reports of their own government.

"Any official will have a hard time trying to Russianize this county, for after all the county business is The People's business and no official or all the officials together will succeed in barring the taxpayers from learning with what efficiency their paid servants are conducting affairs.

"If there be county officials who have such ideas the sooner the public learns it the better, for the quicker that official will be back where he belongs – in private life.

"There is no libel in Hamman's report, for he does not deal with men's characters but with their efficiency or incompetency.

"And there is no libel whatever in the frankest discussion of any official's conduct of public business.

"However, if anyone wants a libel suit, the Bee office is at Van Ness and Calaveras, and the courts are open all day. – Editor Bee.

On April 30, 1924, The Bee proudly noted in a story that many of Hamman's recommendations had been incorporated by the Grand Jury in its report as favorable, thus putting the lie to the claims of District Attorney Lovejoy and the Republican that the jury had negated all of Hamman's suggestions.

Included were Grand Jury recommendations that the county seek more competition on bids, that justices of the peace discontinue the practice of having fines paid on the installment plan, that the County Hospital payroll be pruned, that the Welfare Department be abolished, with its duties to be handled by the supervisors, and that small school districts be consolidated.

The Bee scored several direct hits in this battle. Its costs were in newsprint, with column after column of space devoted to the Hamman reports, and in boredom by many of its readers, as installment after installment appeared. But Hamman and The Bee were vindicated to a large degree, and the Republican was forced to retreat even further.

5

Always On Sunday

The Bee's next major offensive came on September 7, 1924, the day it launched its first Sunday paper, a "real Sunday edition," as it was labeled. It was a major advance in the war, because until then the Republican could boast that it printed the valley's only Sunday newspaper. McClatchy and McLaughlin hit the Sunday field running with promotional stories and house advertisements throughout the previous week informing one and all that the San Joaquin Valley readers would finally have the opportunity to buy a Sunday newspaper worthy of the name. The first promotion came on Page 1 on Monday, September 1, 1924, with an eight-column banner headline, in 96-point type an inch and a third high:

THE BEE TO ISSUE SUNDAY PAPER

The accompanying story ran under the byline of Carlos K. McClatchy. He wrote that The Sunday Bee would not be "a creature of idle thought, born of the moment, but the product of carefully-laid plans, expenditures of large sums, and only comes into being after months of preparation and experimentation." He added:

"The Sunday Bee will be a real Sunday newspaper, not a week-day issue elephantized into greater bulk without change of character.

"The Fresno Sunday Bee will give Fresno and the San Joaquin the kind of Sunday morning paper to which they are entitled."

The Sunday Bee would have:

— "A colored comic section with exclusive characters.

— "A weekly magazine with a front page in five colors by some of the country's best artists.

— "Some of the country's funniest humorists like Sam Heliman and George Ade.

— "It will have what have come to be known as Sunday features, signed articles by well-known leaders, puzzles, illustrated articles on travel and adventure, etc.

— "Columns of cable dispatches of European and Asiatic news.

— "Locally, sports, society and general news covered with that comprehensiveness characteristic of the Bee.

— "In short, it will be a Sunday paper. Fresno needs and deserves such a paper."

The Universal Copy desk at The Fresno Bee (1968).

Robert P. Molander

McClatchy then waxed eloquent on his plans:

"The Fresno Bee in coming to the San Joaquin promised that it would put out the kind of thorough paper to which this valley is entitled.

"The Bee's original promise never included a Sunday paper. But the San Joaquin Valley deserves a real Sunday paper, and appreciating the confidence which this valley has given the Bee, this paper undertakes the task of furnishing it.

"Many will say the Bee is ill-advised to spend the large sums involved in publishing a real Sunday paper at this time. They will say that because they lack the confidence born of knowledge that The Bee has of this valley. The Bee has never faltered, nor wavered, in its firm conviction that Fresno and the San Joaquin Valley have futures of prosperity and greatness before them.

"During the last months when many were gloomy and downcast The Bee was carefully planning the large expenditures for the Fresno Sunday Bee. It does that as its bit toward bringing Fresno and the valley into their own, and if as one of the leaders in that it can accomplish good, it will feel amply repaid.

"For The Fresno Bee backs Fresno and the San Joaquin to the limit. Read The Fresno Sunday Bee and see."

McClatchy wrote another zinger on the day before The Sunday Bee became a reality. He stressed the fact that the Bee would publish a section with a color cover, containing all the news from elsewhere, and coincidentally took a shot at the Republican, which had branded the plans for this new Sunday newspaper as "sensational."

"Tomorrow Fresno will have what she has long deserved and long needed – a real, metropolitan Sunday paper," he wrote.

"Colored comics of characters you know so well. Our Boarding House, Out Our Way, Salesman Sam and Freckles and His Friends.

"The skeptical doubt that The Bee can put out a magazine with a color cover. Buy it tomorrow and see. The San Joaquin from now on has its own magazine section with color cover.

"The Bee isn't satisfied with one wire service. It has four – the only paper in the San Joaquin with more than one.

"Daily The Bee has the Associated Press and the United Press with the two wires covering the world. For the Sunday paper The Bee has the special Sunday wire of the United Press and the service of the

Consolidated Press which maintains a cross-continent wire purely for the Sunday papers.

"Have you ever heard of Maximillian Harden? (He) is the Bee's Berlin correspondent. Each Sunday he will have a special signed article in The Bee. Correspondents in all European centers will cable special articles.

"Telegraph news? If there were any more wire services than the four The Bee has which would give additional news it would put them on.

"In sports, politics and finance The Bee will be the only Sunday paper in The San Joaquin which has a telegraph service carrying signed articles on these subjects.

"Do you like special features? The Bee will have among others George Ade, the famous writer; Sam Hellman, one of the country's best known humorists; Cappy Ricks, written by Peter B. Kyne; the cross words puzzle, the intriguing puzzle which has set the whole East working for its solution; Robert Edgren, the greatest sports writer in the country; the story of Robert M. LaFollette, written by himself, and other NEA features.

"This full-news, full-feature paper will hit the Street with its first edition about 11 o'clock tonight, right off the press. The last edition for home delivery will go to press early in the morning.

"A contemporary by a left-handed inference brands The Sunday Bee with being sensational.

"How awful.

"Yes, The Sunday Bee will be sensational enough to give Fresno a real metropolitan Sunday newspaper to which she has been long entitled and which she has never had – sensational in that it will comb the world for news, purchase the best features, give the children colored comics, and the grown-ups a colored magazine – in the social news, sports, markets, farm news, auto and outing, give to Fresno in a Sunday morning newspaper all the news, the color of life and the entertainment that can be crammed in one paper.

"That's sensational – for it remained for The Fresno Bee to give Fresno a real Sunday newspaper.

"One dime will buy it on the streets – 95 cents will give you The Bee for a month with the Sunday edition delivered on your porch.

"That's sensational, too.

Robert P. Molander

"An evening newspaper, which cleans up the news of the city and the world before it goes to press, combined with a Sunday newspaper entitled to call itself so, all for 95 cents. Not a cent more than other papers without all those advantages.

"That's sensational, too."

The Sunday Bee came out as promised, and was all Carlos McClatchy had claimed it would be. Sports carried the byline of Damon Runyon, commenting on the heavyweight fight in which Harry Wills beat Luis Firpo. Other highlights were News Of The San Joaquin, Social News, Stage-Screen, Auto And Outing, Oil And Mining News, Development, California Country Life (four tab pages to start), for The Radio Fans, and News Of Fresno Lodges. All this was in addition to the regular news, the comics, the special magazine section. There were 60 pages over eight sections. It was, as promised, a "real" Sunday newspaper. Eight years later, in 1932, the Bee was to buy out its last vestige of competition – The Morning Republican. And with that purchase came an attempt at a monumental con job. The Bee would have done well to hark back and read that story by McClatchy on the advent of The Sunday Bee.

In its editions of March 21, 1932, the day it purchased the ailing Republican, The Bee announced, buried deep down in the story of the Republican purchase, that it would discontinue its Sunday edition. The Bee declared it was no longer necessary because all the important news was already in the Saturday paper. It would include the regular features, the comics, the magazine section, California Country Life – all of it. The Republican would be continued by The Bee as a morning paper, renamed The Fresno Tribune, and its Sunday issue would be continued.

It was probably the shortest-lived amputation in newspaper history. On the following Sunday, March 27th, there was no Sunday edition of The Bee.

Enraged subscribers reacted immediately. The Bee's switchboard was flooded with calls Sunday. And there was no letup on Monday. The public, in tune by now to the Sunday edition, would have none of it. One can picture the hurriedly called council of war in Bee offices that Monday. The harried phone operators believed the calls would never cease. The decision quickly was made. A headline at the top of the next day's edition, in bold type on Page 1, read:

Sunday Bee Reappears
To Serve All Bee
And Tribune Readers
The text:

"Came Sunday morning and no Sunday Bee.

"The telephone jangled and rattled with hundreds of calls bemoaning the lack of the Sunday paper which had become part of their routine life.

"The reduction of 10 cents in the monthly subscription rate was no consolation.

"Nor was a large Saturday issue carrying the features of a Sunday paper a satisfactory substitute.

"The Bee since its inception has tried in the best way to give its readers what they wished.

"And with subscribers wanting The Sunday Bee back it comes to life next Sunday as a seven-day paper for 95 cents a month, a combination Sunday paper of The Bee and Republican and Tribune at the same price which the Republican and the Bee each charged before their combination

"For the month of March only Bee and Republican subscribers will pay 85 cents, as previously announced.

"In Fresno and all other cities the Sunday paper will be delivered by regular carrier while in the county auto carriers will deliver to all Bee and Republican subscribers.

"Subscribers, except those served by mail, taking both the afternoon and morning papers will pay only 75 cents a month for the six-day morning service.

"Watch Sunday for an enlarged, improved Sunday paper." The Bee learned a valuable lesson. It doesn't pay to attempt to con the public. The people are too smart.

Robert P. Molander

6

Contesting for Readers

During the early period, both The Bee and the Republican ran contests designed to boost circulation. There were puzzles, with prizes such as wagons for boys, dolls for girls, crystal-set radios for adults, with "easy" instructions on putting them together. Then, September 28, 1924, The Bee announced its blockbuster, the contest to end all contests.

It was heralded on Page 1 and in a double page advertisement inside. The Bee offered $15,000 in prizes, capped with 10 new 1925 automobiles. First prize was to be a Cadillac touring sedan, top of the line and valued at $3,500.

The winners were to be based on "votes," which could be obtained only by selling subscriptions to The Bee. A person who sold a three-month subscription got 1,000 votes. A six-month subscription was worth 3,000 votes, on up to a three-year subscription worth 50,000. All subscriptions had to be paid in advance, and "everyone" would be a winner. Anyone who brought in a paid subscription was allowed to keep 10 percent of the cost. And The Bee kept an ace in the hole – its original offer stipulated that additional prizes could be added during the contest. That was far-sighted. On October 5th, the Republican entered the fray, announcing it would sponsor its circulation contest, with cars also to be given away. Again, the value of its prizes approximated $15,000. It was then that The Bee played its hole card. It would expand its prize list. First, with two more "grand prizes," a Dodge and a Durant.

And, A NEW HOME!

Yes, a two-bedroom home – "a dream home" – on Iowa Avenue in the new Sierra Vista Tract. The home's value, a whopping $8,750, according to The Bee, plus the two additional cars, hiked the prize total of the Bee's contest to $27,000, a figure the Republican never matched.

Boys and girls, men and women, hustled for subscriptions. The Bee never published a list of new subscribers, or printed how many it picked up. Neither did the Republican. But from almost-daily stories, the number must have been substantial. Enough to cover a $27,000 outlay? Probably not, although that figure could have been inflated with full-value costs, as opposed to the prices the newspapers actually paid in the marketplace.

The contest ended nearly three months later, and Basil T. Biswell, an auto supply-firm employee, won the home. The second prize, the Cadillac, was won by the daughter of Sheriff W.F. Jones. The new figure given for the total prize awards was $19,000.

In a key move on the last day of 1924, The Bee announced that Chester Rowell, former owner-editor of the Republican who had more recently been an editor of the San Francisco Chronicle, would open the New Year with the first of a series of editorials of his own choosing. They were to run daily, five days a week, on Page 1 at the top of Column 1. The Bee emphasized that Rowell's commentaries would not be edited, would be exclusive to The Bee, and that The Bee would not be responsible for the thoughts expressed. As it turned out, Rowell's commentaries were not particularly biting, and more often than not consisted of three or more subjects. His first column emphasized that his writings would be from a personal viewpoint, and might at times be at odds with The Bee's editorial policies. The columns were run under a standing headline: Chester Rowell's Editorials.

There were no real conflicts stemming from those columns, with Rowell relying mainly on commentary. Some of his early subjects were on the rebuilding of Europe after World War I, general health, and third terms for politicians. He maintained it was not important whether

Robert P. Molander

a president did or did not win a third term, which was legal in those days.

And he argued against politicians being forced to take intelligence tests, contending they would be as fatal to the politician who wanted to be referred to as "Just Plain Bill" as they would to the office holder who was listed in Dun & Bradstreet. On January 2nd, the day after Rowell's opening column ran, The Bee printed an editorial-page message saying three subscribers had canceled their subscriptions because The Bee had hired Rowell. The Bee maintained that many more subscribers had lauded the paper for having the guts to use Rowell as a commentator. The editorial claimed The Bee had a history of taking strong stands, and that a part of such policy would be to publish ideas, such as those of Rowell, which might conflict with Bee thoughts. It was becoming a stronger paper that was presenting all sides of all issues. "Chester Rowell provides an additional viewpoint," the editorial proudly pointed out.

In its first issue, The Bee had editorialized, in its "Why And Wherefore":

"The primary purpose of The Bee is to tell the news; to tell it fairly, simply and impartially; unfairly to hurt none, no matter how lowly; to favor none, no matter how powerful." It proved, in those early days, that it meant what it said, particularly regarding the portion about not favoring the powerful. It took on, in bold type, a mayoral hopeful, and a mayor, not to mention the Chamber of Commerce. The "hopeful" was Ned Prescott, a 1925 candidate for mayor who was backed by the Republican and who just happened to have been a member of the grand jury which had rejected the Hamman report. He was accused, in a Page 1 editorial written by Carlos McClatchy, with being the major force in the attempt to suppress the Hamman report.

McClatchy's lead paragraph: "The Hamman report, made by the expert employed by the previous grand jury, and suppressed until published by The Bee, did more than anything of recent years to clean up politics in Fresno County." McClatchy then declared that Prescott, who ran a garbage business, was unfit for public office. In return, the Republican accused The Bee of "mud-slinging." The Bee's candidate, Al E. Sunderland, won the election by a margin of 1,300 votes, with some 13,000 of the 21,000 eligible voters casting ballots.

The Chamber of Commerce, whose members were the city's movers and shakers, also wasn't too powerful for The Bee to tackle. The Bee was actively backing a proposal to construct Pine Flat Dam as a water conservation and flood-control instrument. So was the chamber. But its president, L.A. Nares, had land holdings that placed him in opposition to the proposed dam. The Bee editorialized that Nares and the entire Chamber Board of Directors should resign, with the chamber then to be reorganized.

The Chamber Board held a closed-door meeting, but one of those present leaked the agenda to The Bee. Behind those closed doors, The Bee reported, Chamber directors feared that if they resigned, their action would be construed as backing the newspaper's demand for the resignation or replacement of Nares. The Bee also wrote that one of the proposals made at that hearing was for businessmen to boycott the purchasing of advertising in The Bee. This, it was thought, would make this fledgling newspaper back down, toe the line, show it who really held the power in the city.

Carlos McClatchy's editorial answer again was immediate:

"There is no advertiser or combination of advertisers who at any time can control the editorial or news columns of The Bee." The main thrust of the editorial was to urge the Chamber to reorganize for the betterment of the city and county. There was no immediate reorganization of the Chamber, but there was no drop in The Bee's advertising columns, either. McClatchy had reasoned correctly that these hard-nosed businessmen were not buying Bee ads to do him or his newspaper a favor.

The attack on the mayor was a dilly. McClatchy and McLaughlin trained their big guns on His Honor, with the Republican mounting the defense. The Bee lost this major battle, probably the biggest print blowout of the newspaper war, but the loss, though painful, had the effect of increasing The Bee's determination to win the battle.

The skirmish didn't erupt overnight, exactly, but that comes close to describing the way it came about. In 1925, The Bee had backed Al E. Sunderland in the race for mayor. He easily defeated the Republican's candidate, Prescott. But Carlos McClatchy and H.R. McLaughlin quickly became disenchanted with the man they had helped to put in office just a few short months earlier. They concluded that they had

Robert P. Molander

erred, and in a big way. Politics makes strange bedfellows. The Bee had backed Sunderland in the election; the Republican had opposed him. Now, with The Bee attacking the man it had originally supported, it was left for the Republican to take a side. Predictably, the Republican switched, coming out on Sunderland's side.

The first indication came on September 4, 1925. In a Page 1 story, The Bee caustically noted that the mayor was taking a 15-day paid vacation after only four months in office. There was no editorial on the subject, but the implication was clear. The Bee had adopted a watchdog role, and although it had backed Sunderland in the mayor's race, it wasn't about to give him carte blanche.

On October 31, 1925, a police scandal erupted. Thomas J. Niceley, the U.S. prohibition officer for the valley, led a task force that arrested Police Captain Albert D. Trusdell, Detective Sgt. Guy H. Shoun and Sgt. Clifford Sayer, charging them with accepting bribes from bootleggers. The case was to go to the grand jury.

The following day, the Republican quoted Mayor Sunderland to the effect that he had masterminded the police investigation that resulted in the arrests. That afternoon, The Bee, more than a bit irate, quoted Niceley as saying that Sunderland's forces had bungled the investigation, tipping it off to the bootleggers and the involved cops, so that the arrests had to be made early, before the investigation was completed.

On March 13, 1926, the newspaper ran a screaming, black-face banner headline, running over seven of its eight Page 1 columns, demanding: Recall Mayor Al Sunderland. Below that, a drop headline asked:

Shall Fresno Suffer
Three More Years
Of His Reign?

In editorial form, this top story of the day, unsigned but bearing the unmistakable stamp of Carlos McClatchy, scorched Sunderland for the city's "high tax rate," pointed out that he had never defended himself after witnesses in the bootleg trial testified that he had allowed vice to run open with this objective: that fines totaling $60,000 could be assessed periodically to bolster the tax structure. The Bee charged the fines were alternated among the vice lords so that none would be hurt too much, and that all could "contribute." The Bee wrote:

-- "The mayor made no answer on the ground that he would be a witness in the police trials.

-- "The government either failed to call him (in the trial) or didn't dare to call him as its own witness and the mayor said nothing.

-- "And still the mayor remains silent before incriminating charges.

-- "The testimony in that police trial was very damaging to Mayor Sunderland.

-- "The police have had their trial before the federal court.

-- "The mayor should have his trial before the bar of public opinion in a recall."

The editorial continued:

"Month by month the mayor has piled up proof that he has neither the capacity, the judgment nor the temperament to serve Fresno efficiently as mayor.

"Impulsive, stubborn and not sound in judgment, Al Sunderland handles city affairs in a blundering fashion regardless of the charter and the ordinances.

"His violations of civil service rules and provisions have been the boldest of any city administration in California recently.

"His business judgments in city affairs applied three years more will be a heavy load for this city to carry.

"His segregation of city employees into friends and enemies, giving his friends what they desire and refusing enemies their legal rights, has destroyed in the police and fire departments the morale which comes only from the conviction that at the head of the city stands a man, who is impartial and unswayed by outside consideration.

"His reckless disregard of costs of government, his seeming ignorance that taxes must come from The People's pockets, make him a dangerous man to hold power, especially in the days when Fresno needs the quickest return from the depressed conditions that were here last year.

"It was Al Sunderland principally who forced through the high tax rates of last year.

"And if Al Sunderland be in office for the next budget in July, heaven help Fresno."

The Republican came out heavily on the mayor's side, claiming he was a competent office holder, was doing a fine job and that any thought of a recall election was ridiculous and would be an expensive waste of the taxpayers' money. Recall petitions were circulated, with The Bee urging Fresnans daily to sign them. It even advocated having them taken through the city's neighborhoods in the evenings, when working folks were at home. This was done

The recall was ruled to have enough valid signatures, and the petition was filed on June 7, 1926. The next day, the Republican charged in print that 94 of the signatures gathered were invalid. The Bee answered with a protest letter from J.J. Reese, the petition committee chairman, declaring the Republican story constituted an unwarranted attack, that the petition was valid. It was determined that even if the Republican story was correct, the petition still would have enough valid signatures.

The City Commission set the vote for July 23rd. But even the date itself became a matter of contention. With many Fresnans not registered to vote, The Bee demanded it be switched to Monday July 26th, reasoning that would give residents three additional days in which to register. But the majority of the City Commission went along with Sunderland, who demanded and got the earlier date.

Throughout the engagement, The Bee never printed Sunderland's side of the story. The newspaper leveled charge after charge, and Fresnan after Fresnan was quoted, saying the city needed a new mayor. But there was never a mention in The Bee's news pages of anyone who was on the mayor's side. On the other hand there never was a mention in the Republican of anyone who favored Sunderland's ouster. Neither side covered itself with glory. It was an example of news management at its best – or perhaps at its worst. Finally, on July 24, 1926, The Bee allowed Sunderland to "speak" in its news columns. In a Page 1 story, he was quoted to the effect that he had answered all allegations against him in a civil service hearing, all that he was legally required to do. And why, he asked, did "certain special interests which wanted to control local politics and the city" seek to have him ousted from office when he was guilty of nothing and was simply striving to make Fresno a better city?

The Bee answered in an editorial in the same day's paper. The head-line: Face Facts, Mayor Sunderland.

"Why?" it asked. "Because Sunderland is incompetent and extrava-gant," it answered itself, pointing out that Sunderland was "hired" as mayor by The People and they had the right to recall him. (Earlier, The Bee had written that those Fresnans signing the petitions were not necessarily against Sunderland, but were merely exercising their rights to determine on the ballot whether they wanted him in or out. In the editorial, The Bee contended the 3,900 citizens who had signed the peti-tion believed Sunderland was a bad mayor.)

During all this, The Bee was backing John D. Morgan, former police chief and now a businessman, for mayor. (In the event the voters ousted Sunderland, there was the provision on the ballot to name his successor.)

On July 13th, on Page 1, The Bee ran a copy of a ballot, and advised on how it should be marked: An X beside the recall "yes," and another X beside the name of Morgan. And on July 18th, The Bee published a Page 1 story with the heading, Elect John D. Morgan Mayor, Citizens' Plea. The story under it listed many citizens who backed Morgan for mayor. But if there were any residents of the city who would rather have retained Sunderland in office, The Bee never found them or, much more probable, neglected to seek them out. Once again it ignored "the other side of the story."

Coincidentally, or perhaps not, state Fire Marshal Jay W. Stephens came to town on July 18th and, in a speech, declared a recall election would hurt, rather than help, the city. He ripped the "howling minority" that was trying to wreck Fresno. The Republican played the Stephens story big on Page 1; The Bee downplayed it on Page 3. In an editorial, the Bee castigated these "outsiders" who were trying to run Fresno's affairs.

Finally, the election was held, and The Bee was trounced. Sunderland won, 5,789 to 3,532, a majority of 2,257 votes. Percentage-wise, it was near a 62-38 route. The Republican gave the result a banner Page 1 headline, with accompanying story and picture, an editorial advising Fresnans that they had voted properly, and that it was time to get back to the city's business. The Bee editorialized that the people had spoken, and that the newspaper accepted the result "cheerfully." Its only actual solace that day was the fact that its candidate, Morgan, led the other candidates with 4,120 votes. But that didn't matter, because those votes would have counted only if Sunderland had lost the recall. The Bee was left to lick its wounds, but did manage to have the last laugh. Sunderland ran for re-election, with the solid backing of the Republican. The Bee was equally adamant in favor of his opponent, Z.S. (Zeke) Leymel. Sunderland lost, and was never to hold public office again. The margin was decisive, nearly the same as Sunderland's when he beat back The Bee's recall movement. Leymel polled 7,060 votes, 2,381 more than the 4,679 drawn by Sunderland – approximately 60-40 in percentage.

The campaign coverage hadn't changed – the Bee ran laudatory stories daily on is candidate, with only negative mention of Sunderland. The Republican followed suit with Sunderland, largely ignoring Leymel.

7

Radio Station Purchased

As the advertising slogan goes, never underestimate the power of a woman. Even if you were C.K. McClatchy, the powerful owner and editor of The Sacramento Bee in the early 1920s, and especially if the woman in question was C.K.'s wife, Ella.

In probing discussions with his son, Carlos, C.K. described himself as "just a plain newspaperman, not in the radio business, and we are not going to be. That's the end of it, Carlos." The "it" in question was a radio station, an acquisition promoted by Carlos McClatchy, associate editor of The Sacramento Bee at the time. He was one of the first to envision radio's future success, at a time when scientists were still trying to apply Marconi's principles of wireless telegraphy to the transmission of voices and music.

Carlos was certain the scientists would succeed, and foresaw radio as the perfect news adjunct to the newspaper. But he couldn't convince his father, whose reception to the idea was less than cool. And coming from C.K., the denial well might have been taken as gospel – he was not a man to change his mind too easily or too often.

A lively discussion followed, with C.K. eventually retorting, "I can see no more reason why I should operate a radio station than a grocery store in conjunction with this newspaper." End of discussion, he thought. But it wasn't. Carlos had one more iron in the fire – his mother,

Ella. Carlos had told her of his problem, and that evening, over the dinner table, she said, "That is a wonderful idea of Carlos – about The Bee acquiring a radio station."

When C.K. recovered, he answered that The Bee was not going to acquire a radio station. She went on, as if he hadn't replied, striking a vulnerable spot in C.K.'s armor. "Radio's something new. It's the coming thing. I hope you are not getting too old, Charlie, to keep up with the visions of younger men." That did it. Her task completed in a few superbly chosen words, Ella left the men to their conversation, which was moved to the living room of the family home. C.K. took a lot of convincing, but Carlos finally got the job done, and his father acquiesced.

Thus, with Carlos in command, The Sacramento Bee became the first newspaper on the West Coast to operate a radio station. It was tiny KVQ, and it hit the airwaves from The Bee building on February 2, 1922. The station later became the highly successful KFBK. Coincidentally, KVQ went on air the same year – 1922 – that The Fresno Bee started publishing, with Carlos McClatchy again leading the way, as editor. That he was able to keep his hand in on both operations attested to his considerable talents.

Meanwhile, in Fresno, 50-watt Radio Station KMJ had been built by the San Joaquin Light and Power Corporation for short wave use during the building of power projects in the Sierra. The station was a hit-and-miss operation, and the few residents who owned radios rarely were given the luxury of printed logs on what would be presented, or the broadcast times. They turned their sets on, listening contentedly to, and marveling at, whatever happened to come over. Occasionally, the station provided public services, such as the 1925 city election results, which were supplied by The Bee and broadcast at 9 p.m. World Series baseball games also were aired by the station.

On June 10, 1925, The Fresno Bee bought KMJ, rather surreptitiously, as it turned out. The Radio Dealers Association of Fresno, composed of members who were in radio sales, was clamoring for a better local station. KMJ was the only game in town. The association named C.M. Cowan and C.A. Chandler to check the situation, and they made a deal with the owners of the corporation, getting an option to select the buyer.

Cowan and Chandler, granted the option by A. Emory Wishon, president of San Joaquin Light and Power, chose McClatchy as the buyer, in a move pushed by the business-savvy Carlos McClatchy. It's easy to understand why Wishon wouldn't want to sell to the McClatchys. The Bees in Sacramento and Fresno had taken hard stands against private ownership of power firms, a move understandingly opposed by San Joaquin Light and Power and other private power companies.

But the deal was made, and The Bee acquired possession of the station, running daily Page 1 stories through the month of June, boasting of its purchase. The programs consisted mostly of music, but not on set schedules. And news had not yet found its way into the fledgling Fresno airways. This was rectified on October 28, 1925, when The Fresno Bee started its "24 hours of news service." A nightly news summary was begun on KMJ, at 9:15 o'clock. It was to give its listeners "all the news you would read in the morning paper," i.e., the rival morning Republican. Included were sports scores, the day's final report on grape prices, and the weather. Outside news came from United News service.

The Bee was still operating the station from its cramped quarters in the power corporation building, surroundings which became familiar to some Bee staffers, including Carlos McClatchy and Managing Editor Bob McLaughlin, who weren't above playing records over the airwaves. On March 10, 1926, the Bee started operating KMJ from its new studios in the Bee building, via a 100-foot aerial raised on the company roof. Classical and jazz music were the order of the night, with the opening broadcast running from 7-11 o'clock. Many local artists performed, including the Clark Sisters playing their ukuleles. The Bee continued to utilize KMJ for evening sports scores and for late-breaking news. When Gene Tunney decisioned Jack Dempsey in 10 rounds in September, 1926, to win the heavyweight boxing title, the night of the famous "long count," KMJ flashed the result over the air, as "fast automobiles" were delivering Bee fight extras throughout the central valley.

A KMJ "first" came on September 13, 1928, when Fresno's Young Corbett III (Ralph Giordano) fought and won by decision over Sergeant Sammy Baker, the No. 1 world welterweight contender, in 12 rounds at Madison Square Garden in New York City. KMJ broadcast the fight "live" via simulation, with 1,000 seats provided in Courthouse Park for avid listeners. All seats were occupied, and hundreds more fans stood or sat on the turf and listened to the loudspeaker broadcast. Others listened in their homes over their radios.

Another big step forward came in 1929 when The Bee hooked up with Don Lee stations KHJ of Los Angeles and KFRC of San Francisco, giving local listeners "the best entertainment to be had on the coast." That same year, The Bee petitioned and later won approval of the Federal Communications Commission in Washington D.C. to increase its power from 100 to 1,000 watts.

On January 15, 1931, The Bee announced in a Page 1 story that KMJ would become the "New Morning Paper in Fresno." The headline and story:

The Morning Radio
Bee, New Morning
Paper For Fresno

"Good morning, folks. This is The Morning Radio Bee. While you're eating your hotcakes or ham and eggs let us tell you by radio all the news that has occurred the world over since The Fresno Bee went to press yesterday afternoon. Oh, yes, we are prepared to give you a 24-hour news service. The day's news by newspaper presses and the news of the night and early morning by a radio newspaper.

"In some such fashion will the cheery voice of the news crier come into your home by radio starting at 7:15 o'clock Tuesday morning. For a period of fifteen minutes – from 7:15 to 7:30 o'clock – he will give you a special all-night United Press wire and local and valley stories that have developed since The Bee of the day previous went to press. You won't have to bother about reading a newspaper at your breakfast table. A full and complete report in short, terse stories will come to you by The Morning Radio Bee.

"Maybe it will serve as your alarm clock. Maybe the good wife will bless you for getting to breakfast on time to hear The Morning Radio Bee. We know you'll like it and feel sure it will send you on your daily tasks in a happy, satisfied frame of mind.

"Just another service The Fresno Bee has to offer the good people of Fresno and the San Joaquin Valley and it won't cost you a cent, either, in money or time.

"Remember the starting date, next Tuesday morning at 7:15 o'clock on The Fresno Bee radio station. Don't be late."

The first KMJ studio was an office in the power company building, just large enough to hold a piano, the microphone and "two or three midget musicians," according to William F. Bragg, Bee reporter who moved to the fledgling KMJ and who was to become a noted writer of Western novels. Later, the studio was moved to the second floor of the Bee building.

KMJ, while dedicated to its pursuit of daily news, knew it needed to improve its daily fare, in a continuing struggle to offer the listening public an attractive variety. With this in mind, The Bee, in 1926, hired Molly Marshall, a well-known Fresno music personality, to be its program director and music critic. Miss Marshall, a native of Oakland, had attended Fresno schools and studied voice and opera in Los Angeles and New York City. She sang in operas in Los Angeles before moving to Fresno to live.

She soon found it was not difficult to attract talent for the station in its salad days. Nearly everyone who could play any musical instrument or sing a song wanted to be heard over the air. And better yet, they performed free. The following year, The Bee, with the help of KMJ and the knowledgeable Miss Marshall, took a giant step. It was Carlos McClatchy's brainchild, and it hit public print on December 29, 1927. The Page 1 banner, over 7 of the page's 8 columns, read: Mary Garden, Chicago Grand Opera Company, To Give Sapho Here, in smaller type, (Opera by Massenet).

Carlos McClatchy wanted opera in Fresno, and this was to be the first instance of such a coup by anyone in the growing city. The Bee ran daily Page 1 promotional stories on the opera, and KMJ joined in with daily promos. "Sapho" was presented to a sellout audience in the Fresno High School auditorium. (It was such a success that The Bee and KMJ the following year brought in Rosa Raisa in the opera "Norma.")

Miss Marshall was admittedly "scared stiff" at the thought of bringing Miss Garden and the Chicago Opera Company to Fresno, even more so when the train approached, carrying the star and the opera company. But the arrival had been well planned. At the station, Miss Garden was greeted by several men carrying huge bouquets of flowers. These included H.R. McLaughlin, The Bee's managing editor; Ed Higgins, the business manager; Frank Vore, sports editor; Joe Thorburn, a reporter pressed into service, and Fresno Mayor A.E. Sunderland.

Another coup by KMJ and The Bee, led by Miss Marshall, was the appearance of John Philip Sousa and his famous band, both in Hanford and Fresno. While in Fresno, she recalled, Sousa bought $100 worth of dried fruit packages to ship to friends in the East, and he gave a live interview over KMJ, in itself another coup. But Miss Marshall had plenty more. Included among the personalities she interviewed on the air were John McCormack, Feodor Chaliapin, Lawrence Tibbet, Amalila Galli-Curci, Marian Anderson, Ernestine Schuman-Heink, Lily Pons, Jose Hofman, Sergei Rachmaninoff, Artur Rubinstein, lgnace Paderowski, Rosa Ponselle, Richard Crooks, Risa Stevens, Yehudi Menuhin, Fritz Kreisler, Jascha Heifitz and Pablo Casals.

Of particular interest to Fresno-area listeners were the Crockett Mountaineers, a family from Fowler that specialized in hillbilly music. The group broke in over KMJ Radio and went on to the big time in New York and Hollywood. But the Mountaineers nearly didn't get the chance. They were so poor, and shy, that they at first refused to be interviewed by Miss Marshall and Bragg in the family's two-room shack. They finally acquiesced when offered free time over the airwaves, and went on to make it big in the entertainment world.

In a way, it was similar to Bragg's introduction to radio. The McClatchys weren't accustomed to "no" for an answer. Bragg, Bee reporter and deskman, was asked by Carlos McClatchy if he knew anything about radio, and he answered, "No, I don't even own a radio." The quick answer from the boss, "Well, here's where you learn." Bragg stayed on the radio job for "three hectic years." The chief engineer was Norman (Hap) Webster, who had been a radio operator on the Bear, the famous Coast Guard ice cutter. He was to do a creditable job, although he didn't get along well with piano players, contending their use of the instrument's pedals caused signal "bumps" on the air.

Through the years, KMJ switched to an all-news and talk format, with emphasis on local morning, noon and late afternoon news and

Robert P. Molander

feature blocks. Listener call-in shows also were added. And KMJ became the broadcast home of Fresno State College, later California State University, Fresno, football, basketball and baseball games. The station remained successful on the air through the ensuing years, going heavily into news and retaining its No. 1 rating as many rivals came into being throughout the San Joaquin Valley. This continued until 1987, when McClatchy sold KMJ and its sister station, KNAX-FM, started in 1949 as KMJ-FM, to the Henry Broadcasting Company, a San Francisco-based chain.

The second C.K. McClatchy, then president of McClatchy Newspapers, said in a press release, "We've determined the company's future is in newspapers – its primary activity since 1857. We've been in radio since the 1920s and we leave it with mixed feelings, but we believe our efforts are best devoted to the publishing of quality newspaper.

8

The Newspaper War Ends

Throughout this era, The Bee trumpeted its claim that afternoon news-papers were by far the best in publishing the latest news – today's news today. On June 26, 1926, for example, it pointed out on Page 1 that the previous day's paper had featured complete stories on the discovery of evangelist Aimee Semple McPherson alive and well in Arizona (it had been rumored she had drowned in the ocean off Los Angeles), that three actors bound for Fresno from Modesto had been killed in a car accident, that Exchequer Dam had been dedicated, that the sports section had carried stories on tennis at Wimbledon and golf in England, and others, proving "the superiority of the afternoon paper in handling the news from all points of the world – the day's news today."

"The Bee covered at least a half-dozen stories of world-wide, national, valley and local interest in such a manner that the morning paper had to follow without a single new detail of importance."

It was heady stuff, and true, on many days, and it was made possible by The Bee's floating deadlines – usually from 3:00 p.m. to 3:30 p.m. The Bee also claimed its late extras beat the competition, even though they were hawked by the newsboys late in the evening. Extras were run at the drop of hat – for sporting events such as Jack Dempsey vs. Gene Tunney in boxing, Cal-USC in football, and for elections. For

World Series baseball games, there would be nightly extras peddled by the newsboys.

The end was nearing for the Republican. It could have been prophesied as early as 1928. The Bee was on the upswing, the Republican fighting to maintain its circulation, but constantly slipping. It hadn't always been that way. The Osborn brothers had the circulation advantage in the early 1920s, and openly derided the brash newcomer.

The Hotel Californian, which opened its doors in 1923 as the finest in the valley, ran large, special sections in both papers to announce its grand opening. H. Wingate Lake, who leased and operated the hotel, invited the editorial staffs of both papers to a sumptuous banquet to thank them for the jobs they had done in publicizing the opening. The hotel had been built for the magnificent sum of more than a million dollars – $720,000 for the structure, $160,000 for the site and $150,000 for furnishings.

It would certainly have been a lavish party, but it was not to be. As Lake was to recall, he was forced to cancel it after informing McLaughlin at The Bee that Chase and George Osborn told him, "We won't permit our staff to sit at the same table with that damned Bee bunch." Lake was apologetic, but firm. He didn't dare cross the Osborns at that time.

The Bee's first real measure of revenge came in 1924, when on January 19th it bought the fast-sinking Herald, whose circulation had plunged to about 6,000 daily, with declining advertising and with employees racing to the bank each payday before the payroll was depleted.

The Osborn brothers had bought the Herald in 1915 with a loan from their father, and went further into debt to him when he bankrolled them with an additional $1 million so they could buy the Republican from Chester Rowell in 1920. They were draining both papers dry in an attempt to repay the loans, and something had to give. It was the Herald, which they sold for $250,000 to William Glass, owner of the Fresno Republican Printery and former business manager of the Republican. That sale came on July 11, 1922, at the time the Bee building was being constructed. In late 1923, Glass sold the paper to a Los Angeles syndicate, and it was from that group that The Bee bought it. Glass had remained on as editor. The Bee did not announce the purchase price, but it was thought to be equal to, or slightly above, the quarter of a million dollars Glass had paid for it.

Jack R. Goddard, then assistant to City Editor William E. Lockwood at The Bee, recalled the day his paper took over the Herald. "Carlos McClatchy told me to put on my hat and coat, that we were going over to take over ownership of the Fresno Herald," Goddard said. With McLaughlin, they took the short ride to the Herald building, and entered Glass' office. He immediately threatened to challenge the legality of the sale, Goddard recalled, but soon calmed down. The takeover was completed shortly, the Herald employees were given a week's pay each, and the Bee took over the Herald's subscription list. Some of the Herald employees were hired by The Bee, but most of them were left to seek jobs elsewhere. The Herald was a memory.

There was now just one afternoon daily in Fresno – The Bee. It was time to train the big guns on the Republican, and the Osborn brothers. That The Bee bore no malice towards Glass was shown a few years later when it backed him in his successful race for a City Commission seat.

The Osborn brothers detested The Bee, and would never have willingly sold out to McClatchy. But they never were really in the game. They had their big chance to bow out gracefully, in 1928, when an Eastern syndicate offered them $1.5 million in cash for the newspaper. They refused that offer. Then came the Great Depression – they might have survived longer in better times – and they finally sold out for a paltry $250,000, most of which they had to pay out to others. At that. it was better than being forced into bankruptcy, which would have come about in three more months. The McClatchy purchase of the Republican allowed the Osborns to keep their dignity, but little else.

In 1920, when the Osborns had purchased the Republican, it was, under the guidance of Chester Rowell, widely recognized as one of the best-edited and best money-making papers of its size in the nation. But it was never to reach those heights again. According to William E. White, Fresno banker and investment consultant, the Republican had only one good year after the Osborns took over. That was in 1927, when the paper netted a $75,000 profit.

White continued:

"In 1926 when I became manager of the old Pacific Southwest Trust and Savings Bank, the Republican owed us $38,000 and we held a mortgage on their company car and truck-storage garage. They went from bad to worse – gross mismanagement would be my verdict – and in 1930 we compelled them to deposit all their receipts with us and we handled all their expenses and operation costs with overdrafts. These totaled as much as $25,000 every month.

"The Republican finally owed us $25,000 in overdrafts, plus the $38,000 mortgage, was in debt to the Zellerbach Paper Company for $68,000, and we began finding other little bills they owed here and there. We decided that since the Osborns didn't want to sell out on their own, we would have to force them to sell if any of the creditors were to get paid."

White contacted a newspaper broker, who informed him that (in 1932) the only people who were interested in buying the Republican were the McClatchys.

(The Bee would have had a much tougher time of it in the 1930s if the Osborns had accepted that $1.5 million offer in 1928. White recalled that a man entered his office, said he was from Cleveland, showed White a bank draft for $250,000 and said he had a letter of credit for $1 million more, and wanted to buy the Republican. White wouldn't bet his life on it, but he said he had very good reason to believe the man was fronting for Scripps-Howard, a national, reputable newspaper chain.

(The man from Cleveland said he was empowered to go as high as $1.5 million, but the Osborns held out for $2 million, and the deal fell through. It was the Osborns' last shot at viability in the Fresno newspaper world. And they had unwittingly given The Bee a much easier road to travel. Scripps-Howard was on the rise nationally, and would have been a much more competitive foe for the Bee through the years.)

But back to White's recollections:

"I went to a broker who handled the sale of the Herald, and he said other papers weren't interested. They weren't interested because of the run-down condition of the paper and all its mechanical equipment."

The Osborns obviously were desperate, in dire financial straits. Finally, they turned to their enemy of ten years for salvation. The final agreement came with White and a broker handling the transaction for the Osborns in the forced sale. The Osborns didn't even hire an attorney to negotiate the sale, apparently trying to keep expenses to the barest minimum.

White recalls those terminal days:

"We finally arranged a tentative deal with Carlos McClatchy and The Bee, and set a final negotiation meeting in the Californian Hotel. It was attended by The Bee's Sacramento attorney, Alex Ashen; a Fresno attorney, Ed Kellas, representing our bank; the Zellerbach Paper Company's attorney from San Francisco; the broker, and myself. I arranged for the Osborn brothers to remain in an upstairs room until our negotiations were completed. We remained in the hotel room all day, until 9:30 o'clock that night, with the attorneys working out various details of the contract of sale, one provision being that the Osborns couldn't sell the press, Linotype machines or mechanical equipment in Fresno County. When we got the papers all fixed, I called the Osborn brothers to come down from the room where I had them stashed, and they signed the contracts without even reading them. I then called up Ralph Heaton, manager of the main Fresno office of the Bank of America.

"I arranged for him to get down at the bank at 6 o'clock the next morning to issue a cashier's check for $250,000, the price paid for the Republican. Although Carlos said all he was interested in was getting the so-called good will, and circulation not amounting to much, I feel if he had waited a few months, he could have gotten the whole shebang for nothing, since the Osborns were faced with sure bankruptcy.

"When we got through paying the Republican's debts, plus the newspaper broker's $10,000 commission, the Osborns only had $25,000 left for themselves, plus a few thousand they got for the mechanical equipment. George Osborn didn't particularly want to sell – he thought they could still make a go of the paper – but Chase Osborn was anxious to dump the paper, since he never had much real interest in it.

"We wanted to rush the final deal through before Carlos found out what was happening, what shape the Republican really was in – although he was an extremely able man and I'm not sure he didn't know everything that was going on. In fact, I heard afterward that he felt he was doing a fellow publisher something of a favor by saving him from the disgrace of bankruptcy."

The final nail had been hammered into the Republican's coffin. The war was over. The Bee had triumphed, and was to prosper through the years.

ADDENDUM

Mrs. Margaret Rowell Popovich, wealthy wife of former Fresno Bee City Editor George Popovich, was a niece of Chester Rowell, former owner-editor of the Republican. Her father was Milo L. Rowell, pioneer Fresno businessman and a cousin of Chester Rowell. She mused about the Republican sale:

"My father told me he had told the Osborns if they ever were interested in selling the Republican he wanted the first opportunity to consider its purchase, either by himself or through a syndicate.

"Just before the sale was announced by The Bee, Chase Osborn came to our home and asked for my father, who was out of town on business. When my mother offered to give him the name of the hotel where my father could be reached, Mr. Osborn dropped his shoulders in a dejected manner and said, 'Never mind. Maybe I'll see him when he gets back.' I don't know what might have happened had he seen my father, but I'm sure he would have made an effort to keep the Republican going as a separate paper because of its long background with the family."

9

Remembering Carlos[1]

On January 17, 1933, Carlos Kelly McClatchy, the only editor of The Fresno Bee during its first decade, died at the home of friends in San Mateo. The cause of death was listed as double influenza pneumonia. He had been ill only a few days. His wife, Phebe, and his father, C. K., were at his bedside.

McClatchy was just 41 years old but had spent 20 of those years in the family's newspaper business. He started his career as a reporter for The Sacramento Bee after his graduation from Columbia University in 1911. He served as The Bee's capital correspondent in Sacramento and did a stint as the paper's Washington correspondent. After his Army service in World War I, he became associate editor of The Sacramento Bee, a post he held until he moved to Fresno to establish The Fresno Bee in 1922.

In 1923, he was named general manager of the McClatchy Newspapers in addition to his duties as editor of The Fresno Bee. In that capacity, he negotiated the purchases of the Fresno Herald and the Fresno Republican, and, with his father, the purchase of the Sacramento Star.

---

1 Carlos McClatchy's complete obituary is included in the Appendix of this book)

"In the passing of Carlos McClatchy the West loses one of the most brilliant, progressive and dynamic of its newspaper personalities," said the story that ran in the Fresno, Sacramento and Modesto Bees reporting his death. "Coming from a family of eminent California journalists – his grandfather, James McClatchy, founder of the Sacramento Bee, being a pioneer in the newspaper field – young McClatchy, for he was only in his forty-first year, had a remarkable career."

Following his death, the California legislature paid tribute to McClatchy in a formal resolution, and the family received hundreds of letters and telegrams of condolence from around the country. In editorials, newspapers from around California joined in mourning McClatchy's passing.

" . . . he had made himself known as one of the ablest newspaper executives in the West," said the San Francisco Call Bulletin. " ... a brilliant newspaperman," said the Stockton Independent.

"His loss is most deeply realized by his colleagues in the newspaper profession, but will be felt by the whole state," noted the San Francisco Examiner.

Years after his death, Fresno Bee employees and other Fresnans whose paths he crossed, also had some thoughts about Carlos McClatchy:

DON CASTELAZO, editorial – "Carlos was always at the office. He kept to the office, never got out among people. He was a very low-key person. He apparently had these ideas for the paper, all right. He wasn't just a figurehead. When they would put an extra out, Carlos himself would take the papers down the street to sell them.

"Carlos used to pick up people. Kinda befriend them. I don't know where he found them. They used to come up to his office with him. He'd stake 'em to stuff. Sort of like tramps. Give 'em money, things like that. He was very convivial, you might say. He did a lot of drinking. In the office, you could never tell. I never saw him drinking on the job.

"We used to have big parties in Carlos' day. Christmas parties. Top floor of the Fresno Hotel. The whole paper was invited. A couple hundred guests. Dinner, and a lot of bootleg booze. Steak dinner. The cops? They weren't invited.

"Carlos would rent the whole top floor of the Hotel Fresno. The Bee had several of those parties – about two or three of them, as I remember – during prohibition. They'd be on Sunday night, and would last until midnight. No shows or anything like that. No poker games. Carlos would foot the bill for the parties. They were appreciation dinners. We'd get the booze from a rum runner. Carlos got good, imported stuff. Whiskey, gin, mostly gin.

"After Carlos died, and Eleanor (McClatchy) took charge, no more booze was allowed in the (Bee) building. Duke Millard (business manager) used to have parties, right in the building, with lots of liquor, until he got stepped on for that. So did editorial. And the greasy spoon (Babe's) across the alley, we had parties there when we got kicked out of the building. We'd take our own booze over there. Babe didn't care.

"The Bee ran an extra in November, 1924, on Coolidge's victory, It was sold by the thousands. Carlos devised a way to inform the public immediately: He arranged for whistles and searchlight beacons atop the Pacific Southwest Bank building. An operator rode a swaying crow's nest on the spire atop the bank, and flashed a white light, the pre-arranged signal for Coolidge."

JAY CALKINS, pressman – "The press was running, and we were running right along with a 16-page paper on when a gear went out, and we couldn't run any more. We were about halfway through the last edition. They called up the business manager, and he called Carlos. Here comes Carlos down into the pressroom. He says, 'What can we do?' Well, the only thing we could do was to cut down the size of the paper. And we cut it down to eight pages, kicking out the unit that was giving us trouble. Carlos said, 'All right, spare no expense. I don't care what it costs. But get this paper out.' So we printed the eight pages, and I tell you ... it was so late then, that they had the district managers out in the street stopping anyone that would come along. 'Give you $10, take a bunch of papers to Selma.' '$20 to Bakersfield.' Normally they got there by train or bus, but they had already gone. But we got them out.

"When they first started up the Scott press, Carlos wanted to have his picture taken, pressing the button to make the press run. They told him, 'Oh no, you can't do that. You're not a pressman, and only pressmen can start the press.'

"'Well,' Carlos said, 'by gosh, it's my press, and I can start it if I want to.'

"They had a big argument about it. But he was a good, nice fellow, and he did get to start it. They finally decided, well, he wants to start the press and everybody liked him, so they made him an honorary member of the pressroom union. So he pressed the button, and they took his picture.

"Carlos always looked like a bum, right off the railroad jungle. His hair was uncut, his shoes always needed polishing – they were always scuffed up. His pants never had any press in them. He just didn't care much about what he looked like. Anytime you saw him, he was always happy about seeing you. You'd never know he had a dime in the world. If he liked you – and he liked almost everyone – you were in his favor all the time.

WARD GRIMES, reporter – "Carlos was a good guy. He smoked a pipe most of the time. Quite often, C.K. would come down. When the word got around that C.K. was in, everybody would get rid of their smokes. He didn't go for smoking, disapproved of it. He didn't say they couldn't, but everybody snuffed them out when he came in.

"Carlos was very friendly, Once, he was going to Spain. He wanted me to learn Spanish, to go with him as an interpreter. I couldn't learn it, couldn't do it. So I lost that trip. I tried for six months.

"Once, Carlos was arrested for drunk driving. C.K. came down and made him write the story himself. It ran on Page 1.

"C.K. came down three or four times a year, but Carlos ran the paper, and good. Carlos was the typical newsman of that day – aggressive. There weren't any press conferences in those days, and we had to go out and get the stories. He saw to that."

RAY W. HAYS, prominent Fresno attorney – "That man, McClatchy, had the most brilliant mind of any individual I've ever known. I recall that Carlos said the Osborn brothers, owners of the Republican, wanted to get out of the newspaper business and they (the McClatchys) saw a good opportunity to enter a rich agricultural area. Carlos told me he felt Fresno was destined to have great potential growth, and this was at a time in 1921 when we were still just a small country town. Carlos anticipated and visualized the future growth of Fresno better than those of us sitting on Main Street. He seemed to have an inner sight into what

Robert P. Molander

the future held in store for us, and a look around at what Fresno is today (1959) shows he was right.

"It was not long after the Bee had begun operations in Fresno, and the national convention of the American Legion was upcoming in San Francisco. I remember that Carlos had said something about wanting to go to the convention, so I called him up and asked him to go with me, but he seemed reluctant to go. I finally called again when it was nearly time to leave for the convention and asked Carlos if he still planned to go, and would he join me in making the trip by train.

"He finally agreed, but still seemed a bit reluctant about accepting my invitation. Finally, as we took off on the train from Fresno, I opened my overnight bag and pulled out a bottle and said, 'Let's have a drink to our old war days in France.' Whereupon Carlos' eyes bugged out and he smiled widely and said, 'I might as well confess now why I was so reluctant to accept your invitation to attend the Legion convention. I thought you were a damned teetotaler.'

"We intended to spend only three days at the Legion convention, but we had such a good time we ended up staying there for a whole week."

R.R. KUHN, former district manager of Zellerbach Paper Company in Fresno – "I wish to emphasize one thing that pointed to the measure of the man when The Bee took over the Republican. Although he probably could have forced the sale at a price of not over $125,000, Carlos McClatchy, then the editor of The Bee, insisted on paying $250,000, so that all the creditors would be paid in full."

CHARLES McNALLY, composing room foreman: "I met Carlos McClatchy in my first week at The Bee (1926.) Don Stewart, (composing room foreman) said, 'Go down to Carlos' office; he wants to see you.' I wondered what I had done to get in trouble in the first week. When I got there, he shook my hand as a new employee and said, 'Some of your mail got in with mine, and I want to apologize for opening it.' He could just as have well marked it 'opened by mistake.'

"Carlos had a soft spot in his heart for an Irish printer named Jack Sullivan. Sullivan was very loyal to the company, even to the point of selling extras on the street corners on his off day. Jack had a habit of wrecking saloons on Saturday nights after he was discharged from the

Navy in World War I. It was said Carlos had standing bail ready for Jack.

"Carlos had a habit of coming to the composing room at night. One cold winter night he and Jack and a traveling printer, or 'tramp printer,' were standing at the urinal in the composing-room rest room. Jack said to Carlos, 'Look at you with that fancy hundred-dollar overcoat, and that poor soul freezing.' Carlos took off his coat and gave it to the traveler and said to Jack, 'How am I going to get home without freezing?' Jack said, 'You'll find out how the other half lives, and you have only four miles to go.' Carlos took a cab."

ED ORMAN, sports editor – "Carlos didn't have much to do with sports. He was more politically minded. One day Al Madison, who was running a bowling alley, brought up some bowling scores, and he brought me a little bottle of whiskey --white mule or something – and I dropped it on the floor and broke the damned bottle. About noon that day, I got a call from Lockwood, and I said, 'Here goes.' I thought it was about the whiskey bottle. Carlos, Lockwood and Mac were in the office. Carlos said, 'Ed, can you get me a couple of tickets for the game this afternoon (Fresno State College-Hardin Simmons in football.) I don't want any passes; I want to pay for 'em.' I said, 'Oh, yes.' Boy, was I relieved.

"One time, when The Bee was about to knock the Republican out of the box, Carlos had a meeting of staff members. I remember him making a talk at the old Hotel Fresno. He said, 'No one person has created the success of The Bee so far. Everybody has helped.'

"Carlos came to me once and said, 'Do you think you could get Young Corbett interested in training my three boys?' I did. He used to take them out on roadwork. I don't know if he ever boxed with them.

"Carlos didn't like the way we were placing halos around the heads of the coaches. He said, 'They don't create any of their players; they just coach them.' If Carlos were living now, he'd go crazy. The way these guys – TV and radio ... 'You're not supposed to elevate them with a halo around their head,' he said."

GEORGE POPOVICH, city editor – "W.G. Weaver was The Bee's first circulation manager. He didn't last long. Carlos fired him after

Robert P. Molander

Weaver demanded that his divorce suit be kept out of the paper. The suit ran in the paper, too.

"Among the fonder memories of early-day employees are those having to do with the anniversary parties staged with the cooperation of Carlos. It was in the fall of 1923, with the first October 17th anniversary of the Bee's founding upcoming soon, that a group of rugged individualists asked Carlos' approval of, and financial aid for, an office party. A stag. Prohibition was still on the books and devious arrangements were necessary to obtain the necessary refreshments. The parties were devoted to strictly masculine entertainment – stories, a little poker or dice, or just plain-and-fancy drinking. They took their whiskey neat.

"The day Carlos' death was announced in the editorial department in January, 1933, saw tears in the eyes of many a hard-bitten staffer who knew they had lost a real friend and a great newspaperman.

"Typical of his foresight and astute business ability, Carlos, recognizing the inroads of radio broadcasting stations on newspapers, bought the San Joaquin Light & Power Co.'s 50-watt station. Wanting the station to be first-class, he told his business manager to buy a completely new transmitter, which in those days sold for $15,000. Hap Webster, who had made his own radio receivers before he was 12, was hired as the station's first engineer. He told Carlos he could rebuild the station into a strong one with the expenditure of just a few thousand dollars, and would not have to spend the $15,000 on a new transmitter.

"Carlos told him to go ahead, and when the job was finished, a Westinghouse radio engineer told Carlos that the remodeled transmitter was in far better condition, and was better than the one his company had offered for the $15,000. He said Webster had 'added things even our own engineers had never heard of.' The station, KMJ, first went on the air for The Bee on June 12, 1925, with William F. Bragg named to be its first announcer-manager.

"One Saturday night, after I had worked all day and most of the night on a big story involving a federal farm board loan of millions of dollars to the raisin industry, Carlos thought the story so important to the valley economy that he ordered an extra press run and told the circulation manager to deliver the paper to every vineyardist in the valley, whether a regular subscriber or not.

"With the first edition out of the way, Carlos invited me to join him for a midnight supper, having scooped the Republican on the story. When I told him I was on the dog watch until 2 a.m., he said he would speak to the acting city editor and see if he wouldn't let me off. He returned a few minutes later. 'George,' he said, 'there are city editors and then there are city editors. I'm informed they have no one to take your place at this hour so I'll wait until you're through.' And he did, and at 2 a.m. we took off for the juiciest steak dinner a Broadway cafe had to offer, and wound up our private celebration in the wee hours of the morning."

RALPH S. HEATON, vice president and manager of the main Fresno Branch, Bank of America, a man not known as a supporter of The Fresno Bee. He was reminiscing about his early days in San Francisco, where he knew many veteran Bay Area newsmen: "The greatest newspaperman of them all, for my book, is your own Carlos McClatchy down at The Bee. He knows more in five minutes than most men know in a lifetime. And it doesn't make any difference what field you may be discussing. Take my own business of banking. Carlos had as good a grasp of financial affairs as I do, and I've been a banker all my life. He is one of the best-informed men I've ever known."

GEORGE F. SHARP, city legislative commissioner: "Carlos had one of the greatest heads and the best newspaper brains I've ever heard of. It was marvelous to behold, considering the short time he had resided here. One of the greatest things about Carlos was his tremendous drive, as well as his keen brain. When he went into a campaign, he was in it up to the hilt every minute. He figured out angles, dug up facts, made contacts and directed the entire campaign.

"The only time I recall Carlos being put out with me and J.V. (J.V. McClatchy, Carlos' cousin and The Bee's first business manager) was when I got J.V. to sign a petition with me asking the city to install electroliers around the blocks in which the Fox-Wilson Theater and The Bee buildings were located. Carlos was opposed to The Bee asking any favors of anybody.

"In those days we worked for the benefit of all the people and if there was some public issue which Carlos thought The Bee should endorse, he got behind it with every facility at his command. When it came to political campaigning, you couldn't fool Carlos. He was just too smart and the politicians found out he never could be used.

"When I campaigned for re-election, Carlos would have an informal meeting of the clan and he would say, 'How about seeing this person and that man' and so on, figuring out angles that would help the campaign. And he would insist on me going out and shaking hands with every damned voter in town.

"I recall that Carlos helped promote the first major improvements in the Roeding Park Zoo, stimulated the planting of more shade trees; directed the campaigns for public ownership of the water and garbage companies, brought good music to the city and did many other things to build up our community into the fine city it is today (1959.)"

GEORGE S. SMITH, second business manager of The Bee. In the summer of 1923, Smith was recruited to become The Bee's business manager, succeeding J.V. McClatchy, son of Sacramento Bee publisher V.S. McClatchy: "I told them I wasn't interested because I was making good money in my real-estate business. But they offered me a three-year contract whereby I participated in a bonus arrangement on increased advertising, so I took the position. In fact, I was so set in my decision against going back into the newspaper business (Smith had been circulation manager and business manager of the Fresno Tribune and the Fresno Herald for 15 years) that I told Carlos he couldn't pay me enough money to take the job. He told me to write my own contract, so I went to federal Judge George Cosgrave, then an attorney, and told him to put in a high salary and a bonus arrangement, and a clause that I could devote as much time as needed to my real-estate business.

"I was sure that Carlos and James (J.V.) McClatchy wouldn't accept the contract, and sure enough James objected, but only to the clause about still handling my real-estate business. But he said to leave the contract at the Bee office and the next morning he called to say they had signed it without any changes and to report for work the following Monday.

"One of the incidents I recall during my tenure was one of the few times The Bee ever lost a local election. It was the attempted recall (1926) of Mayor A.E. Sunderland.

"While then, as now, The Bee maintained a rigid rule of no interference by the business office with the editorial policies, Carlos did ask my advice on some political matters, although he always made it plain he never had to accept it. I told him that Sunderland was too popular and that he couldn't be recalled, and that a recall move by The Bee would cost us heavily in circulation. The Bee's candidate, John Morgan, an early-day police chief, was defeated easily, as was the recall move. And we lost nearly 5,000 subscribers."

(Smith had been right, and Carlos McClatchy knew in advance of the election that Smith was right, but stuck by his guns and stayed with certain-loser Morgan, who he thought was the better man for the job.)

WILLIAM E. WHITE, banker, investment counselor, after the purchase of the Republican by The Bee: "I'll tell you what they'll say. They'll tell you The Bee is a big octopus, that 'we are killing off our competition.' But those businessmen who tell you that were the same businessmen who refused to give the Republican sufficient advertising revenue to keep it going."

PHEBE McCLATCHY CONLEY, widow of Carlos McClatchy: "Carlos came to Fresno and got things ready for the inauguration of The Fresno Bee. J.V. (Jim) McClatchy came down later with his wife, Hazel. J.V. and his wife didn't stay long. They never bought a home in Fresno. They lived in the Fresno Hotel while they were here. Jim was a great friend of Carlos, and they remained friends after the Sac split. But he never stayed here long, and I never knew why not, whether he was recalled from Sacramento, or whether he and Hazel didn't like it down here.

"They were well-received, as was I. I was very timid about coming to Fresno, partly because I was very self-conscious about our anti-temperance attitude, and I thought – I had a feeling – all the liquor people would be strong for us, and all the others would be against us. Well, that was an illusion, because we were well received by everybody, and anybody who had connections with us entertained us and made us feel at home. There wasn't any evidence that I could see of any resentment against The Bee or any of its attitudes.

Robert P. Molander

"I think they had a feeling that the morning paper was conservative to an extreme degree, and the town was growing, and there was an opportunity for a different point of view, and The Bee immediately started in with a different point of view, so that there were choices for people to take – which paper they liked better – which they had not had before. The evening paper – the Herald – didn't amount to much, and it was failing.

"I think Carlos made a thorough study of the situation, and he was doing that before the decision was made (to start a paper in Fresno.) I'm sure it was his decision to do it. He wanted to expand. Carlos was able to do this one thing, and he was the spark plug, although Sacramento kept a tight hold over what went on. He went back and fourth. (He) was constantly under instruction and cooperation with Sacramento headquarters. But it was his idea, and he was the spark plug that did it.

"He also was the one who got active and busy people, both in advertising and the circulation, which was so important, and he was the one who promoted the activities out in the valley and the various small towns. That was vigorously pursued.

"For a while he wanted to expand as far as Bakersfield, but that was squelched. Probably wisely. He didn't do it personally, but he had a very vigorous staff.

"I was (a sounding board for Carlos.) Carlos talked over practically everything with me. We discussed things. And he accepted me. We reached joint opinions on a great many things. And he even finally arranged that he was going to have a column that he called The Editor's Wife to be on the page opposite the editorials. And it would give me a chance to express things that I was interested in and cared about. They might not agree with the editorial (however, Mrs. McClatchy's column never materialized).

"I knew that he was in close touch with his father at all times, and he had to go back and forth to Sacramento once a week. And he drove and it got too much for him. He was so tired that he couldn't do it. And he was having other troubles, I guess. And anyway, we got a driver, I remember that The Bee supplied him with a driver to drive him back and forth. So it indicates to me that C.K. kept close control over what was going on down here.

"Very many times Carlos would have ideas – he would want to do something new – and it got squelched. One of them was important. Carlos knew the head of that famous Santa Barbara paper, Mr. Tom Stork, had in mind to sell. Carlos was in touch with the newspaper, and with Mr. Stork. He went back and forth. And he wanted, at that time, to buy the paper. For some reason, he (Stork) had it in mind to sell to The Bee. He didn't want to sell to any old person. But he and Carlos were close, and understanding.

"But C.K. put his foot down, wouldn't let him go on with it. And that was a big disappointment to Carlos. I don't think anybody else knew about it. It was just in the family.

"Carlos was very strong in his ideas. However, he wasn't the boss. His father was still the boss, and Carlos had to be curbed in some of his ideas. He never was the boss. Locally, he was. He handled local problems, and he developed the paper, you can be sure of that. He had a hand in policy, but he didn't have the final decision. His father always kept his control."

Shortly after Carlos McClatchy's untimely death, Fresno Bee employees received a letter, copied and posted on bulletin boards, under the name of his father, Charles K. McClatchy. It was dated October 16, 1933. It follows:

"The whirligig of Time has brought around the tenth anniversary of the founding of The Fresno Bee. To you, one and all, under the guiding hand of a brilliant captain who is gone, I owe the fact that said journal has achieved its present enviable position.

"It required faith, patience, pluck, unflinching tenacity, and undeviating loyalty. And these, my friends, you have shown in marked degree.

"For that I extend to you, one and all, my heartfelt thanks.

"And now you will pardon me if from the lips of age comes a few words of counsel to battling youth.

"The Fresno Bee today is staunch and steady. I would have it still further progress and prosper. But I want it – no matter what success may accompany it in the future – never to forget the lessons it undoubtedly learned during its advancing days.

"I want it ever to be kind, and thoughtful, and considerate with all except crooks, big and little. It would be a mighty poor world to live in if we all thought alike. And so I wish its columns ever to be open, within reason, to those who differ with it, no matter if in their difference they resort to caustic denunciation. For a newspaperman who cannot stand abuse has no business in the newspaper profession.

"To those of its force who more particularly are the connecting links between the paper and the public I particularly desire that they should continue in the path they always have trodden – the path of all-around civility, and courtesy, and helpful treatment to one and all. I would like it to be known everywhere that The Fresno Bee will pay as much attention to the righteous plaint of a washerwoman as it will to that of a millionaire nabob.

"And now, when only too many of the great journals of the day are the voice of the House of Morgan and allied interests, I desire The Fresno Bee ever to stand forth as a stalwart and dependable tribune of The People – a newspaper that ever will battle for the right, no matter how weak in worldly power the right may be; that ever will fight entrenched wrong, no matter how panoplied in power the wrong may be.

"Be just and fear not. And may God bless you, one and all. Affectionately, C.K."

C.K. McClatchy's letter closely followed the basic tenets of the Cardinal Rules set down by James McClatchy when he founded the Sacramento Bee. Those Cardinal Rules also became the bible for The Fresno Bee. They follow:

The Bee demands of all its writers accuracy before anything else. Better to lose an item than make a splurge one day and correct it the next.

Equally with that, it demands absolute fairness in the treatment of the news. Reports must not be colored to please a friend or wrong an enemy.

Do not editorialize in the news columns. An accurate report is its own best editorial.

Do not exaggerate. Every exaggeration hurts immeasurably the cause it pretends to help.

If a mistake is made, it must be corrected. It is as much the duty of a Bee writer to work to the rectification of a wrong done by an error in an item, as it is first to use every precaution not to allow that error to creep in.

Be extremely careful of the names and reputations of women. Even when dealing with an unfortunate, remember that so long as she commits no crime, other than her own sin against chastity, she is entitled at least to pity.

The names of rape victims of all ages will not be used except when death occurs or extraordinary circumstances are involved. This applies not only in cases reported to the law enforcement authorities but also in reporting rape trials in open court.

Sneers at race or religion, or physical deformity, will not be tolerated. Dago, Mick, Sheeny, even Chink or Jap, these are absolutely forbidden. This rule of regard for the feelings of others must be observed in every avenue of news, under any and all conditions.

There is a time for humor and there is a time for seriousness. The Bee likes snap and ginger at all times. It will not tolerate flippancy on serious subjects on any occasion.

The furnisher of an item is entitled to a hearing for his side at all times, not championship. If the latter is ever deemed necessary the editorial department will attend to it.

Interviews given the paper at the paper's request are to be considered immune from sneers or criticism.

In every accusation against a public official or private citizen, make every effort to have the statement of the accused given prominence in the original item.

In the case of charges which are not ex officio or from a public source, it is better to lose an item than to chance the doing of a wrong.

Consider The Bee always as a tribunal which desires to do justice to all, which fears far more to do injustice to the poorest beggar than to clash swords with wealthy injustice.

10

H. R. McLaughlin

When Carlos McClatchy traveled from Sacramento in 1920 to check out the possibility of starting a newspaper in Fresno, he took with him the man he needed to make it a success. And when in 1922 The Fresno Bee began its long life, the need was even more urgent. This fledgling newspaper would need a dynamic managing editor, a man who would lead the news operation.

McClatchy knew he had such a man in tow – H.R. McLaughlin, seasoned newspaperman, city editor of the Sacramento Bee since 1911. "Bob" to his friends outside the paper, "Mac" within those boundaries. The appellation would stick until his retirement, even to his death.

The selection, of course, had to be approved by Carlos' father, C.K. McClatchy, but he evidently realized it would be worth the problem of finding a new city editor up north if it meant Mac could help guide Carlos down south. So Carlos was able to pirate this gem of a newspaperman, and together they formed an exceedingly successful team.

It was the second major decision of the period made by C.K. in Sacramento. The first was to give his son, Carlos, permission to start The Fresno Bee. Carlos had convinced him that Fresno was a viable town, one which would grow and which would support a newspaper patterned after The Sacramento Bee. It would be a proud paper not afraid to take hard stands and one which would print all the news, offering

San Joaquin Valley readers a different view of the local and world scenes and a more liberal editorial view than they were accustomed to getting from the conservative morning Republican and the afternoon Herald, as well as the many newspapers in the surrounding valley.

C.K. was putting his trust in Carlos, his only son, who had never been in command of a newspaper, and in McLaughlin, who had never been a managing editor. But C.K. no doubt reasoned that the combination would form a team that would be difficult to beat. That trust proved to be well-founded. The Fresno Bee would grow with the valley, and was to prosper. Respect and credibility were to be earned.

Carlos McClatchy knew he faced a rough road ahead in starting The Fresno Bee, and he wanted someone in whom he had complete trust to run the news side, so he could spend more time with other problems. In McLaughlin, he had that man. And for McLaughlin, it was the chance to make his own news decisions in a city that would have three newspapers, a newspaperman's dream. So he was more than happy to accept Carlos' offer, even though it meant leaving the area where he had been born and worked for most of his life to move to Fresno.

McLaughlin proved the trust the McClatchys placed in him. He worked with Carlos in Fresno for the better part of a year while the two did the preliminary work of setting up the editorial side of The Fresno Bee before it was to begin publication.

This included the selection of a site, getting to know the principal news makers in Fresno, building a team of reporters and editors, supervising the build-up of a filing system for the morgue, and designing the layout of the building itself and its construction. McLaughlin and McClatchy worked in tandem throughout that year, their labors often stretching from early-morning to late-night hours. With their wives, they also socialized together; the relationship remained close through the ensuing years. And through those years, as Carlos McClatchy's personal problems increased, it remained for McLaughlin to take a more commanding role in the daily operation of the newspaper. This he did in his journeyman way, without complaint. He was known in the newsroom as a hard man, but fair – well-liked by the editorial staff. In retrospect, they revered him.

O.M. (Diz) Shelton, later to become managing editor, once said McLaughlin was the best newsman he ever knew. Shelton for years was a reporter who worked under McLaughlin's leadership.

Ward Grimes, another veteran newsman, described McLaughlin as "very gruff, (but) a great guy. I liked him very much. He wanted to raise us from $40 to $50 a week once, but couldn't. (Sacramento vetoed it.) Mac was very well liked."

And Ed Orman, longtime sports editor of the Bee, also had a fond spot in his heart for McLaughlin. Orman was to say: "McLaughlin was so involved with sports as a youngster – especially tennis. He was my boss, really. (As opposed to Carlos McClatchy.) Mac was very critical about sports. Once I covered a Rose Bowl game, and I thought I had written a hell of a story, a fine second-day lead. Mac told me, 'Get the score up in the first paragraph.' I changed it for the next edition. Mac was very fundamental. I think all the workers – the reporters – liked him."

Indeed, McLaughlin never lost his zeal for sports, or for covering sports stories, for that matter. On rare occasions, he would put himself back in harness. One example came on October 26, 1929, when USC played Stanford in a football game at Stanford Stadium. The Page 1 story in The Bee was bylined, By H.R. McLaughlin. (No mention of his title.)

The lead paragraph:

"STANFORD STADIUM: The best team walked away with the laurels in the mid-season 'big game' today and the boys from Troy happened to have that team. They were smarter on attack and defense and made the vaunted Cards of Stanford look worse than the 7-0 score indicated." The reader may pick up the technical misuse of "best," but also should note that the score was in the first paragraph, if not in the first sentence. Mac practiced what he preached.

In those days of tough competition in a two-newspaper town (The Bee had bought out the Herald in 1924), sports was important, to the degree that sports extras were commonplace. McLaughlin and McClatchy were in agreement that The Bee must be first with the story. And being an afternoon paper, The Bee couldn't accomplish that with a late-breaking story such as a sporting event. So it would run the regular editions, then replate Page 1 for an extra, which was hawked through the streets by newsboys who were called back into service after completing their regular deliveries.

Extras on the yearly baseball World Series were published every day except Sunday, as was coverage of all the big fights in the East, such as the famed Dempsey-Tunney bout of 1927, the "long-count" battle pitting slugger Jack Dempsey against finesse boxer Gene Tunney. With such extras, the Bee hammered the message into its readers – an afternoon newspaper brought them the latest news.

Under McLaughlin's direction, with McClatchy's approval, this meant free rein with extras until 1932, when The Bee bought out its sole surviving competition, the Republican. After that, the extras were gradually phased out. The last one of that era came in 1941, on December 7th, when the Japanese attacked Pearl Harbor.

The end of local competition, and the ever-increasing costs of publication, doomed the extras. (The next wasn't to come until more than 50 years later – in 1995 with the "not guilty" verdict of the jury in the criminal trial of football star, O.J. Simpson, in which he was accused of murdering his wife and her friend.) But even without the extras, McClatchy and McLaughlin did much more to spread the news. World Series games, football games, local elections, were broadcast through that relatively new medium of radio. The Bee would have thousands of seats set up in Courthouse Park in downtown Fresno, and presented live broadcasts of the games, or the election results, over loudspeakers.

Fresnans would pack the park to hear the games, or get the results, as they happened. Workers were pressed into service to do the broadcasting, and one of them, on occasion, was McLaughlin. But publishing the daily paper was his first love, and duty. The daily circulation figure under his direction was 16,908 on the first day of publication – October 17, 1922. That figure was given in a "publisher's statement," and was boosted with a cut-rate price for those who took out three-month subscriptions. When McLaughlin retired in 1949, daily circulation had reached 79,107, and the figure for Sunday was 81,113. A more-telling set of figures are those for 1932, the year the Republican gave up the fight, leaving The Bee as Fresno's only daily newspaper. The Republican's final claimed circulation figure was 30,000 daily. That "total" had remained constant since 1922, leading Carlos McClatchy to scoff. How could The Bee's circulation continue to rise, and that of the Republican not drop, he wondered aloud and in print.

The Bee had reached 32,587 daily, and 31,548 Sunday, audited, in March of 1932. In September of that year, with the Republican gone, The Bee's daily figure jumped to 33,037, and its Sunday circulation to 40,843. McLaughlin and McClatchy had done their jobs well.

McLaughlin would do just about anything to enhance The Bee's image. It seems incongruous, in the light of modern newspaper practices, for a managing editor to do what he did in 1925. Whether the idea was his, or McClatchy's, isn't known. But it went like this:

The city held a marble-shooting contest. It was won by 13-year-old Selwin Jackson. As his prize, he was to compete in Sacramento in the state contest, representing Fresno. But his parents couldn't finance the trip or make it themselves, so the Bee took over the sponsorship. In addition, Selwin had to have a "manager" and "big brother" along.

The Bee announced it would pick up the tab, and that the "manager" and "big brother" would be its managing editor, H.R. McLaughlin. Selwin was to call him "Uncle Bob." (The appellation "Mac" was reserved for Bee employees. He was called "Bob" by most others in Fresno. His full name was Hugh Robert McLaughlin, but he was never known to use "Hugh.")

Mac took Selwin to Sacramento, and arranged for transportation, hotel and food costs, plus incidentals. And Selwin proceeded to win the state contest. On that day, The Bee ran a Page 1 story on Selwin's big victory, bylined By H.R. McLaughlin. This time, the byline included, in parenthesis, (Managing Editor of the Fresno Bee.)

But that wasn't the end. All state and regional winners were invited to compete in the national finals in Atlantic City, N.J. The Bee decided Selwin should compete there, too, accompanied by Mclauglin, his "manager" and "big brother." They took the train east to Atlantic City, where Selwin continued his winning ways. He beat his first opponent, and his second, and his third. And McLaughlin's stories were bylined on Page 1. Suddenly, Selwin was in the national semi-finals. But the headline, "Jackson Wins Again," was not to be repeated. He was defeated in that semi-final match. McLaughlin's last story started this way:

"Atlantic City June 4 – In the presence of a cheering crowd of 5,000 persons who had become fanatics in following the matches in the national marbles tournament, Selwin Jackson, student of Fresno

Technical High School and marbles champion of The Fresno Bee, today was presented with a handsome white gold watch and a jewel fob carrying a silver marble. The presentation was made to him as champion of his own league, the western, and a player in the semi-finals.

"The showing Selwin made was a credit to Fresno. Out of sixty-four champions from as many cities in the United States he landed among the last four and by his defeat in the last round of the semi-finals is tied for third place, a position that is the envy of sixty other boys. To beat him, Tommy Raley of Kentucky, who today lost to Howard Robbins of Springfield, Mass, had to set a world's record of thirteen marbles."

Unfortunately, Selwin never got a shot in his final game. "Thirteen" was the game. Howard had the first shot, and he never missed. Wrote McLaughlin, after Howard made his 13th and final successful shot, "Selwin jumped up and shook him by the hand. 'You can't win a game if you don't get a chance to shoot,' said Selwin as he smiled gamely in defeat. ... 'A better boy beat me, that's all,' was the game answer of Selwin."

With all that coverage, one would believe The Bee and the city would sponsor a gala homecoming for Selwin, at the least a parade and brass band. But succeeding issues of the newspaper never mentioned Selwin or his return. It was as if he and his "manager/big brother" had vanished.

Phebe McClatchy Conley, Carlos' widow – she married Superior Court Judge Philip Conley in October, 1958 – recalled McLaughlin fondly. In her Fresno home in 1985, at age 93, this remarkable woman remembered Mac as if she had seen him just yesterday, rather than some 50 years before.

"Mac was my favorite editor," she said. "He was a person who was critically important. All through his lifetime with the paper, he was it. Carlos wanted him when he came down here. They were very close and understanding, and in confidence, too. McLaughlin was able to deal with the reporters and with the actual news end of the paper without any prodding or interference. He was most experienced and secure in that sort of position. This was another case of where we were very close in our family relationships – with Mac and his wife."

When Carlos McClatchy died suddenly in 1933, Phebe lost her direct contact with The Bee. But she said: "I still saw Mac quite often. We were still good friends."

In an interview in her Fresno home on March 22, 1984, she had said: "Bob McLaughlin came from Sacramento. He was the editor, and the working editor. He ran things, and made things go. Of course, Carlos kept very close touch, and he was the promoter, and had the new ideas – outreach kind of stuff. He was the spark plug. But Bob McLaughlin was such a good and competent newsman that he was able to do better in the news, say, than the other newspapers (the Herald and the Republican). And then they fell on hard times, anyway.

"It was a circulation battle, and also a battle to get the advertisers. The Republican lost Chester Rowell ... and was bought by the Osborns. The older son (George) was a substantial, hard-working fellow, but Chase (George's brother) was very handsome and very gay and didn't pay much attention to the paper, and so they were fair game for The Bee.

"They had not had the experience or the training that Carlos had had. Or that McLaughlin had. And Riggins (Ed S. Riggins, who became business manager of The Bee in 1926.) Those three were better working men. They gradually overcame them (the Osborns), and finally bought them out."

Also among Mac's many admirers was Don Castelazo, who retired as The Bee's wire editor in 1972. He first joined The Bee in 1929, hired by McLaughlin as a valley correspondent in Hanford. Then, after being on staff for a year, he was offered a job in the Oakland office of the San Francisco Chronicle. The pay would be $37.50 a week, $10 more than he was making at The Bee. He took the job, but it was in the Depression days and the Chronicle decided it would lop off six hires. This after Castelazo had been on the job just three months. Realizing he would be one of the six to feel the ax, probably the first, he telephoned McLaughlin, asking if he could be rehired. McLaughlin's retort:

"Well you son of a bitch. You know, I told you, if you quit here to get a higher-paying job somewhere else ... we never rehire someone who will do that. But I happen to need a man in Hanford again, so you can come back." Castelazo did, and remained on board for 42 years. After his retirement, he said of the deceased McLaughlin: "He was a good man.

After the war (World War II) McLaughlin went to great lengths to get temporary housing for the new hires. He was quite good at that.

"He was quick in his judgment, and very brusque sometimes, but he was fair, very fair. Mac ran a tight ship. He was a good newsman, very good – smart. He let the city editor do most of the running around. I never saw him (out on the office floor) giving orders to the reporters, anything like that."

Castelazo then went on to offer an exception to that rule: "There was an emergency up in the mountains, an avalanche during the boring of the pipeline tunnel between Huntington and Shaver (Lakes). A lot of men were trapped in there. McLaughlin was right on the ball, got things organized. He got a lot of praise from people. He got his reporters and cameramen up there in a hurry, and caught the Republican flat-footed...

"He liked to party. He always attended our parties in a big way. We had wonderful parties, at our houses. We used to go down to the old Fresno Brewery, just before the war, down on lower Van Ness. And they had a big room there that they used for banquets, beer busts. And Mac would come along. At one party, things got rough, and reporters were ripping off each others' shirts, and throwing them in the fireplace, McLaughlin's among them. So you see, he was just a good guy; a good newsman, a strong newsman."

As mentioned, The Fresno Bee's final "extra" of that era was published on Pearl Harbor Day – December 7, 1941. McLaughlin made the decision to publish it. Don Castelazo recalled he was at home on that fateful Sunday morning, helping his wife prepare a birthday party for their daughter Donna, who had just turned 4. A neighbor came rushing in at about 11 o'clock, repeating the news bulletin he had just heard on the radio. The Japanese had attacked Pearl Harbor. Castelazo jumped into his car and raced to The Bee. Donna's birthday party went on without him.

"Everyone was there," he recalled. "Lockwood was there. McLaughlin was there. Popovich was there. The whole staff was there. Most everyone showed up without being called." (Bill Lockwood was assistant managing editor, George Popovich the city editor.) The decision was quickly made to scrap Page 1 of the already published Sunday paper, and to move the "jump page," to which stories were continued from A-1, from A-9 to A-2. Those pages were switched.

The Bee got a couple of breaks in timing. First, all the lead plates from the Sunday editions, printed in the early hours of the day, were still in place on the press. The second "break" was that gas heaters of the typesetting Linotype and Intertype machines had not been turned off, so that the metal in them was still molten, and hot type could be produced immediately. No four-hour wait for the heating-up process was necessary. In addition, the huge metal pot filled with the molten lead used by stereotypers to make the plates for the press was still hot, eliminating another possible problem.

Printers, stereotypers and pressmen were called in – Castelazo did much of the telephoning – and the extra edition quickly became a reality. The response of Bee workers was overwhelming. Every person contacted, no matter in which department, hastened downtown to The Bee building. Many who weren't needed, such as ad department personnel, showed up as well, as did townsfolk who wanted their news quickly and as complete as possible.

Under McLaughlin's direction, the editorial department swung into action. Castelazo recalled that three "replates" were published, each with more information than the one before. "Teletypes were bringing in the news," he said. "We started putting it together. Making up pages. The first edition came out with some other news on the front page, besides the war news, because we were in that much of a hurry. We kept replating. Three, I think. They were mostly street sales. It was a wild scene."

In those days, permission had to be obtained from Sacramento to use large type in headlines, such as 72-point (one-inch-high letters.) Without asking for permission, McLaughlin exceeded even that, ordering not one but two lines of type, each in 96 points over the eight-column page. The headline read:

Japanese bomb Hawaii;
Declare War On U.S.

The Bee ran a 3-column by 4-inch file picture, depicting an air view of Honolulu. At the bottom of the page was a 1-column picture of Lt.

Gen. Douglas MacArthur, commanding general of U.S. forces in the Philippines, labeled "America's No. 1 soldier."

Sidebar stories on the page had President Roosevelt summoning his cabinet and the Democratic and Republican party chiefs to an emergency meeting, Prime Minister Winston Churchill of Great Britain conferring with U.S. ambassadors, plus local stories on Fresno soldiers who were on duty in the war zone, and the Fresno Air Base personnel and other military men being called to active duty. Remaining on the front page throughout were four small, paid advertisements at the lower corners.

The jump page carried a 4-column map of the Pacific, with Pearl Harbor pinpointed. It would have been better placed on A-1; people were asking one another where this Pearl Harbor was. The jump page also displayed file photos of the battleship U.S.S. Oklahoma, one of many which had been hit by bombers, and another of the Japanese carrier Kaga, a "nest for 60 warplanes." The page also bore a photo of the type of an Army troop transport that had been torpedoed. The page was almost completely "war," except for a couple of small plugger stories and a few small advertisements.

No actual figures were kept of how many extra papers were printed that day. Charlie McNally, assistant composing room foreman at the time, recalled that about 800 were printed on the first run, which was quickly jettisoned for a replate. With the second and third replates, the Bee went all out, printing a total in the three runs of about 38,000 copies, McNally estimated.

Each replate, which included the jump page, had more information than the previous. And as noted, the final replate contained two complete pages of information on the bombing. As far as could be determined, just about every newspaper hustled on the streets of Fresno and the cities in The Bee's circulation area was sold. Fresnans and other valley residents snapped them up at a nickel a copy.

Many probably kept those treasured copies of the December 7, 1941 extras, but The Bee inexplicably did not. None could be found in the plant in a 1985 search, except for the one in the bound volumes. And the Page 1 of that one is missing.

Every employee of The Bee was proud that day. Putting out those extras, they believed, had been a fine example of newspapering at its best. They all thought so, from McLaughlin on down. And despite the sobering thoughts of the day, more than a few congratulatory drinks were hoisted after the hurry-up job was completed. But the powers-that-be in Sacramento weren't so pleased. The following day, as the Fresno employees were busy printing follow-up stories on the bombing, McLaughlin got a phone call from the brass at the flagship paper. No, they weren't all that happy up there. Where did he get the audacity, or the authority, to publish an extra, on a Sunday when the employees had to be called in – on overtime in many cases? McLaughlin was thoroughly chastised. And, no doubt, thoroughly chagrined.

The Sacramento Bee had not deemed the bombing important enough to publish an extra. And probably, the fact that Mac had done it without permission galled them even more.

But Mac was right. Carlos McClatchy, had he been alive, would have backed him all the way. The people wanted to know what was happening far out there in the Pacific. And The Fresno Bee did what it was born to do: deliver the news.

McLaughlin guided the editorial fortunes of The Fresno Bee until his retirement in March, 1949, when he was succeeded by William E. (Bill) Lockwood. He and his wife, Emma Louise, had two sons and three grandchildren.

He was an avid and very good amateur golfer, shooting in the low 70s on his best days. In the words of sports editor Ed Orman, who played golf with McLaughlin on occasion, he had "good irons, short woods." Mac was a member of the Sunnyside Country Club, and played most of his golf there. He was the club champion for two years. In 1928, he was instrumental in launching the annual Fresno City Women's Golf Championship at Riverside Golf Course. The tournament for years attracted women golfers from throughout the San Joaquin Valley. Mac also loved tennis, and played it well, too. Before leaving Sacramento, he was an organizer and charter member of the Sutter Lawn Tennis Club there. In Fresno, he helped organize the Roeding Park Tennis Club, and spent a lot of his leisure time on its courts.

His first newspaper job was as a reporter on his hometown Napa Register. While on that job, he became a correspondent for the Sacramento Bee, and in 1907 was hired by that paper as a reporter. His first assignment was to cover the Western Irrigation Congress, held that August in Capitol Park. He next served in the dual role of courthouse reporter/sports editor. The Sacramento Bee was an afternoon paper, and McLaughlin would wrap up the sports section for the day at 9 a.m., then head for the courthouse and his duties there. His workdays often extended from 6 o'clock in the morning to 6:30 or 7 o'clock in the evening – without overtime pay. The extra work paid off. Early in 1911 he was named assistant city editor of The Sacramento Bee, and six months later became city editor, a post he held until his transfer to Fresno.

Mac's final "extra" was published without his knowledge. It was a replate of Page 1 of October 1, 1947. The occasion was the 40th anniversary of Mac's service with and for McClatchy. The dateline read, "Basque Hotel, Fresno, Wednesday Evening, October 1, 1947. Alongside that, "McEXTRA", preceding McDonald's by decades. Every story on the page was a parody on him. And a two-column overlay, in green, of course, depicted his Irish face.

Across the bottom, in black writing on a green background, were the signatures of Bee editorial employees. They were Tut Jackson, Joe Smith, Ed Schober, Ralph Cole, John W. Anderson, Frank H. Irwin, Delores Williams, Becky Christensen, Gilmore Gilbert, Julius Sanders, Milt Young, Peggy Broad, Beverly Berg, Cy Meanor, Bert Dahlgren, Judson Conger, Ed Orman, Ward W. Grimes, Mary Ellen O'Hare, Hal Coats, Eva E. Burns, O.M. Shelton, Veda Bos, Don Castelazo, Don Stewart (composing room foreman), Bill Lockwood, Marjorie Arnold, Karl M. Kidder, Mike Keyes, Gertrude Bouts, Bob Shuman, Sally Strothard, Wally Erickson (KMJ Radio), Lew Hegg, Omer Crane, Harry Godfrey, Dorothy Hill, Art Buel, Duke Millard (business manager), Jack Burke (Associated Press), Paul Sheehan (Fresno State College), Laura McCardle and Molly Marshall.

McLaughlin died in his Fresno home on October 8, 1952, of a heart attack. He had served as managing editor of The Fresno Bee for 27 years, supervising an era of great editorial expansion. Among those who expressed "deep regret" was Earl Warren, Republican governor of California and one of Mac's longtime friends and admirers.

Robert P. Molander

11

Orders From Above

Through the years from its inception in 1922, The Fresno Bee drew from within its ranks to fill top-level management positions. It followed this practice when H.R. McLaughlin retired as managing editor in 1949. Mac's successor was to be William E. (Bill) Lockwood, a veteran who had been with the newspaper since 1923.

Like McLaughlin, Lockwood had paid his dues. He was city editor of the Fresno Morning Republican when he was hired by McLaughlin as assistant city editor of The Bee in 1923, working under City Editor Fred Moore. Two years later, Moore transferred to The Sacramento Bee, and Lockwood was promoted to city editor, a post he held until being named associate editor in 1937. He was named assistant managing editor in 1946, immediately following a tour of duty with the Army in World War II.

In what was to become custom for a time, it was generally acknowledged that his promotion to assistant managing editor was a designed move preparatory to his becoming managing editor when McLaughlin retired.

Lockwood's "honeymoon" in his new job as managing editor was short, if in fact there was any honeymoon at all for him. The troops were accustomed to McLaughlin, a gruff, fair boss. They loved him, considered him one of their own. Lockwood was following a legend and he never measured up. In fairness, few could have.

Unlike McLaughlin, Lockwood was never to be his own man. He never would win the support of his troops. And having been an Army officer in World War II and a member of the reserves after his discharge, that was hard for him to take.

Lockwood's nemesis was Walter P. Jones, the third editor of McClatchy Newspapers, a man trained by C.K. McClatchy to succeed him after the death of C.K.'s only son, the heir-apparent, Carlos McClatchy. When Carlos died suddenly in 1933, Jones' star ascended. He became a surrogate McClatchy, serving C.K. as managing editor of The Sacramento Bee, then as editorial director of the three McClatchy newspapers in Sacramento, Fresno and Modesto. He retained this powerful role, becoming editor of the three papers when Eleanor McClatchy succeeded her father, C.K., as publisher of the three Bee's after his death in 1936.

C.K. McClatchy had ruled his empire with an iron fist, and he trained Jones to do likewise. But McLaughlin had been so strong, so well-respected by the Sacramento hierarchy, that he could call a lot of his own shots and withstand some of the pressure from on high. He was, in effect, "family." Lockwood was never to achieve that stature. He didn't have McLaughlin's inner strength. It was inherent in his nature, accented by his Army training, to get approval from higher-ups before making any kind of command decision. So he became Jones' surrogate.

In that role, Lockwood got the job done in Fresno, probably as well as anyone could. But editorial staffers lost the feeling they were working for a real, vibrant newsman.

Lockwood was a hard worker, a man known to put in long hours for The Bee, but he spent most of them in his office, an office that actually was located in a corner. He was seldom seen in the newsroom conversing with the reporters and editors under his command.

This boss wasn't one to "shoot the bull" with his subordinates. For most of his reign, there was no assistant to act as a buffer between him and the staff, someone who could soften the blows. Lockwood would accept no excuses, no matter how merited. Two of his favorite, often-repeated sayings were "There's always room for a good story," and "There's always room for a good picture."

These declarations resulted when, in the rush of deadlines, a story or picture didn't make that particular day's paper. Or worse, when W.P.J. asked via the wire why a certain story or picture wasn't in The Fresno Bee. Pity the poor wretch who in Lockwood's opinion had blown it.

A good deal of Lockwood's time at the office was spent in the hard reading of (unedited) galley proofs. Starting early every day, on his order, copyboys were continuously delivering to him these uncorrected copies of news stories from the composing room, stories from all departments that he would attack with his heavy blue editor's pencil. The pencil was vicious. Its favorite target was Dorothy Noble Hill, the society editor. This poor woman knew the city's society movers and shakers, and had lived a privileged life; but she knew practically nothing of writing or editing skills, and could never get the hang of it. She had stayed on the job for years, but she was a battered survivor.

When he had completed his word-by-word reading of those society proofs, there would be as much furious blue pencil marks on them as black type. His editorial wrath wasn't limited to Mrs. Hill. Everyone out there on the floor felt it, from farm editor Mike Keyes (he couldn't have cared less) to copy desk chief Cy Meanor (who handed the proofs out to his copy editors, usually without comment to telegraph editor Don Castelazo (it flowed off his back), to sports editor Ed Orman (he'd grunt and toss them into the waste basket, pretending he never saw them.) For Dorothy Noble Hill, though, it was an ulcer-grinding torture that never ended.

City Editor George Popovich stood up to and, in fact, relished a beef with Lockwood. But he seldom lived up to his oft-repeated boast, over a highball or two, that he "really stood up to Bill" or "really told Bill off" on this or that.

To his credit, Lockwood's blue-pencil zingers didn't go directly to the reporters or copy editors, but to the department heads. However, no one was exempt. Conversely, Lockwood wasn't one to pencil in a compliment on a galley proof.

Walter P. Jones, editor of the Bees, enjoyed golf, gardening and family. But his overwhelming purpose in life was guiding The Sacramento Bee and its offshoots, The Fresno and Modesto Bees. This he did with the full backing of Eleanor McClatchy. Daily, he would spread those three newspapers over the floor of his Sacramento office and scan them, page by page, story by story, word by word at times. Jones hated mistakes, and if they were there, he found them. He was also a bear on story selection and placement, and woe be to the editor who ordered a particular story placed on an inside page when Jones thought it should have been played on Page 1, or vice versa. Daily, The Fresno Bee editors would wire him a menu of its top stories for the day, then wait to see if he countermanded it. On occasion, he did.

And daily, he would send down, via the wire, a list of stories he wanted in the paper. These daily orders came to be known as "Walter P. Jones musts," then "W.P. Jones musts" and finally, "W.P.J. musts." They were rushed by a copyboy to Lockwood's office, and he had them passed on to the departments involved. The staffers often joked there would be a "W.P.J. must" if the sun rose in the West. There was rarely a case of a "must" story that wasn't already in the Fresno plans for proper treatment. The ultimate came one day when Lockwood passed on a W.P.J. "must" to Castelazo, ordering a certain story to be run in that day's paper. Castelazo pointed out that The Fresno Bee had run that story the day before – the exact story, by the same wire service. But Lockwood insisted the order be obeyed, and The Bee ran the story – again.

The kicker came the next day. Jones had seen the story in The Fresno Bee, knew Sacramento had not run it, and ordered its inclusion there. The order mistakenly was relayed to Fresno, where Lockwood complied.

Lockwood was recognized in Fresno as a Monday-morning quarterback. Other than the specific orders from W.P.J., he preferred to check The Bee after it came off the presses, rather than be involved in general news selection. Then he would make his judgments. Again, a major portion of his ire was aimed at the society department, with most of the rest directed at telegraph, farm and sports. Cityside, generally, got off lightly. Lockwood didn't make it clear who would be first in command under him, particularly when he was gone, and this led to confrontations between the editors. Popovich was involved in an almost-daily war with Obie Millar, an editorial staffer who didn't have official "rank" but who filled the category of news editor. He worked with printers in the

Robert P. Molander

composing room, making certain stories were in the proper place, that headlines were correct, deadlines met.

Millar took on himself authority he didn't officially have, and often made decisions in the composing room that conflicted with Popovich's orders. Millar also was known to stomp down the stairs from the composing room to the editorial floor, chewing out individual reporters or copy editors. The results were verbal arguments that could be heard blocks away, with observers relishing them. Lockwood never interceded, never took the obvious step of telling Millar that Popovich had the final word. Gilmore Gilbert was the valley editor. Here again, Lockwood never made the command decision of placing one above the other, and their arguments ran hot and heavy.

On occasion, Lockwood tried to do the politically correct thing. For a few years, he held Christmas parties at his home, hosting the editorial staff. There would be plenty of booze, and most reporters and editors showed up. Some were heavy drinkers, not above accepting a free one or two no matter who was buying. Others treated Lockwood's parties like command performances --you attended, or you might bear the brunt of his wrath on the next working day. Lockwood cut out the parties before his retirement, ostensibly because they got to be too much to handle as the staff got bigger.

During Lockwood's tenure, Bee staffers formed the Fresno Press Club, and he did little to ingratiate himself with them in that regard. He believed, openly, that the club was "an incubator of the Guild," and would have nothing to do with it. The Newspaper Guild was the national union of editorial and advertising personnel. McClatchy, and therefore Lockwood, opposed unionization. Popovich, the city editor, joined right in, though, made all the Press Club parties, and sat in on the poker games.

The Bee brass in Sacramento took a step, which for a long time, assured that the Newspaper Guild wouldn't succeed in its efforts to unionize The Fresno Bee. Fresno salaries were kept at, or 25 cents a week higher, than those at San Francisco and Sacramento newspapers in which the Guild was entrenched.

The arrangement worked until the 1970s, when the Guild finally won an election in Fresno. National Guild organizers had claimed the Fresno editorial staffers of the pre-Guild days were prostituting themselves for the sake of the few dollars they would have had to pay in guild dues.

Few disputed that Bill Lockwood had been a good city editor. He handled the desk well, with just one assistant. He knew what was going on in the city, and deployed his reporters well. He could spot a good picture, knew the value of one. But in the style of the day, most pictures were presented at least a column smaller than they deserved. Graphics were rudimentary. But like any city editor, Lockwood delighted in beating the opposition. He was to do this on occasion, often through the medium of the "extra." One example came on January 28, 1926, shortly after he became city editor. A dozen policemen, including the chief, had been indicted by the federal Grand Jury on charges of accepting bribes from bootleggers They had gone on trial, and the jury had retired at 1:15 p.m. to deliberate. This meant there was no chance of getting the decision in that day's regular press run. But Lockwood realized the verdict could come in that evening, so he had a new Page 1 made up, including file photos of the defendants, leaving enough space for the jury verdict when and if it came in that night.

At 8:20 o'clock, 11 of the 12 cops were found innocent; one patrolman was ruled guilty. Composing quickly put the new story and headlines into type, a new Page 1 was formed and the press rolled with the extra. While Radio Station KMJ, owned by McClatchy, was broadcasting the news of the verdict, Bee newsboys were hawking the extra on the streets. The Republican waited until its regular edition the next morning, and was cleanly beaten.

The following morning a beaming Carlos McClatchy slapped a couple of pieces of copy paper on Lockwood's desk, ordering him, "Bill, I want that printed on Page 1 of the first edition without even a comma changed." The headline and story:

Uxtree!! Uxtree!!

Here's Real Story

Of Bee Extra

"It wasn't the night before Christmas, as the rhyme goes, but it was the night of the Bee extra on the police trial – last night, to be exact.

"The Bee, as usual, was determined to be first on the Street with the news of the verdict. An elaborate scheme for handling details of the complicated verdict had been made, City Editor Bill Lockwood and his assistant, Jack Goddard, had all editorial plans completed, the form was ready in the composing room, the stereotypers were on the job and the press crew was set to go.

"Word of the verdict was flashing from the federal building. The story was briefly told, the page made up and in eight minutes the press was rolling and papers were on the conveyors to the newsboys who were to sell them on the streets. But there were no newsboys. Something had gone amiss. Here was a live, vibrant extra waiting to be read and nobody there to sell it.

"That's the way it looked for a time. But a newspaperman is ingenious, if nothing else. Bill and Jack had put the extra to press with the idea of making it the first on the Street and they weren't going to stop just because newsboys were needed.

"Grabbing a bundle of newspapers and reinforced by (reporter) Eilef Rue they dashed defiantly out on the wet streets yelling their wares. There is a difference of opinion as to the pitch of their untrained 'Uxtree' notes, but it mattered not. They got results and got them quick. They were back in the office in jig time with pockets jingling with nickels and dimes and exchanging experiences. "In the meantime Jack Sullivan and Harold Wilson of the composing room had joined the newsies and as a salesman 'Sully' proved a gem.

"Tom Haughawot of the advertising department and Don Jacobson, former office manager, just happened to drop around at the time, grabbed a bundle of papers, went forth yelling in their cars and soon came back for more.

"By this time the regular newsboys were organized and took over the task of selling.

"But it was the willing hands of the volunteers that gave the Bee its early representation. And such is the spirit with which newspapermen tackle a situation. None of the six mentioned above would have missed the 'kick' of being a newsboy for anything.

"And this story is written without their consent and can't be edited."

In later years, Lockwood was to relate a sequel. As he and the other self-impressed newsboys triumphantly took the pennies, nickels and dimes they had collected back to the office, they were told by Carlos

McClatchy to keep them. And a few days later, each got a $2.50 Bee check from the boss, with an accompanying letter telling him what a fine job he had done under pressure. Lockwood said, "I wish I had framed it to hang with my souvenirs, but there were little mouths to feed in those days and $2.50 went a long way at the grocery store."

Carlos went further. He sent the story to Editor and Publisher, the newspaper trade magazine, which ran it under the headline, "They Got Out An Extra And Sold It Too."

In Bill Lockwood's day, McClatchy employees had to retire at age 65, unless the name happened to be McClatchy, or perhaps Jones. An exception was Harry Conway, managing editor of The Modesto Bee. Conway had been retained on the job for some years after he reached 65. To Lockwood's way of thinking, that set the precedent, and he reasoned that with his 32 years of loyal service he, too, should be given that special consideration. But in 1955, assistant city editor O.M. "Diz" Shelton suddenly leap-frogged over George Popovich, the city editor, to the new post of Executive Editor of The Fresno Bee, second in command to Lockwood.

It didn't take anyone on board long to figure what the future had in store. Shelton would succeed Lockwood, who would be out, and Popovich would remain where he was. As Ward Grimes, seasoned reporter and wise old newsroom sage, put it at the time, "Absolutely. Diz is in; Lockwood is out. You'll see." It came about this way: Lockwood got the word from Sacramento, and summoned Shelton to the corner office from his assistant city editor's chair at the desk he and Popovich shared. The embittered Lockwood told Shelton of his promotion, leaving Shelton to inform Popovich. Shelton returned to the city desk and summarily told Popovich he was taking over as executive editor, and Lockwood posted the notice on the city-room board.

It was a huge pill for Popovich to swallow, and he never did get it down. In his final years with The Bee he was named a Special Writer, relegated to doing historical pieces about The Bee. He soon went on into retirement, never forgiving the brass for dropping him from the short list for advancement, or understanding how they could do it. But the action was long overdue. For many years, Popovich had been leaving the city desk at 11 o'clock every morning, Mondays through Fridays, and heading for the Elks Club, where he had lunch and played poker.

He'd get back to the desk at 1:30 or 2 o'clock, in time to greet the home edition of the newspaper and boast about how he had won again at poker. In the meantime, during those very important hours, Shelton put the paper out, making the important decisions without complaint.

It was to take nearly four years, but in 1959, Shelton was named the new managing editor. Lockwood was out on reaching age 65, despite his novel proposition that a person is 65 until he reaches 66, and that he therefore should have at least another 364 days as managing editor. Sacramento wouldn't buy it.

Lockwood spent a pleasant retirement before his death on July 30, 1969, 10 years to the day after he unwillingly left The Bee. He and Mrs. Lockwood toured worldwide on freighters to such destinations as Tokyo, Okinawa, Saigon, Bombay and Barcelona. He mailed travel stories along the way, and The Bee dutifully printed them. Also in retirement, he was named to the Fresno Housing Authority and Appeals Board, as its president. He also was a member of the Executive Committee of the Fresno Diamond Jubilee and the 1961 foreman of the Fresno County Grand Jury, writing the major portion of its report.

A history buff, he became editor in chief of a historical and photographic work to be titled "Fresno County History," in three parts. But it never was to see print. Thousands of dollars in advance subscriptions was collected and forwarded to the Phoenix company chosen to publish the works. But the firm went bankrupt, and the history died aborning. Most, if not all, of the advance subscription money was lost.

William E. Lockwood was born in Redlands, attended schools there and went on to Stanford University, from which he was graduated in 1917, during World War I. Lockwood entered the Army, reaching the rank of infantry lieutenant. After the war he joined the Organized Reserve Corps. In 1943, during World War II, he was recalled to commissioned service with the Army as a captain, and spent the next 31 months in the European Theater, 18 of them in Germany.

He reached the rank of major. After this second wartime tour of duty, he became a lieutenant colonel in the Organized Reserve Corps, and served as an assistant commandant of the 6238th Fresno Army Reserve School.

The Lockwoods were in Colombia on a South American tour when he died suddenly on July 30, 1969. He was 75. The body was flown to Fresno, and services were conducted and concluded at the Lisle funeral Home. Retired Superior Court Judge Arthur C. Shepard, aging himself but generally regarded in high esteem by the journalism fraternity, gave the eulogy.

There were no special military honors.

12

Shelton Takes Over

On August 1, 1959, O. M. "Diz" Shelton became the new managing editor of The Fresno Bee. The top brass of McClatchy Newspapers couldn't have made a decision more favorably received by the Fresno editorial crew. Diz was one of them. The Associated Press was to phrase the feeling aptly in Shelton's obituary in 1978: "Fresno (AP) – From this age of specialized journalism, one of the 'old school' general assignment reporters has passed. Orville M. Shelton, former managing editor of The Fresno Bee, died yesterday."

The staff knew Shelton was pretty much a loner, that he would be a tough boss. William E. Lockwood, his predecessor, had been, too. But the reporters and editors also knew that Shelton had been there, where they had been, and more. They knew his decisions would be based on solid newspaper knowledge, years of experience, out where the news is made and where only brave reporters dare tread; and in the office, where he had sweated out many years as assistant to the city editor under George Popovich, and as executive editor under Lockwood.

During his four years as executive editor, Shelton sat at a newsroom desk outside Lockwood's office, no walls surrounding him. When he took over the top job he moved into the corner office, but it wasn't long before he had his "outside" desk put back in place and was sitting at it for much of the day, close to the general flow. The corner lost the Ivory Tower image it had borne when Lockwood was in command.

Shelton made himself accessible to just about anyone who wanted to talk business. But let the conversation deteriorate, particularly nearing the crunch deadline hours, and the guest was quick to realize that it was over, that Shelton had better things to do. Tom Kirwan, chief editorial writer under Shelton, put it this way: "I have seen Diz – I know – that people have come up and leaned on him, once they got into his office, which was very rare. Diz would excuse himself, and he'd be gone. They'd be sitting there sucking wind, in the office. And I'd be next door. I'd see them in there. They didn't know what hit 'em."

Shelton abhorred those on the shady side of Fresno's life, and wasn't too anxious to socialize with respected businessmen, either. He was his own, private man.

A local contractor and San Joaquin Valley mover and shaker, a man at ease in dealing with city officials and others in high places, decided he should talk with Shelton. The Bee was no friend to the contractor, and neither was Shelton. Reporters were warned to be wary of the contractor.

The contractor asked a reporter to pass the word that he would like to talk with Shelton, at lunch or somewhere else outside the Bee building (on turf more favorable to the contractor.) The reporter passed the word back to Shelton, who snapped, "Tell the son of a bitch that if he wants to talk to me, he can come to my (bleeping) office." The message was relayed back, but the contractor wasn't to accept the terms.

Shelton did socialize, but with very few, and very select, friends. One was Charlie Marsella, one of the city's top stockbrokers. They'd meet in the Hi-Life, one of Fresno's best watering holes, in the late afternoon, after work hours, down a few belts and discuss the affairs of the day. Marsella never pushed Shelton, never turned the conversation to Bee policies in an effort to earn a favor, or to make a complaint. They got along. They'd sit at the bar, have two or three, and go home. It was an almost daily occurrence. Very few were allowed to horn in on the conversation, join in where they weren't wanted. Mickey the bartender was ready when needed, at a distance when he wasn't. The "circle" was limited to about four men, maybe five. An ideal setting for a man like Shelton

Once in a while, though, Shelton would absent himself from the Hi-Life, and from friend and proprietor Fred Boyd, for a spell. The reason was one common to newspapermen. Let a man discover you work for the paper, insert a couple of drinks in him, and you suddenly become fair game. So it was with Shelton. He was the managing editor, and the buck stopped with him. There was no higher news authority in Fresno. What better man to challenge if your paper had been late in arriving that morning, or if the paper had failed to back your favorite candidate.

Not Shelton – and not Charlie Marsella or Fred Boyd. Those two would take the obnoxious one aside, advise him there were other places more favorable, and send him on his way. And Shelton would drift back in, reclaiming his regular stool.

Shelton was as fair to Marsella as the stockbroker was to him. For a period, Marsella was chairman of the Fresno County Grand Jury, and it was into some heavy investigations. But Shelton never bugged him

The busy Business Office at The Fresno Bee.

about the jury's secret doings. Let the reporters do that. It wasn't fit conversation at the Hi-Life bar, between friends.

Shelton had done it all at The Bee. He started in sports, moved to lodges and churches, to general assignment, to cops, to city hall, to the Legislature in Sacramento, to the city desk in Fresno, and on up the ladder. He was The Fresno Bee's first local columnist, outside of the society department and sports. His column, a once-a-week thing, was titled "Browsing Around," which fit it well. It contained folksy items, a lot of names, humorous anecdotes, some not so humorous. It ran for a couple of years, then was abruptly dropped. It had been started in 1944, during World War II. (Shelton never went to war because he had polio as a youngster and was plagued with asthma. The Bee was laid out (designed) so that Browsing Around and a weekly news summary were on the same leaf, on pages back to back. The underlying thought was that the single sheet could be mailed to valley residents in the armed forces, both in the United States and overseas. The idea had merit, and many soldiers, sailors and marines would discover that leaf from The Bee in the envelope along with the letter from home.

Browsing Around survived the war, but by less than a year. On October 26, 1946, a one-paragraph item sealed its doom. In a command decision, Sacramento ordered it killed. The offending item:

"Memo to Rev. Lawrence Hawley of St. Paul's Methodist Church – That brassiere which was left in the waste basket of your study can be explained. The maid of honor in a recent wedding in the church shed it when, at the last minute, she encountered a little difficulty with the shoulder neckline on her gown and then forgot to retrieve it."

The wedding party complained to Sacramento, and the brass there ordered Browsing killed. They probably thought the column had served its purpose, anyway, the war being over. They didn't kill Shelton, though. In later years, he was to say that he was getting tired of the column anyway, much preferring to spend his time out on the front line. But he always thought Sacramento was "chicken" in axing the column.

Shelton came to Fresno from Oakland, seeking a climate that would be kind to the asthma that bothered him throughout his life. Initially he attended Fresno State College, and Fresno was to become his permanent home. While at State, he established another first. He became The Fresno Bee's first prep writer, covering high school sports on a part-

Robert P. Molander

time basis. His first byline, "By Orville Shelton," came on February 26, 1928, on his report of an all-county basketball game. Later that year he wrote a lengthy feature piece on Fresno boxer Young Corbett Ill (Ralph Giordano), who was leaving for New York to box Sgt. Sammy Baker. By this time, Shelton was a full-time sports writer. A year later, he moved to the city staff. Sports had been an entryway to the newspaper world, but Shelton was more a sports fan than a sports nut, and local reporting was his bag.

During that period, Shelton was courting Alta Larsen. In later days, she would reminisce about how he would come and sit on the front porch of her home, waiting for her to come out. She would tantalize him for a while, make him wait, then join him on the porch to talk. After they married, she made a practice of dropping by the office in the afternoons, waiting for him on a seat at the telephone switchboard. She was there so often that she learned to operate the board, and was hired on an afternoon-only basis to take phone calls. When Shelton got off work, she'd leave and they'd walk or drive home together.

In his adult years, she was the only person who addressed him as "Orville." To the rest of the world he was "Diz." The sobriquet came from his childhood, but he never explained it, at least to those at The Bee. His wife, who survived him, said she didn't know its derivation, either, just that he had been called "Diz" since she had known him. "I think it came from when he was a boy in Woodland," she said. "But Orville never told me how he got it."

Shelton made most of his own decisions on local issues, not deigning to telephone Sacramento with nuts-and-bolts questions as his predecessor had done. But he didn't take the entire load on his own shoulders. At an American Press Institute conference for managing editors, those in attendance were asked to give their theories on management. Shelton's solution, printed with those of others in the API bulletin, was to delegate, and then to delegate some more. Many of his peers didn't agree with him. But again, he was his own man.

His reporters liked and respected him. Reporter Ward Grimes put it this way: "I always had the highest respect for Diz. The day he was boosted from assistant city editor to executive editor, the reaction was good. Popovich (the city editor over whom Shelton had been unexpectedly elevated), screamed bloody murder. But it couldn't have happened to a nicer person. Diz was tops. Shelton was No. 1. He knew his way around. All reporters don't know where to go. He did."

One of the staff's favorite stories about Shelton involved the annual bus trip to Sacramento for the Twenty-Five Year Club Party, held at the home of Eleanor McClatchy. As the bus arrived, Shelton with his wry sense of humor, quipped, "Well...we're halfway home!", much to the amusement of listeners.

Shelton brought Desa Cucuk (later Desa Belyea) in to take over the society department on the long-looked-for resignation of Dorothy Noble Hill. As Belyea was to recall, Shelton told her crisply, "Here it is. Do what you can." In other words, she was on her own. Shape up the department; rescue it from its deadly, dull past. Give it your best shot. I'll be right behind you. I know you can do it, or I wouldn't have hired you. The meaning was clear, and without a plethora of words. That was his way.

Ask anyone who had worked with or for Shelton in the old days, and the answer was invariable: "Diz was a nice guy. He didn't talk much. He'd grunt once in a while. A good M.E."

Political reporter Eli Setencich, later a columnist, recalled the time an election was nearing, and he decided to tour the bars, checking on the local political action, specifically watching the tube, all the while alert for reaction from the patrons. One of his stops was Shelton's Hi-Life. He sat at the bar, ordered a drink and was checking the television set. He looked to his left, and horror of horrors, there was Shelton on the adjoining bar stool. "Oh oh," thought Setencich, "I'm dead." But Shelton grunted a "Hello," and went on talking with the man seated to his left. He saw Setencich's story in The Bee the next day, but he never mentioned it to him.

Another time, on a fine spring Fresno day, the San Francisco Giants and the Cleveland Indians were playing an exhibition baseball game at Fresno's minor-league John Euless Park on the final day of their swing west in the exhibition season. Setencich, a baseball fan, ducked out of the office to watch the game – on company time. On TV news that night, he was shocked to see himself, in full close-up, sitting in the stands. Shelton probably noticed it – he was a fan, too – or was told of it, but again, never was to mention it to Setencich.

At another time, earlier in his career when he was the City Hall reporter, Shelton was at a Press Club bash at the old Santa Fe Hotel, a spot that catered primarily to Basque sheepherders but which became one of the watering holes used by reporters. The food was good, plentiful and cheap. So was the whiskey The meeting was in the back room, and Shelton had left for the bar, sitting alone. A brash young reporter joined him there.

The reporter had an ax to grind. He reported to work at 8 o'clock each morning, taking his chair at a long makeshift table, sort of like a long piece of plywood on legs with four slots on each side at which reporters sat at their typewriters and telephones. Shelton also sat at this table, next to the young reporter. Shelton would enter, sit at the desk, type out a City Hall story or two, and leave the office, not to be seen there again for the rest of the day. He spent most of his time at City Hall. During that brief morning stop at The Bee, though, he often had two things to say to the reporter alongside – "Got a cigarette?" and/ or, "Got a match?"

This got to the young reporter. So that night at the Santa Fe bar, buoyed by a few Scotch and waters, he challenged the old pro: "How come you're so stuck-up?" he asked. "You come into the office like a king, never say a word except 'Got a cigarette?' Or, 'Got a match?' You never even say 'Hello' or 'Good morning.' Then you're gone. What's your problem, anyway?" Shelton grunted, silently drained his glass, and went back to the party. The next morning the reporter went to work with a hangover, wishing he never had been born, or at least had not gone to the bar at that particular moment. The key word was embarrassment. What would Shelton say in the light of day?

Shelton came in, on schedule, not looking like he'd had even one drink the night before. He sat, started typing, gave his standard grunt and said pointedly, sarcastically, "Good morning! Then, with an absolving half-grin, "Got a cigarette? Got a match?" He was handed a Chesterfield and a match, lit up, finished typing his story and took off, again wordless. No "good-by." But things were somehow better. The two got to be friends, sharing a few beers or highballs along the way, often at Shelton's home, along with a mutual love for New Orleans and Kansas City jazz.

In those long-ago days when city hall and local politics formed his beat, Shelton was recognized as the man who knew more about the inner functions of City Hall than those who worked there, including the department heads and the city commissioners He knew where the bodies were buried. He once was offered the city clerk's job by prominent movers and shakers. But he turned it down, knowing that those who gave favors would expect favors in return. And perhaps more important, he had no desire to get out of newspaper work.

In his writing job, a major part of his duties was coverage of city elections. He wrote all the stories that had to do with balloting for city hall posts, including those of the commissioners, in those days before the Bee-backed city-manager form of government was finally approved by the voters.

Television hadn't come to town yet, and election nights were special affairs in the Bee newsroom. All the local politicians, including those running for state and national offices, showed up with their backers, anxiously awaiting the results. They knew they would get them first at The Bee.

The process was an exceedingly interesting phenomenon, truly a thing to behold. The workers in the clerk's office at the Courthouse couldn't tabulate all the final votes for days in that pre-computer period, and The Bee needed them right away for the next day's paper. So college students, editorial copy boys and their dispatch-department counterparts, traveled on motorcycles to election precincts, where they copied results posted outside and phoned them in to The Bee newsroom. In earlier elections, crews were positioned in the elections office at the Courthouse, where they picked up copies of lists of vote returns as they came in from the precincts, and raced them to The Bee newsroom.

This practice continued through the night from the time the polls closed at 7 o'clock, starting with the absentee ballots. Special crews, most of them college students under the direction of fellow-student and entrepreneur Alex (Pappy) Papulias; were stationed at desks on the Bee newsroom floor and in the business office two floors below.

In later years, the base of operations was moved to the basement of the old Fresno County Courthouse, where the sacks of ballots were stored until the official count was made, usually several days later. The results of The Bee's unofficial tabulations were telephoned to the newsroom.

The results were hastened to Shelton and other reporters, who would continually write updated bulletins for KMJ, the McClatchy-owned radio station in Fresno. Broadcasting from the managing editor's corner office, KMJ therefore was always first with the election results, keeping city residents glued to their radios in the nighttime hours.

"Tell radio" was the order of the day, and not only on election day. KMJ had access to all of The Bee's output, often beating the paper with its own stories. In the case of elections, The Bee wouldn't be able to publish the results until the following afternoon's paper. And money-devouring "extras" weren't the order of the day.

(KMJ was not the only radio station that benefited from The Bee's efforts. On many an election night, opposition station personnel were spotted surreptitiously taking notes while listening to Bee election reports coming over their car radios.)

Bee reporters, under the direction of City Editor George Popovich, worked all night and into the morning, when they put the whole thing together and wrote their stories for the day's paper, each bearing the cautious "complete and unofficial returns," or "incomplete and unofficial returns."

Throughout those nights, Shelton would remain at his typewriter, pounding out new lead after new lead, his felt hat sitting on his head all the way. For years, he was an election-night fixture – thin of face and body, felt hat pushed back on his head, a smoking Lucky Strike or Camel, or a bummed Chesterfield, dangling from his lips or burning up in his cluttered ash tray. His fingers themselves almost smoked as he stroked the keys of that old black Royal, updating the stories for KMJ every half hour. Unlike many reporters of that day, he had learned the touch system of typing, and wasn't dependent on just two digits, as was his fellow reporter Karl Kidder.

During all of these seemingly incomprehensible, unbelievable nights of work, the politicians hovered around Shelton, knowing he was first with the most. But he'd motion them away, or snap that he was "busy, damn it!" And, with copy boys consistently updating results on strategically placed blackboards in the newsroom, they could get those results in a minute or two, anyway.

By midnight, Popovich would be gone, not to return until 6 o'clock in the morning. And Shelton was the first one he'd turn to then. Sometimes, he'd get an answer. More often, a grunt.

Phebe McClatchy Conley, widow of Carlos McClatchy, had the highest regard for Shelton. "I knew Diz, but we didn't have a social relationship at all," she said many years later. "We knew him, and in those days I used to go back and forth to the office a lot, so I would see him, stop and visit with him. And he was the one that Carlos depended upon, of course. He was very good, indeed."

Telegraph Editor Don Castelazo would say, "Diz, I always liked. His character was reserved, and yet you could feel the warmth that he had for things. He was a brilliant, brilliant mind."

Speeches weren't Shelton's thing. He refused to make them at almost any kind of sentimental gathering, explaining, "If I go to a party I drink, and if I drink I get sentimental, and if I get sentimental I cry. So I don't make speeches. Or I don't go to them (parties)." He gave this same excuse when he refused a party at his own retirement time, much to the regret of the editorial staff, even Don MacKinnon, an embittered copy editor who could find nothing good to say about The Bee.

Shelton was firm. Wally Henderson was a case in point. He had been a state assemblyman, and was out of office for years. Then, the political disease caught up with him again, and he decided to run "one more time" for the state Assembly in the Democratic primary. This meant that he, like other candidates, was invited to appear before The Bee's editorial board, made up of the paper's top editors, who would make voting recommendations to the public.

Henderson didn't get a vote in that meeting, except for Shelton's. But he overrode the board. The Bee backed Henderson in the primary, though his comeback bid was hopeless. And that's the way it turned out. He was trounced. Some believed Shelton went overboard on that one, that his friendship with the candidate led to his power ruling. Others said he went along with what several believed should be policy – to back the best candidate, no matter what the outcome.

Shelton was strong. Tom Kirwan, the editorial writer, cited the fight to ensure good government, local government particularly, as "probably

Robert P. Molander

the finest sustained policy legacy at The Bee", Kirwan said, "I have to particularly hand it to Diz Shelton, who went along with planning issues on which the powers-that-be were very much out of sync with The Bee – Fashion Fair, leapfrog zoning, St. Agnes (Medical Center) – all those things took a lot of guts for Diz to sustain those policies."

When Shelton moved to Fresno to attend Fresno State College, he knew what he wanted to do – work as a newspaper reporter. During his college years, he was editor of the Collegian, the FSC newspaper, and of Campus, the school's yearbook.

Years later, after retiring from The Bee, he was honored by the state Legislature. The Bee followed up with a story on the honor, and it mentioned the "fact" that Shelton got his newspaper start as a reporter with The Bee. This led Hubert Phillips, an FSC professor of history and political science who was widely acknowledged as one of the best in his field, to type a letter to The Bee. Phillips wrote, in part:

"The Bee of April 16, in its story of legislative honors coming to its recently retired managing editor, said, 'O.M. Shelton, a graduate of Fresno State College, began his newspaper career with the Bee as a reporter.' Wrong. He began it as a reporter and then editor of the Collegian.

"I can speak with some authority on this, for I was chairman of the Publications Committee, which elevated him from reporter to editor. Those of us who had any part in his newspaper career have always been proud that we 'spotted' talent early. It just now occurs to me that perhaps the writer of the quoted story in The Bee does not consider college papers as 'newspapers,' but we at the college in the '20s and '30s will long remember "Diz".

Shelton had an affinity for New Orleans jazz, and revered such giants as Kid Ory, Louis Armstrong, Bessie Smith, Davey Tough, Albert Nicholas. He put together his own hi-fi set when parts first came out, spurning one-piece units. He painstakingly read pamphlets, books on the subject, and bought and assembled individual parts such as the turntable, arm, tweeters, woofers.

He would lovingly sharpen the early-day steel needles, after experimenting unsuccessfully with the cactus variety. The "steels" weren't good for more than a few playings and would dig into his aging, thick vinyl jazz records.

Shelton hailed the coming of the diamond-point needle, and thereafter would use nothing else. An afternoon of enjoyment for him was sitting alongside his set, playing records one by one, listening as in a trance as he gazed into a fish bowl alongside. He once said he didn't pretend to understand the nuances of jazz, but that he listened to it simply because he liked it.

In his later years, Shelton developed another hobby – creating mobiles. He started spending a few weeks each summer in a cottage at Laguna Beach on California's coast, and took up the making of mobiles His first efforts were fashioned from cans, and the word went out that if you were drinking beer, make it Budweiser. Those, he said, were the preferred cans to cut with his tinsnips.

Shelton later expanded to working with wood, forming collages and framing artwork. Many of these adorned the walls or hung from the ceilings of Bee employees and others. Mike Smith, longtime Fresno dentist and buddy of Shelton, had one of those mobiles hanging in plain view outside his office window for at least two decades until his retirement. In that same year, a new office was built for Don Slinkard, managing editor of the Bee. One wall decoration Slinkard chose was a treasured wood collage given him by Shelton many years before.

Shelton continued his hobbies well into retirement. A former reporter turned city editor visited Shelton, and heard sounds emanating from his back yard. There was the familiar buzz of a power saw biting into wood, then a sudden, binding screech, then cursing. "What's the matter, Diz," the visitor inquired. Without looking up, Shelton answered, "Oh, this goddamn saw stuck in the wood. The wood's wet." And what was he working on? "Oh, a goddamn box for the grandkids."

So how's retirement going? "OK. The kids like these things." Then he pointed to a can of something – maybe it was a varnish – which he had just bought. "Look at it," he complained. "Used to cost sixty-nine cents. See what I had to pay for it? A buck forty-nine. Things are really going up. I'll tell you, you better put something aside for your retirement – better get into something that'll bring you some money. The Bee pension won't do it. It's not enough."

"OK, Diz," the visitor said. "How about a drink at the Hi-Life?" "Naw," he answered. "I can't afford it much any more. Besides, I got to finish this goddamn box."

Shelton never liked pomp or ceremony. This was never more evident than on his final day of work at The Bee --December 31, 1970. They wanted to throw him a party, but he'd have none of it. No way. But at least, they'd present him with a few gifts before he left, and they took up a collection on the editorial floor. Presents were bought, and a lifetime "press card" was designed for him. The plan was to do the deed in the afternoon, maybe about 3 o'clock. But Shelton, probably aware of what was going on, snuffed it out. At about 2:30 he put on his hat, slung his coat over a shoulder, walked down the long passageway to the elevator, took it to the first floor, walked out to his car and drove off.

Johnny Lombardi, The Bee's chief photographer, was standing at the juncture of the editorial floor and that long corridor, where the photography department used to be at the old Bee building on Van Ness Avenue. As Shelton walked by, he gave Lombardi a casual forefinger salute, a simple "See ya," and was gone.

"It reminded me of Jimmy Durante's exits," Lombardi recalled softly. "Walking out of the spotlight, into the dark."

About the farewell party, there was no alternative but to acquiesce to Shelton's wishes. George Gruner, his successor as managing editor, had the gifts delivered to Shelton's home the next day. The copyboy who took them reported that no one answered the doorbell, so he left them on Shelton's front porch.

Shelton spent some good years in retirement, fooling around with his mobiles and collages, watching the grandchildren grow up, listening to his jazz records, having an occasional branch and water. But he never was one to take care of his personal health. This neglect became evident in 1978 when he finally was forced to visit his doctor. It looked serious and a specialist was called in.

A few days later, a friend contacted the specialist and asked, "How's Shelton doing?" The answer was immediate: "He's dying." Why? If he had taken care of himself, death wouldn't have come so soon. But intestinal gangrene set in, and his delayed trip to the doctor came too late.

A week later, on November 1, 1978, Shelton died in the hospital. Final rites were held at the Lisle Funeral Home. He hadn't been a churchgoer, but one of the men he had liked and respected through the years was Dean Harry B. Lee of St. James Episcopal Cathedral. Dean Lee offered the eulogy, and said many nice things about the deceased, most of them factual, but with little to describe the man himself.

To quote Kirwan, the chief editorial writer, "Perhaps no one could capture the real Shelton. His managerial style was elusive, as was he. He used remoteness to prime effect, and it stood him in good stead, whether or not that was his purpose. He used his foibles as strengths. I confess there were times when it frustrated the crap out of me."

The funeral home was packed, and most of those present agreed that Dean Lee had done a creditable job. Probably the only one in the house who would object was the man laid out in the coffin.

Unfortunately, the service wasn't packed quite enough. No one attended from Sacramento.

Some years before his death, Shelton and his wife, Alta, were touring the gold country, and they came across a headstone in a Mariposa cemetery. It read:

Stop, traveler and cast an eye
As you are now so once was I

Shelton loved those lines, and said he wanted them on his tombstone. But his request, if indeed he ever made it to his family, wasn't heeded. Which was too bad. They would have fit his subtle humor to a "T".

Robert P. Molander

13

George F. Gruner

Like Diz Shelton, the man he succeeded as managing editor of The Fresno Bee, George F. Gruner was the people's choice. But early on in his career at The Bee, a good bet would be that he'd never ascend to the top spot. There was too much riding against him.

Gruner had served in the Army in Europe in World War II and worked for the Oakland Tribune as a reporter/rewrite man. After nearly three years in Europe, he was back in his home state, contacting newspapers in search of a job. The Fresno Bee had an opening on the copy desk, and he filled it.

He was to become the last of the in-house editorial employees to make it up to the top post as managing editor. (Don Slinkard was to become managing editor, but this after the top job was retitled executive editor.) In 1955, on Gruner's first day on the job at The Bee's copy desk, he was introduced to the man sitting next to him on the "rim" – one Jim McClatchy. Jim McClatchy? Gruner spent the rest of the day trying to figure who this man was, finally discovering that yes, Jim McClatchy did, indeed, have close connections to the McClatchy clan – he was Carlos and Phebe McClatchy's first-born. And he was working his way up the McClatchy ladder, learning the trade.

After a short period on the copy desk, Gruner, because of his previous cityside experience at the Oakland Tribune, became the first choice as a sub on the city desk run by George Popovich. When an opening came up, City Editor Popovich chose Gruner to become an assistant city editor, working under him and alongside No. 1 assistant city editor Diz Shelton. But it didn't appear that Gruner could rise much further. It was "gospel" that the city editor should be one who had served time in Sacramento, covering the state Legislature, with particular emphasis on news of Fresno and the San Joaquin Valley.

Gruner didn't fit those requirements, but two others did. Gordon Nelson was considered the top reporter on the staff. He'd covered the Legislature and politics, plus water, which was intertwined with politics. And there was Charles (Chuck) Hurley, who was covering the Legislature. He was in the running, even though he had never worked on the city desk, directing reporters or editing copy.

When Popovich lost his job on the city desk, Nelson was chosen to succeed him. He proved to be a fine city editor – hard-working, thoroughly respected. And Hurley was covering the Legislature in Sacramento. Gruner had two strikes against him – running behind a city editor who was about his age, and another, who apparently would succeed Nelson because he covered the Legislature.

But suddenly, Nelson quit to go to work for himself, then for Congressman B.F. "Bernie" Sisk. As expected, Shelton, by then managing editor, chose Hurley, who had the Sacramento background, to succeed Nelson.

Hurley turned out to be a poor choice, thoroughly disliked by the staff. After getting the job, he never seemed to want it, or to do what was required in it. Not too long after he was elevated, Hurley summoned now-first-assistant Gruner into an office and said, "I'm working too hard. I'm not going to work this hard any more. You're gonna have to do more." Gruner was nonplused: "I figured, well, what the hell, you know, the whole thing is – my attitude is that everybody bails hay, and you do what has to be done to get the paper out. It's the fun, you know. Getting the paper out."

Suddenly, Hurley opted off the city desk, and out of The Fresno Bee. He headed to Sacramento to work for the State Democratic Committee. And Gruner, without making a move on his own, got two jumps up the ladder of the hierarchy. Nelson and Hurley, were gone. Gruner suddenly was the logical choice to take over the city desk. And he got the job. The

Robert P. Molander

"people's choice," the one the staff had wanted, was in command. Many who were preparing applications to other papers, now tore them up.

The city editor's job is considered one of the most demanding in any field, and probably the most demanding on a newspaper, particularly on the editorial side. It's been said that five years on the job are about all a normal person can take. The unflappable Gruner served there for nine years.

In 1970, when it became known that Shelton would retire the following year, Gruner was made assistant managing editor, serving under Shelton. The following year he took that final step up, becoming managing editor. In those days, an "executive editor" was subservient to the managing editor. Since then, managing editors in newspapers across the nation have been named executive editors as the persons in charge of the newsrooms. The responsibility, the control, often the salaries, remained much the same. Gruner was one of those who became executive editors, and Don Slinkard, another savvy newsman who had served under Gruner as assistant city editor, city editor and assistant managing editor, was elevated to the managing-editor post.

Gruner would say that Slinkard was the perfect right arm – the man who kept him in check, slowed him down, prevented him from going overboard at times. Slinkard would regret that he was city editor for only about eight months, but he was more than capable of handling his new job. A good choice, and like Gruner, one that was highly respected in the newsroom.

One might wonder about key employees in the organization – those who were "irreplaceable." The reporters felt they fit that bill. So did the editors. But two others also fit the description, Frank Brown and Don Castelazo.

Brown was an editorial employee who worked with the printers in the composing room. Lines of hot type had to be assembled in page forms, and snap decisions had to be made. The system wasn't explicit, as it later became with the advent of computers in the newsroom. Pages were not dummied precisely. The editors would tell Brown which stories and photos would go on Page A1 and B1, and he'd fit them in, telling the printers which story to place where. He was a whiz at it, making snap decisions by looking at type, not hard copy. And reading type was an experience in itself. As one looked at the page of type, the printed words were both upside down and backward.

Brown was largely in control of the inside pages. He would quickly tell the printer working with him to, put this two-column head here, that photo there, this story here, etc. He wasn't allowed to do the actual work himself. In fact, he couldn't even touch the type. The ITU (printers union) wouldn't allow it. If he did, the printer working with him was entitled to dump the whole page of type on the floor.

The second key man was Don Castelazo, an old-line telegraph editor. He'd enter early in the day, be told how many pages there would be in that day's paper, and estimate the "news hole" – the number of columns of news type he'd need for the day. Then he'd start selecting stories to fill the space, tear them off the many wire-service teletypes used by The Bee and pass them along to the telegraph desk, where they'd be edited and topped with headlines.

He and Frank Brown would communicate, and "Casty" would tell him which were the "must" stories, (those that had to get in that day's paper) and the "use" stories (those which were almost as important.) The remainder would be used if space was available, or put into Brown's "holdover" file, to be used the next day, the next Sunday, or be killed.

Reporters in those days were taught from Day One that they wrote the news; they didn't make it. Tom Kirwan, editorial pages chief, broke that policy with the following commentary on the Op Ed page, January 17, 1992:

Old newspaper days: Remembering Casty

"The death of Don Castelazo the other day, at age 84, was an occasion for mourning by those who go back a ways with The Bee. It's not just that he was a good and kind man. He also was a symbol of our old newspaper days when pencil, paper, paste, ruler, scissors and typewriter were primary tools and type was set in lines of lead.

"Don – or 'Casty' – worked for the Bee for 43 years, from 1929 until his retirement in 1972. For 16 years he was the telegraph editor --the very title evokes the past – and that's how most of us remember him.

"The newsroom in the old Bee building (now the Metropolitan Museum) was, well, gritty – noisy, grubby, paper-strewn.

"It was an afternoon paper in those days, with brutal deadlines and a level of intensity that started revving up about 6:30 a.m., peaked around 11 a.m. with the first edition, and didn't really ease off until early afternoon.

"Casty was the vortex, sorting out and choosing copy from the wire service teletype machines, keeping track of new lead paragraphs and adds and inserts, plucking out what was needed from the growing heap and moving it over to the copy desk for editing.

"The newsroom was not a smoke-free environment then, to put it mildly. Casty smoked a pipe. I'm not sure it was a calming influence. He was known to set wastebaskets on fire.

"Casty was a diminutive man and worked on his feet, his shears flashing, his time and motion refined into a kind of journalistic ritual dance that gathered force but never spun out of control. There was maybe a millisecond for contemplation.

"How he did this so well and so equably was, and remains, a mystery to me. The whole business of putting out an afternoon paper with the old technology, with reasonably coherent results, was a minor daily miracle.

"Don Castelazo was one of the chief miracle-workers."

Walter P. Jones, top editor of the three Bees, exercised complete control from his Sacramento offices, checking competition newspapers such as the San Francisco Chronicle and the Examiner, ordering stories be run, often to the chagrin of his editors afield, who figured they knew the value of a story.

When Jones retired, the editor's position was passed to Carlos' son, the second C.K. McClatchy, and things got more independent in the hinterlands. C.K. didn't exercise the type of control favored by Jones; he granted each of his papers more autonomy. And he didn't object to a different look to the three papers. Until his time, one often could have switched the Page 1 mastheads and, except for a local story or two, not been able to differentiate one paper from the other.

One change instituted by Gruner was the elimination of the "ears" on Page 1 of The Fresno Bee. Consulting with Fresno staff people, he concluded he wanted Scoopy off the front page. This would have been considered heresy in the earlier days. After all, the company had paid Walt Disney himself to draw Scoopy as the emblem of the Bees.

With some trepidation, Gruner approached C.K. with the suggestion. C.K., with little hesitation, approved the idea, after saying, rather firmly, "You're going to keep it on the editorial page, aren't you?" Gruner hadn't given that a thought, but he quickly nodded "yes." And the Page 1 Scoopy soon was gone. Gruner wanted to change from the old-fashioned style, to lighten up the "flag" – give it more air, more white space. And it worked. (Later administrations returned Scoopy to page 1, on various occasions and in various costumes.)

Gruner was a member of the "Bee Four." The others were City Editor Jim Bort and reporters Bill Patterson and Joe Rosato. Their claim to fame? Each served 15 days in jail in 1976 rather than reveal the name of a confidential news source.

The background: The Bee in 1974 ran a series of articles detailing secret grand-jury testimony which led to the bribery indictments of a city councilman and two others. The stories quoted a "reliable source,"

The Fresno Bee's "jailbirds" (from left to right: Joe Rosato, George Gruner, Bill Patterson, and Jim Bort), address the press on their way to jail.

Robert P. Molander

and revealed the contents of an investigative grand-jury report. That report had been sealed by court order, and The Bee's stories indicated someone had violated that order.

A few days after the articles were published, Superior Court Judge Denver C. Peckinpah subpoenaed Bee reporters and editors to a hastily convened court inquiry. Peckinpah's mission was to determine who leaked the Grand Jury testimony. He agreed it was legal to publish the stories, but that his concern was who gave The Bee the report. Gruner, Bort, Patterson and Rosato were taken before the court. Asked the identity of the source, each declined to answer, basing the refusal on the state Shield Law that allowed newsmen to protect confidential sources. The judge took the position that the law did not apply to the courts, a separate branch of government.

McClatchy spent a small fortune defending the foursome in unsuccessful appeals to the California Supreme Court and the U.S. Supreme Court. The case was to become one of several confrontations between the press and the courts. Gruner, Bort, Patterson and Rosato were sentenced to an indeterminate stay in the county jail, after being warned by Peckinpah that they'd remain in custody until the source was revealed. Their stay actually was in what was called the county prison farm, a jail annex, away from the tougher county jail.

After 15 days, it was the testimony of psychiatrist Paul Levy, that they'd never reveal the source, that they were defending a basic tenet of their profession. They were released from custody by Superior Court Judge Hollis Best. The source never was revealed.

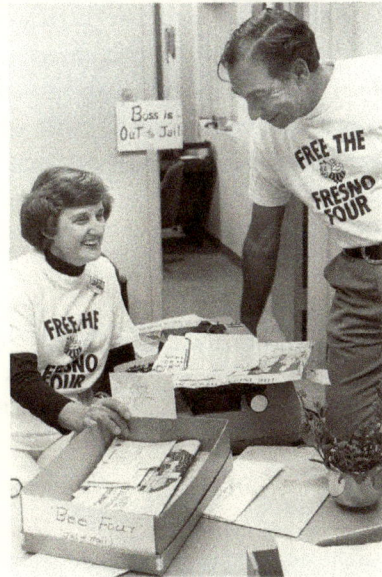

City Editor Bob Molander and Mary Zaninovich (Adm. Assistant) share a joke about the boss being out to jail.

The case got national attention, and with just cause. Roger Tatarian, former editor-in-chief of United Press International and later a professor of journalism at California State University, Fresno, wrote, "This is the biggest gang bust of newsmen in the 200-year history of the United States. Judges in other jurisdictions have occasionally bagged single journalists, but here a single court racked up four in one shot."

There were court actions for a year and a half, reaching the U.S. Supreme Court three times. On September 2, 1976, the final word came down from the highest court: Petition denied. It would not be heard. Case closed. Go to jail, Bee Four.

It was not an unpleasant 15 days, as jail terms go. Lt. Bill Cunningham, a friend of many Bee reporters over the years, was in command of the prison farm, and he didn't carry a whip. Custody was on a "trusty" basis. A friend of the newsmen even showed up with a large net, along with golf clubs and golf balls, so Gruner and Bort, the golfers of the group, could practice their swings. The four as civil prisoners were not assigned any work detail.

And the regular prisoners treated them with respect, in a more-or-less jovial manner. "I gotta go feed the dogs in case one of you guys tries to escape," one shouted to them on their first day in custody. Congenial inmates offered marijuana joints, which were politely refused. And one, a jail house artist, drew a cartoon showing them hanging from ropes, with the caption, "Hang In There, Bee Four." The Bee later published the cartoon.

The four were constantly on the phone, answering calls of news gatherers throughout the nation and even overseas. They also read the hundreds of letters they received, most of them on the positive side. And they had scores of visits from family and Bee friends, including C.K. McClatchy, top man at McClatchy Newspapers, who had OK'd the heavy court expenses.

The case led to a new policy that if a reporter was given a tip on a possibly inflammatory story, he was to give an editor the source's identity so the decision to publish could be shared.

Gruner had his lighter side. One oft-recited tale involved veteran Bee reporter Ward Grimes, who wound up his career writing stories on real estate and development. In those waning years, Grimes answered as few telephone calls as he could, letting others pick up the ringing phones. Grimes' desk was alongside a pillar in the new room. He moved it behind the pillar, so he couldn't be seen from the city desk, where the city editor and his assistants sat. Then, when the city desk got a call such as an obituary, and looked around for a reporter who wasn't busy, Grimes couldn't be seen from his strategic post behind the pillar.

Gruner, an assistant city editor at the time, wasn't above stretching out and peering behind the pillar, and telling Grimes to answer the phone. But the favorite story of the time involved checking the paper when the first copies rolled off the press. Gruner would assign reporters to check the sections of the paper – one the A Section, another the B section, etc. But when the copy boys arrived with the papers just off the downstairs presses, Grimes would disappear into the men's room down the hall. And there he's stay, relaxing on the "throne," for about 10 minutes or so.

Gruner solved that one, too. One day, as the papers arrived and Grimes disappeared, Gruner took a copy of the paper into the men's room and tossed it over the stall door, behind which Grimes was seated: "Ward, check the C's," he said as he walked out.

Through the years, The Fresno Bee was proud of its record of credibility. It has stood up for what it believed was right, the consequences be damned. This included backing political candidates who would probably lose, provided the editors believed those candidates were more fit for the office than the opposition.

A good example of that credibility came with the 1980s race for a municipal court seat, involving the incumbent and a challenger. Under The Bee's policy, all serious candidates were allowed to meet with the newspaper's editorial board and present their views on why they should be elected. The Bee then would publish its list of recommendations.

It was close in the meeting room. The board members were trying to keep in mind the McClatchy Newspapers admonition that The Bee will back the better candidate, no matter whether it thinks that candidate has a chance to win. In this race, it was believed the challenger had no chance, that the incumbent would easily get the public vote necessary to win. Gruner stepped in and asked the other board members present: "Which one would you rather appear before if you were in court?"

That got them all thinking and, following more discussion, the vote was 6-1 in favor of the challenger. Gruner joked that with that majority he didn't have to cast his vote. That's the way it ended up – 6-1, with The Bee endorsing the challenger. The election result? The thinking had been right. It was the incumbent by a wide margin.

Then there was the case of Sharon Levy, wife of Joe Levy, owner-operator of Gottschalk's department store, continually one of The Bee's heavyweight advertisers since the newspaper was founded in 1922. Mrs. Levy decided to run for a seat on the Fresno County Board of Supervisors. She, as other candidates, was interviewed by The Bee's Editorial Board.

Most of the board, in the days before women's rights became paramount in the nation's thinking, wondered about a woman in public office, and the vote was 6-2 against. But Gruner was nothing if he wasn't independent. He overruled the verdict, ordering that The Bee recommend Levy in the election.

She won, and turned out to be an excellent supervisor, including stints as board chairman. Gruner's insistence that she get the Editorial Board's backing, he said, had nothing to do with advertising; she was simply the best candidate.

An unidentified figure appeared in print in The Fresno Bee in those days, bylined as "The Shortender" to protect the real identity of the reporter. He operated in the shadows, and his byline would show up two or three times a year. One of his major "busts" was the Plantation Club, a tavern in the building across the street from the old police building on Broadway. In it was an elevator, complete with operator who scanned those entering, It carried gamblers upstairs a flight, where they were greeted by the sounds of rattling dice and shuffled poker cards. They also found football parlay cards.

Another coup was several houses of prostitution the Shortender unveiled in one night of work. Many, police and the underworld alike, wondered who this figure was. But The Bee never identified him.

At 4:42 o'clock on the afternoon of May 2, 1983, a severe earthquake, measuring 6.5 on the Richter scale, ravaged the town of Coalinga, 25 miles southwest of Fresno. The Bee's staff effort in covering the earth-

Robert P. Molander

quake was of Pulitzer Prize quality – an assessment later agreed to by news experts from across the nation. A Pulitzer Prize jury in the category of local coverage selected The Bee's effort as the best in the nation for 1983. But sad to say, the experts were overruled. The "award" to Fresno came from the Pulitzer jury; the Pulitzer Prize Executive Board, which had the final say, instead gave the top award to the Long Island Newsday.

On that fateful May 2nd, Bee editors had completed their 4 p.m. review of the news, submitted by the various departments, and had made plans for the front page, (The Bee had switched to morning publications by then), when The Bee building began to shake. Earthquake!

Anyone who had lived in California for a few years knew what it was. But knowledge of the epicenter was yet to come; it was near Coalinga on a previously undiscovered fault line. Telephone calls to the area were fruitless. Lines were down. So Bee editors dispatched reporter-photographer teams, via the highways by car, and aboard small, chartered planes. Time was of the essence – the Bulldog (first edition) deadline was just four hours away. The Bee staff did a job worthy of a Pulitzer Prize. Page Al was completely remade, and was "all quake." Five other pages were completely "quake." Besides the main story, there were sidebar pieces on the role of the Army National Guard, the Lemoore Naval Air Station, blood bank donors, the fault-line system, Coalinga as a town, emergency services which responded, and the embarrassing fact that the California State University, Fresno seismograph machine failed to record the earthquake because it had run out of paper.

In the aftermath, one member of the Pulitzer jury, chagrined because its recommendation had been overridden, sent The Bee a copy of its nomination to the Pulitzer Board: "The Fresno Bee was four hours from its first deadline when a powerful earthquake struck Central California shortly before 5 p.m. on May 2, 1983. When it was determined that the epicenter was near Coalinga – 25 miles northwest (sic) of Fresno – and that the enormous damage had occurred in the town, Bee reporters headed by plane and car for the disaster scene. Despite darkness and confusion several Bee reporter-photographer teams reached Coalinga, and though all phone lines were out, managed to file first-hand accounts and fly their photos out so that the Bee's first edition had six full pages of stories and photographs.

"It was an outstanding example of a newspaper mobilizing in the face of a major calamity with its reporters and photographers taking risks and using great resourcefulness to provide its readers with accurate, detailed and well-written accounts. The Bee's coverage was skillfully edited and over the next few days, the Bee maintained the pace and quality of its coverage, focusing on the aftermath and recovery efforts.

"A highlight of the first-day coverage was that besides vividly describing the damage, the Bee told residents of the valley all they needed to know about what to do and what to expect in the 24 hours immediately after the quake rocked the area. The Bee staff did a superb job under pressure and followed through with the kind of earthquake-related coverage which informed and enlightened its readers – first-class performance all around. The Jury voted this entry as its first choice."

The stories reflected the finest effort by The Bee staff in the area of spot news, where quick reaction to unforeseen events was the test. The prize instead went to a series of stories developed over a period of time.

Robert P. Molander

14

Dropout In Charge

Back in 1922, George Popovich told a bare-face lie. He said he was 18, and he was only 15. He had dropped out of Fresno High School; he had to get a job. The Railway Express Company was hiring, but wanted "men only." Popovich was well over 6 feet tall, thick of beard, and probably passed easily as 18, and he was hired as a wagon driver. The pay was $47.50 a week, he claimed later. However, Popovich was prone to exaggerate, and that does sounds like a huge salary for a wagon driver in those days – especially for a kid who was supposed to be just 18.

He also recalled the work was spread over six days a week, with long hours and no overtime pay – still a princely amount, if true. But he soon was to toss it in, whatever it paid, and instead took a job that gave him the unprincely sum of $16 a week, but one that at least filled his needs.

The Fresno Bee was about to begin publication, and was hiring. Popovich had this burning desire to be a newspaperman, he said later, and the new job was as a copyboy, the lowest rung on the editorial ladder, for The Bee. He applied for the job and got it.

Popovich took an early retirement in his later years. He was to be the last earthly survivor of that initial 1922 editorial crew, dying on April 11, 1979, at age 71, some 57 years after The Bee's first publication date.

He survived that long despite three heart attacks that he boasted would have doomed lesser men.

Modesty was never in the lexicon of George E. Popovich.

Popovich was a high school dropout, but he quickly realized he wouldn't get far in the newspaper game if he remained uneducated. So he became self-taught, spending his evenings at night school studying English and typing, and in the library reading "every book I could find on the newspaper business." He worked as a copyboy for six months, after which City Editor Bill Lockwood promoted him to cub reporter.

His education continued. Shortly after joining the editorial staff, he was granted a bit of the wisdom of Carlos McClatchy, the newspaper's editor: "Young man, now that they've made you a reporter, I want to give you some sound advice. For the best basic foundation in the English language, I want to have you read the Holy Bible and the complete works of Shakespeare." It was heady stuff for a 16- or 17-year-old, but Popovich complied. Many years later, he was to say, "I read the Bible six times from cover to cover, and struggled through Shakespeare's works over a six-month period."

First with, and later without, the support of veteran reporters and deskmen, Popovich rose through the editorial ranks. He started covering lodges and churches, advanced to the police beat, the city hall beat, financial and farm reporting, political writer, and covering the legislature for The Fresno Bee in Sacramento. In 1937, when Lockwood was promoted to associate editor, Popovich was elevated to city editor.

The old hands hadn't hesitated to help Popovich along in his formative months on the newspaper, but it didn't take them long to realize that advancement was his thing.

One reporter of that period said, "When he was a cityside reporter, Popovich wasn't popular with the reporters. He was too arrogant, had no consideration for the other reporters as individuals. He was cocky. But he was the first Fresno Bee reporter to cover the legislature in Sacramento. "He became city editor, and there was no love lost then, either. They didn't like George."

This was true of many, but there were other reporters who did admire Popovich, despite his rough edges. He knew a good story, how to deploy

Robert P. Molander

reporters on one. And he would protect them, on occasion, from the picayune displeasures of Managing Editor Lockwood.

Popovich could change faces in an instant. In those days, a reporter was given the daily task of picking up the mail in large pouches at the Post Office, and the news envelopes from outlying San Joaquin Valley towns and cities at the Greyhound bus terminal. The trip had to be started at 6:30 in the morning so that the valley and city desks could pass on the news to KMJ, the Bee's radio station. Its first news broadcast was at 7:15 a.m., Monday through Friday.

One morning, Jud Conger, the reporter who regularly made the Post Office and bus station pickups, had the day off, and a young reporter whose first year with The Bee was just up was assigned to make them. He didn't have a car, but there was an office Ford available, and he lived in an old apartment house just a block from the newspaper.

He had a few too many drinks the night before, and didn't wake up until 6:30 in the morning – hung over. He didn't take the time to shave or shower, dressed quickly and raced to the office, took the Ford, made the news pickups and drove quickly back to the Bee, praying all the while that Popovich would be late. No such luck. Popovich was sitting at the city desk, glaring. It was 7:15. There'd be no early valley news for KMJ that day.

Popovich's husky voice could be heard blocks away: "Where the hell have you been? We missed the damned radio broadcast. They don't have any valley news. Don't you like your job? Do you want to work here? Drinking all damned night. You better shape up, kid." And he stomped out of the room.

In those pre-cafeteria days, editorial staffers would cross the alley between Van Ness Avenue and Fulton Street to Babe's, the "greasy spoon" where they bought breakfast. Popovich went there that day for his morning helping of ham and eggs. The reporter sweated him out for half an hour, wondering where he'd work next. Popovich finally returned, headed for his desk and called across the intervening space to the reporter, "Hey kid, your raise went through."

He never mentioned the matter again. And the reporter was never late again with the morning mail, either.

The Fresno Bee building in 1968.

Popovich knew News. He knew Fresno County was always at or near the top of agriculture earnings across the nation, and Popovich saw to it that the agricultural picture was covered thoroughly. He wouldn't hesitate to battle mightily over which stories should be on Page 1, and if his reporters came up with a good farm or water yarn, you could bet it would make the front page.

He felt the same way about business stories. If a new plant was coming to town, it made Page 1. If a bank opened, it made Page 1. Growing population figures made Page 1. If a story showed almost any kind of progress in the city or surrounding valley, it made Page 1.

Weather stories were out there, too. Every day. No exception. He demanded them, got them. But they were the bane of reporters. A weather story on Page 1 every day. That might be OK in the East, where weather patterns varied almost daily. Or in the Fresno fall and winter, when unseasonal rainfall might severely damage the crops.

Robert P. Molander

But in the summertime, those stories were sheer drudgery, deadly dull: Fair and warm, fair and warmer, fair and unseasonably warm. But never HOT! It never did get "hot" in Fresno, if you believed The Bee, even though the temperature might get to 115 degrees. It wasn't Popovich's rule; it came all the way from Sacramento, from the company president, Eleanor McClatchy. She abhorred the word. Once, on an infrequent visit to Fresno, she stopped by the telegraph desk, said "Hello" to the rim rats (copy editors), probably intending to pass right on by. But Don MacKinnon, at a loss about how to respond and later wishing out loud he had said nothing, volunteered that "It sure is hot." That's all it took. Even though it was late afternoon, in August, and the mercury had topped the 100-degree mark. And the cooling system in the old Bee building on Van Ness Avenue never did work too well.

But MacKinnon, now sweating more than the weather required, got a two-minute dissertation. The valley weather was perfect for its intended purpose, to help the crops. Exceedingly warm temperatures. Yes. Warm temperatures are good for the valley, and for the bodies who lived in it. But don't call it "hot."

Popovich loved to gamble. Preferably on the turn of a card, but he tried it all. In the early days, gambling was widespread in Chinatown, in West Fresno. There was chuckaluck, in which the gambler bet on the throw of three dice. There was the "numbers" game. And although police of the day insisted there was no "numbers" operation in town, worthless tickets could be found daily, strewn in the gutters of Chinatown, tossed there by losing bettors.

There was over-under. The gambler threw the dice, and bet whether his roll would total over or under the magic number of 26. Push (26) paid the house. It was Popovich's favorite dice game and he, like other aficionados, always lost over the long haul. He'd groan. He hated to lose, even though he was playing a loser's game, with the odds in the house's favor. And worse, he hated to be thought of as a sucker. But to him, over-under was almost as irresistible as a poker game at the Elks Club.

Ward Grimes described Popovich shooting the dice from the leather cup at the sideboards of the small, circular green-felt table: "He'd just shake them and shake them. He'd get mad and throw them. He was a nut on that. Then we'd go in the back and buy our lottery tickets. It was all illegal, but they'd pay off the cops." Grimes said he saw the payoffs, in nickels, dimes, quarters, half-dollars, small bills, nothing that could be traced.

In retrospect, it was strange, this gambling, or rather, the lack of any stories being written in The Bee about it. The Bee was openly against police corruption, police brutality and payoffs to cops. But veteran reporters of that period said gambling was rampant, and the wonder is that The Bee allowed it to continue without making it public. Or that its city editor or his reporters were a part of it, knew of it, without revealing it in print. Opium dens were also involved, and they were never shut down by the police, or revealed by The Bee. Reporter Grimes, no lover of Popovich, told how he would take his boss to Chinatown, showing him its innermost secrets, initiating him into the gambling joints, at the city editor's request.

Grimes claimed to be close to the Chinese, and trusted by them, to the point where they'd seek him out for protection from the tongs. He'd inform the police, he said, and they would do what they could, or wanted to, which usually was very little. The way Grimes told it, Chinese hatchetmen would be dispatched from San Francisco, perform their gory duties, and return to The City. The bodies left behind would be buried without fanfare, or cremated, with the ashes shipped to China to be interred with their ancestors.

The Chinese handled their own problems and the police were more than content with that arrangement. The few who pleaded for outside help largely were ignored.

Through the years, there were consistent rumors of a literal Chinese underground – laboriously dug tunnels beneath their "city." Most outsiders insisted there was no truth to the rumors of these tunnels, but Grimes insisted he had seen them – been in them. And had taken Popovich with him. "Chinatown had an underground then," Grimes said. "That's where the opium dens were. They had bars, not to keep you in, but to keep the cops from getting in. They'd push a button and a light would go on. That was the warning system. I was in there, tried it once, two puffs (of opium.) It didn't do anything to me.

"They were paying the cops off. They'd have raids every once in a while, but the word would filter down and they'd know about the raids in advance. The raids were just to let the cops look good."

Robert P. Molander

These were fascinating stories. Editors and reporters knew of them. Popovich knew of them. But they never saw print.

Popovich lost his touch in his later days on the city desk. He still kept up with the news, getting to work at 7 o'clock in the morning, taking time out for breakfast at Babe's, but invariably leaving the building at 11 o'clock. His assistant city editor – Tut Jackson, until he was shelved on to the copy desk for drinking too heavily, and then Diz Shelton, until he was elevated to executive editor over Popovich – did the brunt of the work on the city desk.

Popovich would leave a general plan for the home edition. In those days, the copy deadline for the afternoon paper was 1:30 p.m. By then, Popovich would have been gone for two and a half hours, at the Elks Club for lunch – and his daily poker game. He'd never say he was going to play poker. But on his return, he'd leave no doubt. "I really took the boys today," or "I beat them one hand for $35," or "I had a bad day today. Broke even." To hear him tell it, he never lost.

Popovich had a drink or two on occasion, but booze never got to him the way it did to many reporters and deskmen. He was fond of saying that a drunk could never win at poker. He was a gracious winner. If he won, he'd buy magnanimously – drinks, a sandwich, both. But he was a terrible loser. Beat him in a hand, or a round of golf, which he also loved despite an incurable slice, and he wouldn't speak to you. After losing a golf game with a reporter or two, he'd explain, "Eleanor (McClatchy) always told me not to beat the boys at golf. Said it would be bad for employee morale."

On one of those golfing rounds, with a reporter he had picked up and driven to the golf course, the reporter missed an easy putt on the 17th hole and threw his putter to the green. Popovich was bending over, surveying his putt, and the errant putter bounced up and hit him a glancing blow on the head. He didn't say a word, then or through the 18th hole. Then he ignored his regular pit stop at the coffee shop, slammed his golf clubs into the car trunk and drove off, leaving the reporter stranded.

He didn't mention the incident at work the following day, or in the future. It was as if it had never happened.

In the early days of Popovich's reign on the city desk, it was strictly a man's world. There were no women reporters. There was Molly Marshall, who did reviews of plays, and there were society department ladies who wrote about engagements and weddings. But no "real" reporters, the kind you sent out on a fast-breaking story.

Then came World War II, and men suddenly were at a premium. Popovich needed a reporter. But there weren't any out there. Most of the men were at war. Then the light beamed. Upstairs, in the composing room, was Eva Burns, a grammarian whose desire to become a reporter was as intense as Popovich's had been at age 15. She had been hired by Don Stewart, the composing room foreman, as a copy holder. She worked with the proofreaders who checked galleys of editorial proofs, on the lookout for typographical errors, misspellings or factual mistakes.

The proofreader would read his proof aloud, and Burns would read along silently from the editorial copy, and they'd check each other. But she soon was bored with this. Stewart went to Popovich: "Why don't you give this girl a chance, George?" Popovich was hurting, so he talked with Burns. She was scared to death, but she desperately wanted to become a reporter. As she recalled it:

"It was 1942, and they couldn't get a man for love or money. And George said, 'Goddammit, I hate to hire a woman.' Right to my face. But he hired me. As a reporter. At $30 a week. That's the same I had been making as a copy holder, but a lot more than the $16 I had been making before in a department store. So I told him that would be all right. Gee, I would have taken the job for nothing."

Thus, Burns became the first female cityside reporter hired by The Fresno Bee. She was to become the first of many, until years later there were about as many women as men reporters, doing all kinds of stories and covering all kinds of beats.

It took World War II to set the scene, but Burns – she would have been referred to in print as Mrs. Burns in those days – broke the barrier. The women were on their way, and Popovich, recalcitrant as he was, nevertheless started it all in Fresno. In reality, he did go it one better. Before his retirement, and with Lockwood's permission, he "stole" June Muller, a fine reporter who just happened to be a woman, from The Bee's society department. The selection proved well-founded. He

Robert P. Molander

was able to put her on just about any story, and she came back with the goods.

Muller had worked for the Oakland Tribune as a copy girl, then for the Contra Costa Gazette as society editor and general-assignment reporter. She became a reporter for the Post Enquirer in Oakland and "quit the business" in 1946 to become a housewife. In 1951, after the untimely death of her husband, she went back to newspapers and gave The Fresno Bee a shot "because it was between San Francisco and Los Angeles and seemed a good place to start again," she said years later.

She didn't succeed immediately. Managing Editor Lockwood turned her down. His given reason? She didn't know the area. So she took a copy of The Bee back to Oakland, rewrote the local stories in it and mailed it and the rewrites back to Lockwood. "That's when he hired me," she recalled from her retirement home in Coronado.

She was hired as a society reporter, but soon tired of writing engagements and weddings. Six months after being hired, she went to Popovich with an ultimatum. He needed a reporter, and she told him, "I go city-side in two weeks, or you can consider this my two-weeks notice." Whether or not she was bluffing, and she probably wasn't, she got the reporter's job.

Muller never was assigned a regular beat, as most reporters were then, but covered a wide variety of stories. Many were features. She also was art editor, film critic, jazz and entertainment critic, and worked on special sections, on the copy desk, and put in an occasional shift subbing on the city desk. She left to become a reporter for the San Francisco Examiner. Muller was handed good general-assignment stories; Burns usually was stuck inside the office. She wanted to do more than church and lodge news, her primary beat, but Popovich "protected" her, against her wishes, treatment he never afforded Muller.

"Sometimes, George didn't want to send me after a hot one," Burns said. "But you're sitting in the office, and you're the only reporter they have, what do you do? So he'd send me out, but he didn't want to. He thought I'd get hurt. George was a darned good newspaperman. Sometimes he used to call somebody a son of a bitch. But I loved him just the same. I used to go home and be mad at him sometimes, but you have to remember, he let me do those things I wanted to do. He tried to keep me from going on some of the hot ones, and then he'd send me.

"I had more freedom than other girls in similar positions, because I went around and visited other newspapers, and some of them never got to do anything but the churches and lodges. One time he yelled at me clear across the room, 'Dammit, where the hell is my so and so story?' I did an awful thing. I yelled clear across the room, louder than George, 'In the basket, on your desk. Where the hell did you think it would be?' He looked at the basket on his desk and said, 'Oh, sorry.'

"George was all right by me."

Police brutality was not uncommon in those days. Some cops were mean, and they took it out on the denizens of West Fresno, the other side of the tracks. Mostly, this meant the African-Americans. The Italians, Russians, Germans who also had communities within the community there weren't bothered much. And the Mexicans, largely, hadn't arrived yet. Many of those on the force were recruited from the overall West Fresno community – blacks excepted.

Reporters of the day saw police brutality – needlessly pushing a black until he fell down the stairs of the old Police Department building on Broadway, and laughing at his plight. Sticking him in the gut or kidney, where it wouldn't show externally, with a heavy billy club. Punching him with a clenched fist until his face bled.

These indignities were talked about and laughed about at the police station, and in the editorial department of The Fresno Bee, to a lesser degree. Unfortunately, that's the way it was. No one complained, least of all the blacks. It was their lot, and they accepted it.

Back in 1922, when The Bee was founded, it had adopted the Cardinal Rules as first set forth by James McClatchy when he founded The Sacramento Bee, and confirmed by his son, C.K. McClatchy, when he became editor in Sacramento. The 14th, and final, Cardinal Rule: "Consider the Bee always as a tribunal which desires to do justice to all, which fears far more to do injustice to the poorest beggar than to clash swords with wealthy injustice." A noble rule. But The Bee didn't heed it in these cases.

It wasn't until the civil rights movement of the 1950s and '60s that The Bee, along with other laggard newspapers in the nation, finally took up the battle for African-American rights. They no longer could be ignored, picked on, beaten up for no reason other than their color.

There were common incidents of rights being violated, again primarily against the blacks.

George Popovich was more than disappointed; he expressed shock when he was passed over and Diz Shelton was promoted from assistant city editor to the new post of executive editor, an obvious step towards the top editorial job of managing editor. Popovich had assumed it would fall to him. But now, he had gone as far as he was going to go and he knew it. The writing was on the wall. But not wanting to throw in the towel, he did make one more try. He contacted the brass in Sacramento, trying to sell the idea of his becoming a sort of company greeter, one who would wine and dine top news sources and business contacts who could be helpful to The Bee and the community. With his personality, he reasoned, he'd be perfect for the job. But The Bee's leadership wanted him out of the city editor's chair. His first heart attack hastened the move, and he was named a special writer, doing feature stories on Fresno history and the personalities who had helped build Fresno.

In 1958, Gordon Nelson, a county newsman and former Marine, became city editor, and The Bee's image changed forever.

One Sunday morning Popovich was late for a round of golf and was speeding to the course. He was pulled over by a Highway Patrol officer on a motorcycle, and the cop approached the car, ticket book in hand. But before he could start writing, Popovich said sternly, "I'm George Popovich, and I'm the city editor of The Fresno Bee. We write a lot of good stories for you guys; we're always on your side. Do you know that? And I'm late."

The shaken officer backed off: "All right, Mr. Popovich, but please try to drive a little slower." Popovich gunned the car out, grinning and saying, "I sure told him, didn't I?"

A second heart attack hit Popovich in 1962, and on his doctor's advice, he got out of the newspaper business. An old friend, Hugh M. Burns of Fresno, was a powerful state senator, and Popovich became his administrative assistant. But a third heart attack, this one in 1971, forced him to quit all work, and he spent the rest of his life, until his death in 1979, having lunch and playing poker at the Elks Club, or playing golf at the Sunnyside Country Club, of which he was now a member. After his first marriage, which ended in a bitter divorce, Popovich wed socialite Margaret Rowell, whose uncle, Chester Rowell, had owned the old Fresno Morning Republican and the afternoon Fresno Herald, both eliminated by The Bee in the circulation war that lasted from 1922 to 1932.

She and Popovich had a nice home alongside the Sunnyside Country Club. After that marriage, he held such titles as partner in the Rowell Company, vice-president and director of the RowellChandler Company, director of the Fresno Boys Club and director of the Sunnyside Property Owners Association. He had made it big, but long-time acquaintances firmly believed he would have chucked it all for that managing editor's job at The Fresno Bee.

15

Everybody Knew Ed

Few Fresnans of his day ever heard the name Edgar Orman, and fewer still ever heard the names Edgar Weber Orman strung together. But "Ed Orman" was a household name in Fresno, as well known in print as any other person in the city's history.

In the eyes of his readers, Orman was "The Fresno Bee Sports Department." His Sport Thinks columns – five every week – were the bible of the local sports community. If Ed Orman wrote it, it was gospel. Whether it be on a high school basketball game, a college track meet, an international prize fight, a professional baseball or football prediction. The sports world was his realm, and if he wrote it, you could bet on it.

Orman was a crusty editor, and he ruled his fiefdom with an iron fist. He was far ahead of his time in his hatred for cigarettes, cigars or pipes. There would be no smoking within the sports department confines. And there wasn't, if he was around. Sports reporter Tom Meehan would practically swallow his cigar when Orman showed up unexpectedly. But Meehan couldn't hide the smoke screen, or escape the lash of Orman's instant fury. In his defense, Orman suffered from severe allergic reactions, particularly in the spring and summer when he was outdoors covering sports events, such as a night baseball game. He'd return to the office, his eyes a bloody red, his breathing belabored.

Any scoops in the department belonged to the boss. If a reporter came in with one, he wouldn't dare put it in a story without telling Orman first. And more often than not, the item would first be seen in an Orman column.

Throughout a lengthy association, Orman and Sports Writer Omer Crane never got along. Orman had no legitimate reason, or the will, to fire sports writer Omer Crane, and Crane never took his problems to a higher court. In fact, when it was finally decided that the department needed an assistant sports editor, Crane got the job. But the bitter feelings never abated.

The Fresno Bee grew over the years, and Ed Orman played a major role in that growth. He was never one to shirk work because of the hours needed in the ever-expanding sports field, and he kept his finger on everything that was going on. Overtime pay was almost unheard of in his early days, but that didn't seem to bother him. He worked split shifts for most of his career – in at 6:30 in the morning, getting out that day's editions. That meant laying out the paper with yesterday's or last night's local news, and with the outpourings of burgeoning professional sports.

That chore would be completed about 9 o'clock, after which he'd get on the phone and pick up tidbits for his next-day's column. Names were the thing in those columns, culminating with his Christmas Day feature, replete with just about every sporting name in the local arenas – athletes, coaches, fans. The sports gentry would await those columns eagerly, and the "names" not included were crestfallen. His Christmas presents – names in his column – were more sought after than the ties and socks that adorned the decks under the Yule trees.

After the column was written, Orman sometimes would take a few hours off, then cover an afternoon high school game, especially in his earlier days. And it wouldn't be uncommon for him to cover a night game or a late meeting on the same day. These were grist for his column mill – a quote here, a tip there. They were everywhere, and no one in the entire editorial department got more of them than he. Oftentimes, his problem was not what to put in the column, but what to leave out because of space limitations. After the death of the Morning Republican in 1932, when it was purchased by The Bee and put out of business,

The gang's all here.
Fresno Bee men at company golf tournament.

Orman's was the only game in town. It was Sport Thinks or nothing. But the fans rarely were heard to complain.

Local sports celebrities beat a well-worn path to his corner desk next to a west window, ostensibly to shoot the bull but in reality seeking entree into the column. To court The Fresno Bee Sports Department was to court Ed Orman, and he had no lack of suitors. Hunters and fishermen gravitated to Bert Dahlgren, golfers to Omer Crane, prep athletes and coaches to Bruce Farris. But let anything big come up in any field and it was Orman's. The scoops were his domain.

Orman was a solid backer of local sports, and didn't hesitate to join boards and groups which were instrumental in furthering local athletics, or in selecting top athletes for awards. One example was the Greater Fresno Youth Foundation, which was organized to take over the local baseball franchise when the St. Louis Cardinals dropped their Fresno farm club. Orman was a major backer of the foundation, in print if not financially. His participation was contrary to McClatchy policy of the day – you never blew your own horn, or became overly visible in the public eye. Orman was the exception.

He also was in the forefront when the West Coast Relays were started in 1927. The one-mile board track at the Fresno Fairgrounds was destroyed by fire and there was moaning and gnashing of teeth from the auto-racing gentry, but Orman later was to call it "a blessing in disguise." He explained:

"It paved the way for the establishment of the prestigious West Coast Relays. Al C. Joy and Gerald F. Thomas were the leaders of the Raisin Festival Association, which had its festivities and big parade every spring. The auto racing was a part of it.

"Participation of communities in the festival diminished, and Joy and Thomas proposed an athletic event to substitute for the parade and auto race. We, in cooperation with Fresno State officials, came up with the idea of a gigantic collegiate athletic event. And so the West Coast Relays were born."

Fresno State College, to become a university in later years, was one of his favorite subjects in print. There was a wealth of story ideas at FSC, and Orman milked them dry. His columns ran the gamut – football, basketball, baseball, track. Sometimes the minor sports, as they emerged.

But his was a male world. Women were for the kitchen, or child-bearing. There was an occasional Babe Didrickson Zaharias, a Mickey Wright, a Helen Wills. But they were in the vast minority. Sports was a man's world, and Orman covered it as such. So did most other sports-writers in the nation.

Orman was also a "homer." He rarely wrote anything derogatory about the home team. His coverage of the Fresno Cardinals and later the Fresno Giants minor league baseball teams amused the staff. If the home team won, the game story or column might mention "our Fresno Cardinals," or "our Fresno Giants." If the team lost, it would be "the Fresno Giants."

The "homerism" wouldn't be honored, though, if he didn't get the story first. Once in a while a radio station, even including the Bee's KMJ, would get a beat on a story. Orman would call the news source and blast him for letting radio have it first. The source would immediately slide into Orman's private doghouse, likely to remain there for a long spell. He never was one to forgive and forget. And the source's team, if he happened to have one, might suffer in print. Orman wouldn't stand for being beaten on a story by "those radio jerks" or "those radio bastards." He was to grow to hate TV even more, but fortunately for his mental health, it hadn't been on the scene for too many years before he retired.

If Orman had any favorite subjects, they were auto racing and boxing. He reveled in the friendship of the giants of those sports, and would interview them every time they were in the area.

He built up a large collection of photographs depicting him and the athletes he interviewed – Jack Dempsey, Joe Louis, Max Baer, Rocky Marciano, Billy Vukovich, Bob Mathias. Bee photographers learned to make these prints for Orman's library. In retirement, they adorned the walls of his den.

He was a great admirer of J.C. "Aggie" Agajanian, longtime racing impresario known as the "Dean of Indianapolis Car Owners." Aggie owned or sponsored racing machines from 1948 to the 1980s, and his top cars at the Indy 500 races invariably bore the number 98. A Californian, he cultivated and was greeted warmly by sports writers across the nation, and was a frequent Fresno visitor. He'd get the red-carpet treatment when he entered the Bee sports department, wearing his trademark white Stetson cowboy hat. He was prominently mentioned in countless Orman columns.

Orman would have given an arm and a leg to cover the Indianapolis 500 races in person, and The Bee gave him that opportunity on the expense account. It paid off. He was there in 1953 and 1954 when Fresno's Billy Vukovich won back-to-back Indy 500s, and on Memorial Day, 1955, when Vukovich was killed on the track.

"Vuky" was a special friend of Orman, and had reaped gallons of ink in The Bee as he graduated from local midget racing to the nation's major tracks. On this day, Vukovich was leading the 500 again when he was forced to pass to the right, something he had said a driver on the track never should do, was involved in a multi-car crash and was killed. That day, The Bee ran an 8-column banner headline on Page A-1 – "Vukovich Dies In Racing Crash." The accompanying story was by

Orman, telephoned from Indianapolis. He later was to say it was the toughest assignment of his newspaper life. Besides the fact his friend was killed, he was forced to dictate his story over the phone to The Bee, to a secretary who took it on a typewriter, with precious little time remaining before deadline.

After Orman retired from The Bee, he was hired by the Fresno Guide, a shopper publication, to write a series of columns titled "Down Memory Lane." He went to a couple of Indy 500s, relaying feature stories from the track. His other Guide columns were reminiscing on old-time sports in Fresno, and were well-received, especially by the senior set. But one critic likened it, say, to the San Francisco Giants trading Willie Mays to Cincinnati in his old age. How could The Bee let him go?

Orman claimed credit for originating the nickname for Fresno State sports teams – The Battlin' Bulldogs. It survived through the years. He also was instrumental in bringing Fresno's first professional sports team to town. The year was 1941, and Orman yearned for good local baseball. He was a friend of Phil Bartelme, agent for the legendary Branch Rickey, the owner of the St. Louis Cardinals of the National League. John M. Euless, a local Realtor and businessman, was a baseball nut, and Orman introduced him to Bartelme. The threesome convinced Rickey that Fresno would be a good city for a franchise, and the Fresno Cardinals were born, a major cog in the fledgling California League.

The big problem was coming up with a place for the team to play. Euless and Orman pushed through construction of Fresno State College Park, a joint college and public effort. It was completed in a matter of weeks, and its components included some pilings from Ratcliffe Stadium, plus materials donated by lumber companies. The field was to become John Euless Park.

The Cardinals were successful in Fresno for many years, but things got tough after the 1956 season and word came that it would be the last for the St. Louis offspring. The Greater Fresno Youth Foundation, started earlier by Orman and other baseball fans, including major Fresno businessmen, decided local ownership would be the best solution. Thus the Fresno Sunsox were born, and played the 1957 season. But without a major league connection, good players were hard to get. The team lost games and money. Then, almost miraculously, the word filtered in from the East that the New York Giants and the Brooklyn Dodgers were moving west.

Another friend of Orman was Garry Schumacher, director of public relations for the New York Giants. Orman let it be known that Fresno, in the heartland of California's fast-growing San Joaquin Valley, would indeed be the perfect city for a Giants franchise. The Giants bought Orman's plan, and on December 13, 1957, Orman broke the story: "You will be following the Fresno Giants, not the Fresno Sunsox, next year." It was probably the biggest coup of Orman's lengthy career. The Fresno Giants remained a constant in Fresno for 21 years, becoming the longest-lived minor league baseball franchise in the nation.

People in Fresno automatically equated Ed Orman with sports, but that's not the way he started. After reading his columns over the years, it would be hard to believe that this writer to whom proper grammar was a relative stranger was The Fresno Bee's first education writer. But he was. Interspersed with sports stories after he came aboard in 1924 were pieces on the city schools system. His first byline, though, was in sports. It came on August 30, 1924. He had covered a prize fight the night before. Joe Bell of Pittsburgh stopped Tony Bonillas of Los Banos in the second round. Referee Gene Jewett halted the fight.

It was the next year – May 6, 1925, to be exact – that Orman made the front page for the first time. It came on the first story of a series on the condition of the city schools system, stressing the lack of proper buildings, the inadequate facilities for expanding enrollment. The Bee followed the series with editorials that backed changes, and on November 10, 1925, the voters passed two bond issues for improvement of the existing buildings and the construction of new schools. The improvements were exactly those called for by Orman in that series.

Orman disliked having his columns changed in any manner, by anyone. And generally, no one wanted to read them in their original form, either. Most sportswriters under him, with the possible exception of Omer Crane, wouldn't change a thing. In addition, a person could get "wet" reading one of Orman's pieces. In those days, succeeding takes (pages) of a typewritten story or column were pasted together before it was sent to the composing room to be cast into type. Orman would slap on huge gobs of soggy paste, and a column of three or four takes would wind up soaking wet. So if time permitted, the person assigned to edit the column before it was sent to the printers would "hang it out to dry."

If time was of the essence, it was sent to composing untouched. There, copy cutter Hal Jacobs would ease the wet mess out of the pneumatic tube which had carried it to the composing room, curse mildly and hang it up to dry. If it was too close to deadline, he would cut it back into takes and send each to a different typesetter. This, of course, negated the need for pasting it up in the first place, but evidently no one ever pointed that out to Orman. Or, possibly, he was too stubborn to acquiesce.

One afternoon, he asked a cityside reporter with whom he had become friendly to read his column over and "send it up" to composing to be put in type. The reporter took Orman at his word. He checked the column carefully, changed some words, made some corrections, rewrote a couple of paragraphs, even changed the lead paragraph a bit. And he sent it up. That's the way it appeared in The Bee the next day. The reporter asked Orman if it was all right.

"Yeah," growled the sports editor. "It's fine." But that particular reporter never was asked to copyread Orman's column again.

Orman could boast of many outstanding achievements during his long career. He covered the 1932 Olympic Games in Los Angeles. He sat ringside at nearly all of Young Corbett III's bouts, including the match in which Corbett outpointed world champion Jackie Fields in San Francisco to win the welterweight title, and Corbett's later title defeat in New York by Jimmy McLarnin. Corbett was a Fresno southpaw whose given name was Ralph Giordano. After a couple of matches, he adopted the name of Young Corbett Ill. Italian names weren't the ring rage in the early 1920s.

Orman covered horse racing when it first was legalized at the Fresno District Fair. He covered several Rose Bowl football games, including three that coach Pappy Waldorf's University of California football teams lost to the Big 10 in the 1940s. There were also East-West Shrine Games at Kezar Stadium in San Francisco, baseball World Series in Chicago, Los Angeles and New York. Scores of fights were reported under his byline, including some featuring boxers such as Joe Louis and Rocky Marciano. He sat ringside the night heavyweight Max Baer fatally injured Frankie Campbell.

There was a humorous angle to Orman's coverage of the Corbett-Fields bout at Radio Park in San Francisco, but one which he didn't appreciate. Radio Station KMJ, owned by The Bee, wanted instant coverage. The Bee complied. Duke Millard of The Bee's business office was to pick up Orman's blow-by-blow account from ringside via Western Union, and broadcast it to Fresno-area fans over KMJ. The whole town was listening. The logistics worked well, but Millard, a true ham, magnified Orman's round-by-round information, interposing his own thoughts along the way.

"Corbett won the decision," Orman said in later years, "but the way Duke replayed it, it didn't come out so well for Corbett. The Italians in Fresno were up in arms, and were going to lynch me. They knew Duke was getting his information from me. They thought, before the decision was announced, that Corbett lost. It was the way Duke replayed it. He favored Fields." Orman took care of the problem in succeeding issues of The Bee, assuring the local fans that their hero had indeed won.

Ed Orman was on board before black athletes were allowed to compete on major teams, particularly in the South. There were none, of course, in professional baseball. Orman always believed he played a part in breaking the national color barrier in college sports. The facts tend to bear him out.

The year was 1946, shortly after the end of World War II. The Fresno State College football team had a game scheduled with Oklahoma City University in Oklahoma City. Two members of the FSC squad were Jack Kelley, a halfback, and Millard Mitchell, a guard. They were black – in the language of the day, "colored." And Oklahoma City didn't want to play a team whose roster included colored athletes.

The schools dickered back and forth for weeks before the game. It was on – it was off. FSC's position was simple: Kelley and Mitchell played, or the game wouldn't be played. Oklahoma City countered that there would be no game involving blacks. Orman ran daily stories in The Bee. Local fans were in an uproar. It probably wouldn't have amounted to much, except that the wire services picked it up.

This was 1946, the year before Jackie Robinson broke the Major League color barrier with the Brooklyn Dodgers. The public was in the mood for a change. African-Americans were making themselves heard. It was two days before game time and the hassle hadn't been settled, but the FSC squad took a charter plane to Oklahoma City just in case. Kelley and Mitchell were on board. So was Ed Orman.

He spoke with the Oklahoma City public relations man in the Biltmore Hotel there, and the man told Orman, "Well, I'll tell you, Mr. Orman. You can put 'em out on that field out there but we're not going to be responsible for what happens."

FSC officials and coaches were in a bind. Should they stand for right, or bow to might? Certainly, given the mood of the day, Kelley and Mitchell would be lucky to survive the game. The decision was made. Common sense ruled. Because of the certain physical danger, Kelley and Mitchell would sit on the bench in street clothes. And FSC was trounced, 46-7. With Kelley and Mitchell in the game, it no doubt would have been lost anyway, but probably not by that overwhelming score. The pair were first-stringers, acknowledged as two of the finest players on the Bulldog squad.

United Press and The Associated Press, alerted by Orman's stories in The Bee, covered the game, and it made newspapers throughout the nation. Not many cared about the game itself, except the immediate cities and their fans, but the issue of barriers to blacks was one everyone was reading about, and which many cared about.

There were pros and cons everywhere. The game became the subject of columnists across the nation. Years later, African-Americans were accepted as football players at the University of Oklahoma, and in succeeding years at other major institutions in the United States, particularly at such previously major all-white bastions as the University of Alabama and the University of Mississippi. Certainly, the end of racial bias in sports would have emerged, no matter what, but Orman and The Bee surely did their bit to hasten it along.

Orman was an organizer, and his word carried a ton of weight locally. He was instrumental in organizing the Fresno County Athletic Hall of Fame, and the Fresno Hot Stove Dinner, which was to attract top baseball players including Tom Seaver, a Fresno product, but also such

Robert P. Molander

luminaries as Johnny Bench at the height of his catching-slugging career with the Cincinnati Reds. Orman was there when the West Coast Relays got its start in 1927, and attended and wrote on every one of those track-and-field extravaganzas for the following 50 years.

It cost him physically to cover those out-of-doors events, particularly in the spring. He'd return to the office after covering a Fresno Giants baseball game at night, his eyes a blood red, his nose a sieve. He never could find a cure for the allergies that plagued him throughout his career and into retirement, but he never let them stop him from covering an event he thought was important enough for his typewriter. It was because of those allergies that he banned smoking in the sports department, putting him years ahead of his time in the clean-air movement.

Orman got deathly ill with cancer before his age-65 retirement. He was taken periodically to San Francisco for special treatment, and actually "died" there once – for about three minutes. He was revived, and eventually beat the disease. Managing Editor "Diz" Shelton saw to it that The Bee carried him on its payroll for many months after his sick leave ran out, earning his undying gratitude.

Ed Orman got his start as a newspaperman by peddling the Brazil Times in his native Brazil, Indiana. He wrote sports stories for the high school newspaper, and, despite his diminutive stature, played basketball, becoming captain of the team in his senior team. The team made the state finals, held at Purdue University. He was a four-letter man in high school sports, also playing baseball and competing in track and football. He played baseball in a semi-pro league and earned a tryout with Terre Haute of the Three Eye League. He didn't make the team and decided to move to California.

His first stop was at Venice in Southern California, where he worked doing it all for a weekly newspaper. Then he migrated to Fresno and a stint in the circulation department of the Fresno Morning Republican. He wanted to write, and was hired as a reporter by H.R. McLaughlin, managing editor of The Fresno Bee, in 1924.

In 1959, still employed as The Bee's sports editor, Orman was honored for his 35 years of writing sports in Fresno with a dinner at the Sunnyside Country Club. It was attended by some 300 sports fans of the area. Seated at the head table were, among others, Pappy Waldorf,

University of California football coach and San Francisco 49ers scout; Buck Shaw, coach at Santa Clara and the 49ers; Bill Schroeder, Helms Athletic Hall of Fame figure; and Rube Samuelsen, Pasadena sports editor, influential Rose Bowl figure and an acclaimed public speaker. City and county officials were also in attendance.

Orman, as required, sought permission from William E. Lockwood, The Bee's managing editor, to attend his own party. Lockwood told him it would be all right, but that he couldn't accept any presents of appreciable value. The word was out that the party givers intended to give Orman a new car, but if true, that never came about. He continued to drive his old jalopy.

There was another, more gala party for Orman. It came in 1974, after his retirement from The Bee, and was held in the Elks Club, of which he was a member. Tickets were sold throughout the city, and 450 attended. Everyone who was anyone was there, even though Orman wasn't with The Bee any more, and didn't have the column in which to laud friends and slice up enemies.

Still, he was hailed as the "dean" of West Coast sports editors, which he indeed was. Famed local wit Al Radka was master of ceremonies, and the party was attended by the mayor, police chief, scores of coaches, California League officials, fellow sports writers and editors from near and far. He got trophies of every kind from the sports gentry.

Coach after coach took the microphone at the head table, heaping tons of praise on the honored guest. The fact that the affair also was attended by The Bee's new sports editor and its executive sports editor, plus the sports reporters of the day, didn't faze these coaches. The Bee would never be the same, would never be as good in the sports field as it was in Orman's day, they opined.

In his day, Orman had held every one of the speakers in his steel grasp, and they knew it. But they didn't hold that against him. Orman was their sports editor, and The Bee would never be the same without him.

Orman was elected to the Fresno Boxing Hall of Fame, as a writer, not a pugilist. He also was named to the Fresno Twilight League Baseball Hall of Fame, again as a writer, and was the first president of the California League Baseball Writers Association. But he had what he considered some unfortunate moments with The Bee:

For many years, he was generally considered and generally labeled the sports editor, but later revealed he never got commensurate pay.

In 1963, he traveled to Los Angeles and covered a Yankee-Dodger World Series game. A couple of days later, the word came down from Sacramento: There would be no more out-of-town sports trips for Fresno without prior approval from Sacramento.

On a day off in the early 1960s, he was sitting in the press box at a San Francisco Giants baseball game. Announcer Russ Hodges, looking for fresh blood, asked him if he'd do an interview on the air. Orman was well aware of Bee policy, of not blowing his own horn, but Walter Mails, a Giants official, said he'd get an OK. He telephoned The Sacramento Bee and got Fred Moore, who called Bill Lockwood in Fresno. Lockwood denied permission and the word got back to the San Francisco press box. No on-the-air interview.

Orman, like most other retired Fresno Bee employees, contacted in 1985, bemoaned the minuscule pensions received by old-time staffers. "You can't live on them," he said. "I had over 100 overtime hours – compensating-time hours – when I retired, that I didn't turn in. They were so good to me when I was sick, I didn't have the nerve to turn in that overtime. They treated me real good, you know."

16

Women On Board

In 1951, Desa Cucuk (later Desa Belyea, after her marriage to George Belyea) graduated from Fresno State College, where in between her studies she found time to write weekly college columns for The Bee. She was offered a full-time job in the Society Department, and therein lay the rub. Her answer was quick, and empathic: No way, Jose. First, she didn't intend to be stuck with writing social news – weddings, engagements, that sort of thing. And second, this talented San Joaquin Valley native wanted to head for the city, in this case, The City – San Francisco.

She quickly found a job she wanted there – writing public relations for CARE. She soon rose to the position of director for the Northern California region for CARE, and was there in 1956 when Gordon Nelson, successor to George Popovich as city editor of The Bee, dropped by. He wanted to know if she would be interested in returning to Fresno. It seemed that The Bee's venerable society editor, Dorothy Noble Hill, was going to pack it in. The job was Belyea's if she wanted it. Again the answer was short and quick: No, she wouldn't return as "society editor;" "women's editor," maybe.

The Fresno Bee, at its birth in 1922, ran a daily Women's Page, centered on engagements and weddings, with a local column, Social News by Margaret Strother. In 1928 Carlos McClatchy and Bob McLaughlin decided to expand it. The section went to two pages daily, four on Sundays. It featured the syndicated Dorothy Dix, billed as "the most appealing woman writer on human problems in the world. Her column goes into 30 million homes in all parts of the world. Her insight into human affairs is remarkable, her philosophy so full of common sense that her comments interest all classes."

Also included were Diana Dare's Beauty Talks, featuring luminaries such as Mary Pickford, Lady Diana Manners, Mrs. Howard Chandler Christy, Alma Gluck, Marion Davies, Pola Negri, Pavlova, Peggy Hopkins Joyce, Ruth St. Denis, Gloria Swanson – a different celebrity every day.

Editorial Department Women in 1960. Eva Burns (lower left) was The Fresno Bee's first woman reporter.

Robert P. Molander

There were cartoons, recipes, style and illustrations by "the experts of the Drygoods Economist, the outstanding magazine on fashions in the United States." Added were a baby column, sewing tips, and Matrimonially Speaking, a column touching on the "everyday little problems of husband and wife." A big package, but still aimed exclusively at the women. Men were non-existent, as far as the society department was concerned.

Belyea agreed to visit Fresno, not too confident of what lay ahead. Did she want to return to the boondocks? She was granted a short interview by Orville M. (Diz) Shelton, the managing editor. He also told her to just shape the department up, lead it into the modern world. "Here it is; do what you can," said Shelton. "We think you can do it. We want something different." Nelson told her: "We want to move into the 20th Century. The section isn't keeping up with the rest of the paper."

There were no real guidelines. They offered her the job as a matter of necessity, and in faith. She took it, knowing The Bee had a long way to go. The society format had been simple: cover practically every wedding in town, every engagement. Do big stories on them with pictures. Some club news – who poured tea, who wore white gloves. Dorothy Hill used to cover all the big parties. She'd run them on the cover of the Sunday paper – three or four pictures, and a story. Or, the front page might feature the three or four "weddings of the week." That was about it.

It didn't take Belyea long to surmise the local coverage was basically limited to Fresno's "400," high society; the "in" clubs, women golfers, the country clubs, nothing on the little people. She thought, "The average reader might read about the weddings. That was about it. Nothing else."

Not so, she discovered. Dorothy Hill hadn't been all wrong. It didn't matter whether Miss or Mrs. Average Woman was a part of high society; she still enjoyed reading about it.

Belyea started with a four-woman staff – herself, Lizbeth Solling, Wanda Coyle, and Diane Webster. They worked as hard as the male reporters and editors, but for less-than-equal pay. Much later, in 1984, Belyea made a speech on "Women in the Newsroom." In it, she recalled how, in her early days on the paper, the women reporters were paid quite a bit less than the men. In 1959, after some controversy, the women were raised to equal financial status with the men, and were given retroactive pay along with the raises.

"We were so happy, and so grateful to the company." Belyea recalled. "And instead, as Wanda and Diane said, we should have been suing them. We should have been mad that we had been discriminated against all this time, and instead, we thought, 'Oh, aren't they nice.'"

The first break from the old system didn't really come about until a few years later, in the early 1960's. That's when it was decided that the "society" sections of all three Bees – Sacramento, Fresno, and Modesto – would be labeled "Women's Activities." The editors were ordered to broaden the coverage, get more feature stories. But there was still the sticking point: Stories had to be limited to "women's news." It was still pretty much club news and a baby column, a health column, some fashions. But they were deadly stale. Belyea and her staff were intent on reaching more women, and to increase the number of feature stories.

Success was a long time coming. The '60s did see more features, but not much else changed. Then, in 1970, The Bee sent Belyea to Reston, Virginia for an American Press Institute seminar for women's editors. It was to change forever the section coverage. "I really had my consciousness raised," Belyea said. "We had a couple of women speak; the women's movement was just getting started. They were very impressive – Washington Post, Washington Star, the New York Times' Charlotte Curtis.

"They kept talking about how we could do more, how women – not just the women's pages – should be different, how women's lives were changing. Women were becoming more active, and they were asking for equality. Everything was starting to come into place, and the Equal Rights Amendment was coming up."

The staff got larger with the addition of Linda Koch, Pam Dugan, Sandy Tompkins, each a young, vibrant female. They and their predecessors were ready to help make the changes being demanded by women throughout the nation. Had they been men, they would have been labeled "young Turks." The Fresno Bee's women's department, later to finally become officially the features department, got into background stories about abortion and rape, once censored subjects.

One story in that period raised eyebrows, caused a lot of comment and helped bring about progressive results. It involved rape, or rather, a "pretend" rape. At that time, women, instead of being considered victims of rape, were often blamed as having induced the rapists to act – in effect, of seducing their attackers. In the eyes of the public, the police, and the courts, they were thought to be the instigators, rather than the victims.

Belyea had the story set up through channels. High-ranking police knew what was coming, as did hospital officials. So did the ranking Bee brass. Tompkins called the police one night to report she had been raped (she hadn't). She was interviewed, taken to the hospital for examination. One specific she recalled was how those directly involved – police, hospital personnel – were so impersonal. No compassion, no comforting words. And there was the discomfort of being forced to describe the attack to a male officer. "Sandy's reaction was that the treatment was pretty good," Belyea recalled. "In general, we were trying to encourage women to report rape. At that time, you didn't generally report it. It was also just to see how those who reported it were treated. Were the police sympathetic, or were they taking the other tack?"

In ensuing years such stories, which resulted in increased public interest and to fairness, led police departments throughout the nation, including Fresno, to designate trained female police officers to handle at least the first contacts with the victims. Rape-counseling services were born. And the blame shifted from the true victims to the perpetrators.

The department was still a haven for women – female reporters, female editors. But that was about to change. The first male to enter the sanctum, albeit in a roundabout and not necessarily voluntary way, was Woody Laughlin, a cityside column writer whose five-efforts-a-week output was growing in public favor. Woody wrote about the common man, and often the less-than-common-man – a hobo he would run across, a woman down on her luck and being forced into prostitution to feed her children. His column gradually migrated into a full-time women's department feature.

But the real turnabout came when Guy Keeler asked to be transferred to the women's department. Keeler was an energetic young cityside reporter who had been hired to work the night beat, a 4 p.m.-to-midnight or 5 p.m.-to-1 a.m. beat, five shifts a week. He would check police and sheriff's offices for late breaking stories, and would cover night meetings of planning boards or special gatherings. It wasn't a beat a young family man would want for long.

Keeler had a nice touch for feature writing, and wanted to do it on a permanent basis. As it happened, Belyea was heading in that direction, and was quick to accept Keeler's bid to join her staff. Then, Dennis Pollack asked to leave the editorial staff and move into "sox" (as the department was still being called, much to Belyea's displeasure.) And Eddie Lopez wanted to join from of all places, the sports department. Belyea picked them both up.

In line with the new wave of ideas, Belyea started writing a weekly column, intended to make women more aware of things they could do apart from being "just homemakers." She said, "Women would come up to me and tell me that I got them thinking about what they could do – to run for public office, things like that," she said. "I called it 'Monday Memo.' They could still do things outside. They could be volunteers, they could do anything they wanted to do.

"I usually played up some woman who had done something special, not necessarily Fresno but anywhere in the country. Just to kind of raise their consciousness. At the end of every year, I would do a roundup of what Fresno women had accomplished. It would be like, Linda Mack, the first woman on the Fresno City Council, or whether a woman was the first to do something in Fresno. I did a lot of those first woman things.

"About that time, I thought we ought to change the name, and we made it Contemporary Life. It was a mouthful to say, but it was what we wanted to say: We wanted to talk about what was happening in people's lives. And we started writing about men in the '70s. For a while, we ran a man's view once a week.

"We made the name change to 'Tempo' in 1978 or '79. I still liked the name 'Contemporary Life,' but it was primarily because it was an awkward lag, (too long) and 'Tempo' was sort of upbeat. With 'Tempo,' I think we went into straight features."

Then came a period of wondering. Had The Bee gone too far in changing over the women's department? Belyea worried that it had lost its

Robert P. Molander

hoped-for identity, become neither fish nor fowl. Was it possible to find an ideal mix? There still was no really strong area for women. Equal rights, the abortion issue, were being covered so well, she reasoned. There was Dear Abby and Irma Bombeck, each well read, but the attempt to make it a more general section resulted in nobody having a real feeling for it.

An advice column was instituted. Penny Raven, a socialite with access to the "400," was brought in to write about the parties. She stuck mostly to socialites, rather than being a "people columnist." This didn't go over so well, Belyea recalled, because it was like waving a red flag in the eyes of most Fresnans, and, "There's not a real 'society' in Fresno anyway."

With reporters spending more time on features, and with space in the section so limited, something had to give, and it was, of all things, that gallant old bastion, weddings.

The American Press Institute gave Belyea the novel idea – charge the subscribers for their wedding stories. The idea seemed heretical – a real newspaper never paid for news, did it? And weren't engagements and weddings "news?" There'd be rioting outside the Bee building!

It took years before The Bee would buy the idea. But it finally was deemed the only way out. If Sunday space was 30 columns, 15 were set aside for engagements and weddings. It was an impossible situation. Something had to give. First, in a Band-Aid solution, Belyea ruled that wedding announcements more than two weeks old would not be run. But that didn't work. Irate mothers stormed The Bee, complaining to Belyea, George Gruner, the managing editor; Roger Coryell, who headed up the business side of the paper; and even to Eleanor McClatchy in Sacramento.

"It was the worst thing I ever did," Belyea recalled. "It really was. We raised it (the deadline) to a month, and then we had people coming in six weeks later. There was just no way around it. Plus, they wanted pictures, and how did you decide who gets a picture and who doesn't?"

So the concept of "paid weddings" was tried, and amazingly, there was no adverse reaction. Even the first day it was done. In fact, the paying public actually liked it. Mainly, it was so well accepted because people didn't know any better – they frequently thought they would have to pay for the announcements anyway, often contacting the department with statements like, "I'll give you $50 to get this story in the paper; I'll give you $100." Staffers would jokingly say they could retire with all the bribes they were offered. Gruner and Coryell went along, and the final decision was made: The public would pay. And it did. Willingly.

In later days, Belyea would wonder if The Bee had made the right decision. The announcements were run as the families wanted, but were poorly written, in the eyes of the department, and were not edited. Belyea believed she had created a monster, one that should be shoved back to the classified-advertising section of the paper. But the stories remained in the women's department, later named the "Features" section, just where the public wanted them. And they were expanded to include births, graduations, military service, almost anything the public would pay for.

The department really hit its stride in the Contemporary Life section of the '70s, expanding quickly. It was ahead of the rest of the paper in design and attractiveness. Included rather quickly over the decade was coverage of the community, all kinds of women's issues, both statewide and nationally. It was an exciting time for women nationwide – the height of the women's movement. A lot was happening, and Belyea was keeping abreast of it.

"I'm really proud of what we did during the '70s," Belyea said. "That was the highlight of my career," a career that included her elevation to assistant managing editor. The Sunday department was combined with Contemporary Life. The arts, Forum, TV, and consumer reporting were added. A weekend section was started, as was a Home and Garden section. Church pages were folded in. Finally, the department took on Spotlight, a special Sunday tabloid section specializing in entertainment. The Food section was already there.

The department had burgeoned from one little women's department into a total package of everything that was "feature."

Featuring the shaping of a fast-growing city.

Robert P. Molander

17

Depression Days

Fresno Bee employees often complained through the years that their newspaper made the money, but that the profits were routed north to help support The Sacramento Bee. Top management in Fresno knew of these local, widespread rumors, but did little or nothing to dispel them. But in fact, those Fresno beliefs, no matter how they came about, were to a large degree not too factual. The Fresno Bee, like many newspapers throughout the nation, was not in the best financial shape, what with the stock market crash of 1929 and with the Great Depression of the 1930s taking their toll.

Consider advertising rates of that period: classified ads at a contract rate, 10 cents a line; open classified rates, 20 and 25 cents a line. Display advertising, $2 a column inch, even lower under contract rates. Add the fact that since its inception in 1922 The Fresno Bee for a decade was battling two established local newspapers, the morning Republican and the evening Herald, for supremacy, and that the ensuing war often necessitated lower advertising and circulation rates than were practical for survival. So if "Fresno money" actually was funneled northward in the later years, it could have been labeled "payback time," for The Sacramento Bee had, in fact, picked up a large share of the tab for Fresno's battlefield expenses

Bill Ennis, a Fresno Bee ad salesman in those days, recalled, "The early 1930s were times that separated the salesmen from the copy boys. The Great Depression was in full swing, and advertisers were very reluctant to spend money for space in any media, especially a new paper. They were tough times." So tough for The Bee that a practice despised by the editorial side became common: An advertiser would be accommodated with a late ad, even including the morning of publication of the afternoon Bee. The ad would be accepted, and inserted into the paper. And if that meant cutting or eliminating a news story, so be it. The ads came first.

The Fresno Bee had a succession of business managers, many more than the editorial side's long-serving managing editors. The first was J.V. McClatchy, who left soon to return to Sacramento. He was a son of V.S. McClatchy, who with C.K. McClatchy owned and operated The Sacramento Bee until he was bought out by C.K. in the summer of 1923. J.V. was succeeded by George S. Smith, formerly with the Fresno Herald and the Fresno Tribune. Smith was instrumental in The Bee's decision to locate in Fresno, having done a study which showed the paper would sell a minimum of 700,000 inches of advertising in its first year. As it turned out, even that seemingly lofty estimate was surpassed in Year One.

Smith hung on for three years before he quit to devote full time to his private, expanding real-estate business, which he had started before joining The Bee and which he continued to operate during his three-year tenure with the newspaper. Smith was at the business helm of The Bee when the Fresno Herald was acquired by The Bee.

He also was there when he had to make a decision that was very unpopular with the workers. In its earliest days, soon after its building was completed, The Bee, with the blessing of Carlos McClatchy, planted a garden on the roof. It had grass and flowers, and employees enjoyed having lunch up there, seated at lawn tables and chairs on Fresno's balmy days. "Heavy rains caused the roof to sag and crack several of the 6-by-8-inch beams in the composing-room ceiling," Smith recalled. "The contractors removed more than 100 tons of dirt and lawn which had been installed to provide a recreational spot for employees during the summer months." Unfortunately, in a turn not anticipated, the rains had turned the dirt into heavy, roof-crushing mud.

Following Smith, the next in line for the top business-side job was Ed S. Riggins, former publisher of the San Mateo Daily News Leader and assistant business manager of the San Francisco Chronicle. Smith died suddenly in 1935 after having served eight years with The Bee. Included in his tour of duty was the purchase of the Fresno Republican. Increased advertising in The Bee, plus boosts in circulation, both led by Riggins, along with continually better news coverage, sealed the Republican's fate.

Fresno's next business manager came up from the ranks. R.W. "Duke" Millard, a native Oklahoman, took over from his post as advertising manager, which he had held since his hiring in 1928. Millard was a bear of a man, in stature and in daily behavior. He was as quick with a pun as he was with a dry martini, along with being a very hard worker. In the parlance of the day, Duke worked hard and played hard, keeping each in proper perspective.

His crews generally loved the man. He never hesitated to go to bat for them, whether it be for raises in pay or better working conditions. And he sponsored an annual Christmas party, replete with booze, in the expansive business office. This practice was halted by Sacramento, in line with Eleanor McClatchy's wish that there be no drinking on McClatchy property. (She relented on this rule a bit when she had sherry wine served at the annual employees' 25 Year Club get-togethers at her Sacramento home.)

Millard's influence was felt even in editorial, not in story selection but in overall appearance. In the early 1950s and before, editorial staffers had the unseemly habit of crumpling used copy paper and tossing it on the floor, rather than in the waste baskets provided. One day, Millard took an almost-unheard-of trip to editorial, and while walking through the department, expressed disgust at the paper-strewn floor.

"Why the hell don't you clean this up?" he roared. "The place looks like a pigpen." Bill Lockwood, the managing editor, took the little-used path of paying attention to the ad department, at least to its leader, and went along with Duke's "suggestion." After that, the editorial staffers, unwilling as they were to acknowledge anyone or anything from the ad side, used the waste baskets. After all, Millard did sign the paychecks.

Duke enjoyed a good laugh. One of his hands, Max Armstrong, later to become business manager of The Fresno Bee, recalled a party in Sacramento, with Duke dressed as an Indian, war paint included. One of the guests was Governor Earl Warren, a favorite of The Sacramento Bee and of Eleanor McClatchy. Warren and Millard knew each other from Millard's time with the Long Beach Press-Telegram. They were good friends. Warren congenially said, "Hi, Duke." Millard responded in kind. "Eleanor happened to see it, saw Duke with that damned war paint, and she just about split her seams," Armstrong said with an appreciative chuckle.

"Duke was a sad case. In my heart I can only say good things about Duke, but I realize that he violated all the rules of employee-employer relations by his go-to-hell attitude. But yet I would say that the guy had more good ideas in a minute than most of those people in Sacramento had in a lifetime. And though I'm strongly in favor of what Eleanor did --she went out to his house and fired him, and I don't blame her a damned bit – it was his go-to-hell problem that did him in."

Yes, Eleanor McClatchy did fire Millard, but it wasn't one of those delegated jobs, or one done over the telephone. She was driven from Sacramento to Fresno and got the job done, in person, at his home. Here's how it went, according to Armstrong, his successor, Carter Roberson, and a simple notation on Millard's personnel file in The Bee's editorial library:

It was late evening on July 16, 1959. Millard was the business manager, the most powerful position in the newspaper's business department. He had telephoned L.R. (Matt) Matushak, the company controller, at his Sacramento office. It was through Matushak that Millard got his orders in Fresno. A June 11, 1958 memo from Matushak in Sacramento to Millard, did make it appear that Matushak was on Millard's back. The memo:

"On June 2nd you placed a long distance call to O'Shea in Modesto in the amount of $1.35, and on June 6th, $1.25. In processing long distance telephone tolls, Gus Kortstein called this to my attention and wants to know if this is a Modesto charge as he thinks the Modesto Bee will object if it could have been handled in a simpler manner, say by letter or perhaps teletype."

End of memo, on two matters totaling $2.60, addressed to the head of a multi-million-dollar corporation link in Fresno.

The evening conversation with Matushak wasn't to Millard's liking, so he stewed about it and, after hitting the gin bottle for a few more drinks, he again telephoned Matushak, this time at about 1 a.m. on the fateful following morning, July 17, 1959. The earlier talks had to do with Sacramento-designed policy, particularly over the lack of wage increases for department heads. Armstrong and others had been known to prod Millard about these pay increases, including their own.

Fortified internally, Millard made the second call, "reading Matushak down one side of the wall and up the other, and of course cursing him,

Thousands of "Parade" magazines stack up in the Bee mail room.

and finally told him what he thought of him and the organization," according to Roberson. That was it. Matushak reported the matter to Eleanor McClatchy, and she ordered her chauffeur to drive her to Fresno, post haste, that morning, and to the Millard home. She rang the bell, and he, who hadn't made it to work yet, opened the door.

Without fanfare, she informed him in no uncertain terms that he was fired, and to clear his office of his personal belongings. As soon as she left, Millard telephoned his secretary, Lois Hammond, telling her to put his files in boxes. She did, and had them delivered to his home. But unknowing, she had all of his files boxed and sent, including the business files.

This got her in trouble with Miss McClatchy, who was about to fire her, too. But Armstrong intervened, saying Hammond had been a valued employee through the years, was still loyal to the company, and had inadvertently made a mistake in sending Millard the business files. Miss McClatchy relented, and Hammond wound up first as secretary to Roberson, who at the time was the national advertising manager, and later as a secretary in the Personnel Department, winding up with a full retirement and pension.

Besides being tough when he had to be, Millard was known as a man who could switch quickly to guile when it served his purpose. Along those lines, he used at times a unique method of dealing with crafts-union leaders at contract time.

Sitting conveniently across Van Ness Avenue from the Bee building was the home of the Fresno Aeriè, Fraternal Order of Eagles – the Eagles Club, as it was popularly known to Bee employees, who were known more than once to sneak across the street to the Eagles bar to visit Ed, the friendly bartender, and down a relaxing beer just after deadline. Millard was from Oklahoma, and had worked for the Oklahoma Times before heading west. Coincidentally, it seemed there was an influx of printers from that same paper to The Fresno Bee. Although no one ever claimed that Duke had brought them in, it was quite a "family."

As Roberson and others tell the story, Duke would invite the president of the local chapter of the International Typographical Union (ITU) to join him across the street for a quick one. The sojourn inevitably would turn to contract negotiations, as Millard intended. The two

Bee employees enjoy a Christmas lunch.

would negotiate over drinks, and ultimately, on more than one occasion, according to Roberson, "Duke would walk away and they would come up Van Ness slightly unsteady, but Duke would have a signed contract in his pocket."

At another time, when Duke was still in good graces up north, there was a party in Modesto, the geographical central point of McClatchy's trio of newspapers. Millard and three of his employees – Roberson, Ken Poulsen and Al Gaad – rode up in an old, black company Ford, circa 1946. They got there OK, and the afternoon was generally spent partying and playing softball. The field was a cow pasture, with Roberson at one point sliding several feet in cow manure while trying to catching a fly ball.

The fun over, Millard gathered his crew and headed down a two-lane road toward Highway 99 in that old black Ford. "Duke was going 90 miles an hour down this narrow road through the vineyards," Roberson said. "And I remember being so scared – we all were scared – that Gaad and I got down on the floor and tried to hide from whatever could happen. And in spite of our pleas, Duke kept going awfully fast.

"Well, we made it back to Fresno and we went to Millard's house. He wanted to show us something, and we sat on the floor in his living room, and he pulled out of his pocket about $1,100 in small bills which he had carried to Modesto and back from the night before, when he won the money in a craps game at the Sunnyside Country Club.

Ralph Wayne (Duke) Millard moved to Cayucus, a beach community on the California coast, following his firing by Miss McClatchy. He took a hand in that community's civic life, and at one time was known as the "Unofficial Mayor of Cayucus." In Fresno, he had been active in club activities, including being president of the University Sequoia-Sunnyside Club, which catered to the well-to-do businessmen and golfers, and the Las Palmas Masonic Lodge, plus Scottish Rite bodies, and also was a member of the Rotary Club. But none of that helped him on his final day at The Bee. His Bee profile, kept in the paper's editorial library, contained one forlorn note: "Dismissed by Miss Eleanor McClatchy on July 27th, 1959."

Millard was succeeded by the quiet, nose-to-the grindstone Charles F. Sells, a man who also had made his way through the ranks, but one who wasn't quick to make friends. Known to be an interim, or fill-in business manager, he served until his retirement in 1966, when Max Armstrong, an ambitious man who had been waiting, somewhat impatiently, for his chance, got the top job.

Armstrong had been hired in 1936 as a salesman, and had filled all the jobs up to the top one. He was raring to go, but soon after his promotion it became apparent to him that the umbilical cord to Sacramento hadn't been loosened, let alone cut, and that he wouldn't be able to call his own shots. He became bitter. In his words, years later: "I never had too much autonomy – none at all. It was very disheartening, to know that everything that you did – damn near everything – had to be cleared in Sacramento. I had to work through John Hamlyn, the attorney; or Matt Matushak, the controller; or Eleanor, the president; or the board of directors. And I had to go up there every three or four months, at least, and sit in on a board of directors meeting, and I never got an opportunity to ever let down my hair.

"It's just hard to believe that anybody would be given the responsibility of a multi-million-dollar business with no damned authority. It was absolutely ridiculous. It was just a pathetic way of running a business. I'm not saying this to criticize Eleanor, because, hell, she wasn't a businesswoman – she just got shoved into the job. In fact, I remember the first time in 1946 she had a meeting, and she said, 'I know there are a lot of you people – a lot of you out there – who think you could do a better job in running this better than I can. But I've got the job."

In private, Armstrong charged that the lack of independent policy maintained through the years created an atmosphere of doubt and stifled any ambition on the part of the business managers of any of the three papers. "We (the business managers) used to get together, but we couldn't get anything done. We all suffered from the same disease, or problem. We just couldn't get an answer on anything."

Armstrong contended that his predecessor, Sells, left him a problem when Sells retired. "I didn't know it myself until the day I took over the job," Armstrong said. "Sells never told me anything about it, and Eleanor didn't say anything about it. Fresno was several hundred thousand dollars in the red. It was in red ink. We were losing, in the red, the last two or three years before, when Sells was in charge. I thought, hell, I was going into a solid business. I learned to my disappointment and dismay that it was not that at all, it was a losing proposition – red ink."

Armstrong claimed that Sells hurt him by keeping The Bee's financial condition a secret, forcing Armstrong to discover it for himself. "I didn't even know the profit-and-loss figure. I was damned nice to Carter Roberson when he took over the job. (Roberson confirms this.) I went the last mile, because I didn't want to be guilty of the same thing that Sells had done to me."

Armstrong said he turned things around – putting the paper $713,000 in the black in his first year, $1,156,000 the next and $1,400,000 the next-- by getting department heads to cooperate, lowering expenses of the various departments, and cutting the number of employees through attrition, firing none for economic causes. "I just told the department heads that we all had a problem, a mutual problem," Armstrong explained. "I didn't tell them we were losing money, I just told them we had a mutual problem, and we've got to correct it. So they fell to, and it got to be a sort of a mutual experience, because everybody just performed in a way that you would expect.

"We didn't have budgets in those days; they didn't know what a budget was. I cut expenses, and gradually cut the number of people without firing anyone. We just didn't replace a lot of them, because we had a lot of excess fat around there. It was terrific, in all departments."

The Bees had a strict editorial policy over the years – no free advertising. The editorial department employees loved it, although at times it resulted in quirky decisions. For example, a car in a story couldn't be labeled a Ford or Chevrolet, on the theory that it could help sell those brands of cars. But an expensive foreign car? Or a sea-going yacht? The Buick Open, a professional golf tournament in Flint, Mich., was arbitrarily renamed The Flint Open in the McClatchy papers. A Chevy or a Ford became just an unnamed car. If the police were seeking a 1950 Chevrolet used in an escape after a bank holdup, for example, it became a "1950 American-made, blue, four-door car." Not the most brilliant description.

Advertising employees of the Bees didn't like the policy, simply because their advertisers didn't like it. And that was good enough reason for them. But to a degree, they also had common sense on their side. Armstrong, the boss, particularly disliked it, seeing no harm in giving an advertiser a break in news coverage, such as a photo once in a while that could be disguised as news.

"It was absolutely, almost unbelievable what went on, in the way of an advertising standpoint, of trying to get publicity for Gottschalks (The Fresno Bee's biggest advertiser over the years) or anybody," Armstrong said. "It was nauseating. In fact, I wrote down a word here, in big letters – HATE! That's the only damned word I can think of that describes the feelings of the merchants in town towards The Fresno Bee."

Gottschalks department store, as The Bee's major advertiser, thought it should swing some weight. So did Armstrong. And one perk Gottschalks wanted was permanent positioning for its ads on Page A3 of the Bee. Roberson recalled that Armstrong, as business manager, was informed that company policy from Sacramento would be enforced: No advertiser would be permitted a guaranteed position for its ads. When

Armstrong passed the ruling on to Joe Levy, president of Gottschalks, "all hell broke loose."

"So Gottschalks punished us by transferring some advertising to the Guide, (a free shopper) and by withholding some other advertising," said Roberson. "Ultimately they came back. They still pretty much had Page 3 or what we would sell as the equivalent, somewhere in the first seven pages, or the back page. Weinstocks complained about favoritism when they first came to town. There were others who would gripe, sure. Later on, after Roger Coryell came on as general manager, when they signed a multi-page contract, it was almost understood that a great number of their ads were going to appear on Page 3. I can't say it was a guarantee, but it was pretty-well understood."

Armstrong and those same advertisers who were incensed at this lack of what editorial considered free advertising were exceedingly angered at any news-page mention of an advertiser who had done something considered wrong, such as being arrested on suspicion of drunk driving. The "victim" would telephone early the next day and plead that his name be withheld, often threatening to pull his advertising from the paper if his name were printed.

When the City Desk refused the plea, as it inevitably did, the caller would contact the Bee salesperson who handled his account, demanding that the salesperson intervene. The salesman would inform his boss, and the plaint would eventually reach the business manager, and he'd see what he could do about it. But eventually, after a few such futile attempts, he too would quit trying. And, to the everlasting credit of the editorial department, the names would be printed, even though the practice might cost the paper in lost revenue from pulled ads.

Editorial would print the offending names. Period. No favors for advertisers that non-advertisers wouldn't get.

Armstrong and most others in the ad department never could understand this editorial position – that the fact a businessman was a big advertiser in The Bee entitled him to nothing more or nothing less than a person who had no advertising, no imagined "pull" of any kind with the newspaper. They reasoned that because a person bought space in the paper, he was entitled to favorable treatment.

"Good god," Armstrong moaned. "It started with a little simple thing like drunken driving. I would get calls from an automobile dealer or some of those other guys who hit it up too much and got drunk. They'd say, 'Jesus Christ, I can't have my name in the damned paper. Drunken driving!' They would try to work on me or Millard or anyone around there. We, of course, didn't try to do anything. Anyway, it just made the merchants in this town realize that The Bee had them in the palm of their hand. And it was just a hopeless experience on my part to try to get anything done. It was the most unpopular paper I ever worked for.

"Every time I went any place, or anybody from The Bee ever showed up, we were the target of a lot of ridicule and snide remarks, low blows, and every damned thing you could think of. I belonged to the Kiwanis Club for years. Hell, I'd go, and get it up there. Sooner or later, some creep would bring up the McClatchys or The Fresno Bee."

Armstrong pointed out that many grocery ads were exclusive with the Fresno Guide at one time. The Guide also built up its classified ads, and added some of Fresno's biggest advertisers, such as Gottschalks, although not exclusively. "As advertising manager, I would call a guy like Tony Justenson (an owner of supermarkets), for instance. He wouldn't even see me. One time, over drinks, I did get him back in the paper, and the next damned day he was arrested for drunken driving, and they ran this usual story about it. And he quit The Bee. The Bee just ran roughshod over these people. They had a city editor there – George Popovich – he contributed more to the dislike of The Fresno Bee – he and Bill Lockwood, when Bill was city editor – than any two people that I know of. Millard and I used to go out and make a few friends, and they'd end up undoing what we tried to do. Through refusing to even consider a story. Hell, they wouldn't even be polite to an advertiser who went up to see them."

The editorial policy was simple: The advertisers weren't buying ads to do The Bee a favor. The reader deserved his 10 cents worth of news, and that meant all of it – 100 percent. And if "all the news" happened to include the name of a big advertiser, so be it. Here's how George Gruner, former executive editor of The Fresno Bee, put it:

"We used to run (the names of) drunk drivers. We ran a list of those who were arrested for drunk driving in the previous 24 hours. We listed

Robert P. Molander

everybody. We had people who tried to keep that out of the paper, who'd call up and plead, 'It's going to be the end of my life, etc.'. We'd say we're sorry, we can't pull it.

"The convincer was that our owner-editor was arrested for drunk driving, and we ran his name. He never said boo about it. That was Carlos McClatchy. And that's always the greatest defense. The greatest thing the paper ever did – the bravest thing, if you will – was to run the boss' name. That fact established the editorial integrity of the paper more than any other single act. Of course, we had many other arrests of Bee employees of relatively high standing, who were well known in the community. We ran them, too."

Another matter that incensed Armstrong in his early days with the paper was that of salaries, which he contended were too low. "Hell, I went to work there, and I chased Millard around his house one time when I first came here in 1936, to get him to give me a raise, from $27.50 a week to $30 a week. I finally got the damned $30, but I had to go through a lot of hell to get it. I'm sure Duke had to get a Sacramento OK to get it. When they first started this business of meeting the going wages on different newspapers on the West Coast, I would get an OK to raise salesmen's salaries $2.50 a week. Next week I'd get another damn note to raise them again – $2.50 a week. They were trying to get up to a decent level, because they were very much underpaid people. Then, of course, they were trying to keep the unions out of there. It was quite an experience."

The Fresno Bee had little serious competition following the demise of the Republican in 1932. What little it did have came from the Fresno Shopping Guide, a weekly throwaway (free) paper that was started after the Republican was taken over by The Bee in 1932. Few in the upper echelons at The Bee took the Guide very seriously as a competitor, except for Max Armstrong. At one time he believed, literally, that the Guide could have put The Bee out of business.

The Shopping Guide and its successor, the Fresno Guide, remained in operation for 47 years, graduating at times to twice-a-week publication, to three days a week for a spell, and, towards its end, even publishing five days a week. Predictably, the Guide competed for local advertising by giving businessmen lower rates than those charged by The Bee. But through four changes of ownership, and despite constantly leveling charges at The Bee, it never achieved credibility or sufficient paid circulation.

The Guide started its attack on its opening day, May 14, 1932. A headline read, "Monopoly Smoked Out in War on Shopping Guide." The story charged that The Bee was behind a campaign to slow circulation of the Guide, including arranging, with the assistance of the police chief, the arrest of a 13-year-old newsboy. The Guide's owner, William Paris, purposely went out on the "delivery line" himself and was arrested, as planned, under a city ordinance barring the distribution of handbills.

In another edition, the Guide wrote: "Inasmuch as there is only one daily paper in Fresno which usually tells only one side of a story, we wish to put before the public the side that is not told. We are not necessarily expressing our own opinion, but give both sides an opportunity to express their viewer opinions. This service is open to everyone, including The Fresno Bee, should they desire to reach the many thousands of Guide readers who do not subscribe to their paper."

The Guide indicated it would publish a Sunday paper, but it never got off the ground. In 1958 it asked its readers to pay its carrier boys 25 cents a month, saying the payments would enable the Guide to continue publication. It was not announced how many subscribers complied. On February 8, 1968, control of the Guide was sold to new majority stockholders: Mr. and Mrs. A. L. Funch Sr., owners/developers of the Fig Garden Village shopping center in Fresno; and to powerful John Bonadelle, the area's largest home builder and longtime opponent of The Bee.

Under this ownership, the Guide was to publish on Mondays, Wednesdays and Fridays. Bonadelle announced he was prepared "to meet and defeat each Bee sally." But this, too, never came to fruition. Later that year, the Guide plant on H Street in downtown Fresno was hit by a midnight blast. Police said six or eight sticks of dynamite exploded at the entrance door. An almost simultaneous explosion damaged the Army Induction Center a block away. No arrests were reported in either case.

The Guide continued publication, and on Nov. 25, 1976, announced it would become a daily paper. It claimed 85,000 daily circulation, but The Bee, after a check with the California Newspaper Publishers Association, announced the paid circulation of the Guide was 21,514, with 60,210 unpaid. The five-day-a-week publication was short-lived, and it was cut to twice a week. Then, in November, 1979, the Guide called it quits as a "newspaper." It became The Fresno County Reporter, the publication's last gasp. and went out of business a few months later.

Max Armstrong hadn't anticipated this turn of events. In fact, in the late 1940s, he informed Eleanor McClatchy that The Fresno Bee could be in big trouble. He was running scared. "This company could never get it through their noggin that they damned near lost this Fresno Bee to the Fresno Shopping Guide," he said. "There was a guy here named Bill Paris who owned the Guide and, believe me, he was a firecracker. He knew what the hell he was he was doing. And he was an experienced newspaperman. Later on, his son-in-law, Bill Spaulding, took over the Guide.

"They offered me a job one time, and I told Eleanor about it. When I took on this job (with The Bee) they gave me a lousy damned salary, considering the responsibility I had. I told her in a letter, 'For your information, John Bonadelle has offered me a job in running the Fresno Guide. And the Fresno Guide, for your information, is just about to take over The Fresno Bee.'"

Armstrong estimated the Guide had about 90 percent of the grocery advertisements in the Fresno area, The Bee the remaining 10 percent. "I'm talking 1945, when the Guide was its strongest," he said. So he conducted a test on his own: On a Saturday afternoon, disgusted at seeing the multitude of grocery ads in the Guide, he went to his office "and got on the damned phone." He telephoned "50-to-100" homes, at random, asking housewives: "This is an independent survey. Would you tell me where you make up your list of groceries, your shopping lists?"

"Would you believe that damned near 75 or 80 percent told me the Fresno Guide? That was the damnedest thing I've ever heard of. I repeated that to Eleanor. They had the idea that they were coping in Sacramento with the Sacramento Union, which was a daily newspaper. And here we were, worrying about what they called a damned little weekly or semiweekly. But after my experience in calling those 50 or 75 or 100 people, on a Saturday afternoon, I became convinced that they (the Guide) had the readership. The point I want to make is, this company has no idea how damned close that Paris shopping guide came to dominating this market, and to costing them a hell of a lot more money than it did. Bonadelle wanted to make it something live, but he couldn't."

An increasingly sore point with Fresno Bee management was the mail room, which was charged with distribution of the newspaper to the delivery trucks after it came off the presses. A few of those mailers, as they were called, came to Fresno from the Detroit area. Their leader was Ed Downs, who was planted in Fresno as an agent by the International Typographical Union, of which the mailers were an arm. And Downs did organize. After several fairly physical confrontations around and about the mail room, the Mailers Union muscled its way in and threw out the old union.

The Fresno Bee had a very liberal sick-leave policy – every permanent worker was entitled to five weeks of sick leave a year. In the eyes of some employees, its only fault was that it wasn't cumulative. But in the eyes of management, its major problem was that scores of employees, particularly the printers and the mailers, considered sick leave as a part of their salary packages and used all of it, every year. "The abuse of sick leave through the typographical union and the mail room union – it was understood that they were going to use it on an annual basis," said Roberson. "And there were indeed printers there – at least one husband-and-wife team – who each drew the five weeks plus their vacation every year. By the time they got their days off, they were only there about three-quarters of the year."

There was a humorous story (to most) along those lines. A printer, his present year of service nearly ended, checked with the Personnel Department to determine how much sick leave he had used up. "All but three days," he was told. So in the following week, the printer took off three "sick days." When he got his next paycheck, he was chagrined to find he had been docked three days pay. He stormed into the Personnel Office, complaining bitterly. But he was told by the same person who had informed him he had three days remaining, "I'm sorry; I made a mistake. But it wouldn't have made any difference, would it? You were sick, weren't you, and couldn't work?"

There were cases in which mailers were working other jobs, such as pulling shifts at San Francisco newspapers nearly 200 miles away, while

Robert P. Molander

they were supposedly sick off the job at The Bee. But the beginning of the end to the power of the unions came with the arrival of Roger Coryell at The Bee in 1973. He was the first "general executive" of The Fresno Bee, at a new management level. Coryell might have been termed the paper's first publisher, except that he wasn't given dominion over the Editorial Department. Over everything and everyone else at the paper, he was "The Man."

Coryell was charged with applying pressure on the unions to reduce their domineering attitudes and to get rid of what were termed terrible work practices, particularly by the typographical and mailers unions. At one point, the mailers union was going to put up a picket line, complaining over the intended use of a new inserting machine, one which would greatly speed up the insertion of pre-printed sections of the paper in the mail room after the main sections rolled off the presses. Coryell challenged the union, and supervisors and high-ranking company officials spent a night preparing for a strike, but it never came about. There was no picket line, and normal production continued.

Another time, Ed Downs, the mailers union boss in Fresno, notified management that his union wouldn't allow the use of a new inserting machine unless the company agreed to hire two more mailers to handle it. Up in Sacramento, Irwin Potts, McClatchy's director of newspaper operations, heard of it on a Saturday, before the big Sunday run. He leaped into his car and raced to Fresno. Storming into the mail room, he ordered that the device be put into operation, and used, for the following edition. Downs backed down, and the order was obeyed. Potts drove back to Sacramento. Downs blustered, but his power in Fresno was fast diminishing.

The crafts unions, and later The Newspaper Guild, which had organized the editorial staffers, were still operational, but lost most of their clout. During this period, there was a sharp decline in national advertising, brought on with the advent and increasing popularity of television. Classified advertising grew, and became almost as great as display advertising. Advertising was also affected by the coming of pre-printed inserts, which at first had to be manually inserted into the paper but later were put in place through the use of insert machines. Some of these inserts were also pre-dated, so they had to sit around in the mail room for awhile, resulting in storage problems.

Through the 1950s, the Bee attempted to recover the lost national ads and overcome the hefty TV competition, and helped the Fresno area become a test market for some products. Many test runs were held in Fresno for food, personal products, cigarettes and alcohol. But the growing TV disparity was never overcome.

The profit picture of The Fresno Bee was far from overwhelming in the 1940s, '50s and '60s. The costs of page composition had a lot to do with this. The composing room, manned by the printers, was still on hot type at the time, with all pages made up from lines of type fashioned from molten lead by linecasters or typesetting machines. But in the early '70s, the so-called Scanner Agreement was signed by The Bee and its printers. It marked the beginning of computerized typesetting at The Bee, and the beginning of the end for the dominance of the printers and the newspaper's other crafts.

One particular ITU demand, unwillingly acquiesced to by the company, had to do with what was called "bogus type." At the time, "mats" were in use. A mat was a matrix of fiberboard-like material in which a full-page or partial-page ad was impressed under great pressure, curved and then placed in a form, with molten lead poured over it. The result was a lead plate which was mounted on the printing press.

The printers maintained that any advertising for which The Bee had received a mat must be reset or duplicated in its complete form, because the ads had not been set into type by them. So their representatives demanded, and got, the "privilege" of setting these ads into type. The resulting ad proofs were then corrected, if need be. Then, when they were ready for publication, they were tossed aside – thrown away, to be melted down. It wasn't unusual to see printers working full graveyard shifts on "bogus." In the company's eyes, these full shifts were a travesty.

In 1971, the Bee plunged into the future of "cold type" with the purchase of an electronic scanner that could "read," copy for classified ads and news stories. When working properly, (and it had many bugs) it would far exceed the capacity of printers. A fast printer could set seven lines of type a minute. The scanner could do much more with far less time expended. And it didn't require coffee or cigarette breaks.

The ITU agreed to the scanner purchase. Among the contract provisions, the practice of reproduction (bogus) was ended. The Scanner Agreement led its demise, but more particularly it led to more advanced computerized typesetting, and to sharp curtailment in the number of crafts employees of The Bee.

In one of the contract provisions, The Bee guaranteed 121 lifetime situations (jobs for life) for that number of printers who were already on board. Some 40 older printers were bought out with cash payments averaging $5,000. Until then, there had been some 165 guaranteed jobs in the ITU at The Fresno Bee. The elimination of those 40 jobs meant sharp reductions in salaries. Initially, the 40 job cuts resulted in yearly savings to The Bee of more than $1.5 million, including salaries and fringe benefits.

As time went on, as computers came into being and printers got older and retired, or in some cases were bought out, they weren't replaced, and the list of guaranteed jobs for those who were there when the Scanner Agreement was signed, fell to 25 or fewer.

Still, those in power in Sacramento felt a lot more could be accomplished economically. In 1973, a national business-analysis firm, Haskin-Sells, was hired to conduct a thorough audit/review of the operation of all three Bees, and project what would result if the McClatchy newspapers continued with the same type operation. Representatives of the firm arrived in Fresno and went through the figures, the history, the local five-year projections, held interviews with managers, looked at what was projected in the way of manpower costs, then made recommendations. This process was also followed at the Sacramento and Modesto Bees.

The recommendations called for major overhauls, topped with the addition of a new layer of management – a chief executive officer of McClatchy Newspapers. The first of these was Bob Birkenheimer, who held the post for two years. He was succeeded by Irwin Potts, who was taken on board in 1975 as director of newspaper operations, became vice president in 1979, executive vice president in 1985, president in 1987 and chief executive officer in 1989, after the sudden death of C.K. McClatchy.

Potts was to supervise major growth in the company, from the three papers in being when he was hired to the 28 daily and weekly newspapers at his resignation as CEO in 1996, and his move to the position of chairman of the board. He was succeeded as president and CEO by Gary Pruitt, who had been the first publisher of The Fresno Bee, as company officials moved along the lines suggested by the Haskin-Sells report. From that period on, The Fresno Bee underwent major changes. Bob MacMichael, a planning director, was hired by McClatchy, and budgeting began on a much more thorough basis than before.

Budgets were produced, for annual and five-year plans, under Potts' direction. MacMichael made many trips to Fresno from his Sacramento base, giving needed suggestions during the planning stints. The Haskin-Sells report also resulted in "holds" on hiring in many of The Bee's departments, including national advertising, which was Carter Roberson's charge.

"It decreased the number of employees," Roberson said, "and rightly so. It had grown through a series of estimates based on earlier revenues, which were quite handsome but which in the middle '50s declined dramatically with the advent of television. But any department that wasn't showing profitability was subject to review. I'm sure overtime pay was also affected."

It was a new regime for The Fresno Bee. The newspaper would join many other corporations in the nation, under brilliant but tough CEOs such as Potts, in adopting policies aimed at producing much more and better work, with fewer employees. It was a tough pill for employees and their unions to swallow, but it had its intended results.

In 1960, the daily circulation of The Fresno Bee was in the 107,000 range. In 1976, 16 years later when the population of the Fresno metropolitan area was booming, the daily circulation of The Fresno Bee was still in the 107,000 range. Obviously, something had to be done. In December of 1976, The Fresno Bee undertook probably its biggest step since its inception in 1922. It switched to morning publication. This major step was taken after several meetings of the McClatchy brass. Not too coincidentally, that included Irwin Potts, although the final decision rested in the hands of C.K. McClatchy.

It meant full morning delivery of the Bee. And it was not a step taken lightly. In fact, it was one taken with much trepidation, especially by

Fresno editors. The local wisdom was that Fresno was an "evening paper town." It was thought that the community patterns, especially its reading habits, were keyed off a paper delivered in the evening. But Potts was firm in his decision to go forward, asking only how soon the Fresno changeover could be accomplished. Estimates of up to six months were made by the Fresno editors, who were shocked by Potts' final word:

"We'll do it in 30 days."

His assessment of the staff's capabilities proved correct – the changeover was accomplished in his 30-day time frame, and The Fresno Bee became the second major newspaper in the nation to convert from evening publication to mornings. The first was The Modesto Bee, also under Potts' direction.

The initial thought in Fresno had been to beef up the Saturday paper only, and run it as a morning paper. It was the lightweight paper of the week, never carrying its own slim poundage, having suffered a heavy decline in advertising sales. Its news ration, outside of Pages Al and B1, went mainly to the church pages.

But the final decision, pushed by Potts, was to go all the way, every day. One of the first benefits was in the increase in major real estate and automotive business ads published on Saturdays. Because of that influx, other businesses joined in, also buying Saturday ads.

Another great improvement was in the Wednesday food section. It hadn't been doing so well, either. But now, with housewives able to scan the Wednesday paper early and take off on their jaunts for good grocery buys, the Wednesday paper also took off. A few stores even switched their ads to Tuesdays in attempts to beat the Wednesday advertisers.

Also surprising to many Bee executives was the fact that the production forces went along with morning delivery, not complaining about the way their lives were turned around. "We were apprehensive about making the change," said Roberson. "Much of the discussion had to do with how the labor force would accept the change – the pressmen, and the mailers, and the typo union, because you certainly were changing their hours. And that part was accepted reasonably well, surprisingly."

A major fear had been how the circulation department would accept the biggest change. Mailers were accustomed to loading delivery trucks in the afternoon, but now would have to work in the wee morning hours instead. Would they strike? No. Even that came about better than most insiders had predicted. There were few beefs.

And despite hundreds of complaints from readers that they didn't want a morning paper, that they would cancel their subscriptions, relatively few carried out those threats. Circulation started to rise immediately, increasing by thousands each year, and reaching more than 175,000 in the advancing years.

Potts and C.K. McClatchy hadn't been afraid to assume the risk, and they were proven right. The Fresno Bee was on the rise again.

18

Farmers Don't Approve

The question was raised in 1983 by C.K. McClatchy, editor of the McClatchy Newspapers, in Fresno from Sacramento on a working visit: "Why do the farmers hate The (Fresno) Bee?"

In reality, it was a long-standing love-hate relationship.

In the earlier days, The Bee published a Sunday farm section – California Country Life – consisting originally of four tabloid pages and growing to an eventual 60 pages, on occasion – until its virtual demise in the 1980s through loss of advertising. It was filled with contemporary, and most often complimentary, stories on agriculture, relating to the industry at large, what was happening with farm groups, with the women's auxiliaries and youth organizations such as Future Farmers of America and 4-H Clubs. It drew high praise; the farm community loved it. And subscribed to The Bee, to a degree, because of it.

On the flip side, The Bee covered breaking agricultural stories in the regular news section of the daily paper, and many times these stories were negative to the farming community. Nobody else in Fresno covered that aspect of the news. Radio stations, and later TV, stayed unabashedly on the side of the farmers; they needed the advertising dollars.

Fresno is the heart of a vast agricultural belt. The San Joaquin Valley is a near-desert, but with water brought to the fields in irrigation canals,

The Three-Man Farm Department at work. Farm Editor Leo Dollar (left).

instantly becomes a lush paradise for farmers. Cotton and grapes became paramount crops, along with a myriad of others.

It was to this farm community that California Country Life was specifically aimed. At its zenith, this publication won four consecutive first-place annual awards for best of its type in contests sponsored by the California Newspaper Publishers Association – 1971 through 1974. In 1975 it won the silver, and reverted to the gold in 1976, a total in that period of five out of six first-place awards and a second-place.

The section wasn't merely a puff piece for the farmers. At Cal Poly San Luis Obispo, for example, professors would use this Sunday farm section as an ag text for the students. The university paid for a dozen subscriptions of The Sunday Fresno Bee until Duke Millard, the paper's business manager, ordered that 12 copies of the Sunday paper be given weekly to Cal Poly.

During its glory years, Country Life had two editors – Michael James Francis Keyes, a true Irishman from Dingle Bay; and Leo Dollar, a college-bred American.

Robert P. Molander

Keyes, "Mike" to his legion of friends, came to this country from Ireland with his family at the age of 12. He was graduated from Notre Dame University with a bachelor's degree in teaching. He helped pay expenses by working for the South Bend Tribune while at Notre Dame. After he graduated, he took a teaching job in a South Carolina high school. The story goes that he taught math and history, with a stint of Latin thrown in, although that one is hard to swallow, considering his Irish brogue and the Southern-twang of his students.

Later, he taught for a year at The Citadel. But having had his fill of what he termed "dealing with brats," Keyes decided to return to the newspaper field. His first West Coast job was as a copy editor at The Sacramento Bee. He moved to The Fresno Bee the following year, taking a job on the copy desk. Carlos McClatchy, who was running The Fresno Bee, decided he wanted more farm news, and in 1931, California Country Life was born.

It started as a single sheet, folded once into four tab-size pages. Keyes was named the farm editor. During its expansion days, it was to include – in addition to the more than 50 percent agricultural news – book reviews, a radio log, building and development stories, home and garden, and home of the week. Its main story would be a feature, with photos, on Page 3, usually concerning processing stories, packing, fresh and frozen fruit packs, livestock, poultry.

Bee agricultural reporters relied heavily for expertise from the farm advisers who were part of the California Agricultural Extension Service. The valley counties supplied the office buildings and vehicles, and the farm advisers were paid as university staff members, often reaching professor or Ph.D. status.

Any feature having to do with agriculture would fill the bill for Country Life. Wire news on agriculture was also included. But Fresno State College, founded in 1911 as a teacher's college and farm school, was the major beneficiary of the section. Keyes and Dollar were ordered to run at least one Sunday feature story, complete with photos, on some activity on the FSC campus. The general rule was that The Bee promote some FSC activity weekly – no exceptions.

But at least in one instance, the "rules" seemed to get bogged down. The general rule of the newspaper as a whole was that no company or product would get "free advertising" in the news columns. One day, Leo Dollar came up with a story that he reasoned, correctly, was big news. John Deere, the farm-tractor giant, was coming out with a new cotton picker that would work two rows at a time, rather than just one. Dollar wrote the story, but it was killed by managing editor Bill Lockwood, because it was "advertising." Dollar argued, logically but not successfully, that Cadillac, Ford and Chevrolet got stories every year on their new-model automobiles. Why not John Deere?

Mike Keyes was a part of the "Front Page" lifestyle of the day. He was a major factor in keeping the suppliers of his brand of whiskey in business, and every Saturday during the fall football season he would hold radio parties in his home. The featured game was the Notre Dame Fighting Irish vs. the sacrificial lamb of the day. Several Bee staffers were a part of the Mike Keyes/Notre Dame Fan Club fests – Dollar, Diz Shelton, Don Castelazo, Bob Shuman, Lew Hegg, Duke Millard, Don Steward, Bob Molander – the list was long. The booze was free. The only prerequisites were penchants for John Paul Jones and Notre Dame.

Keyes would hold fort while standing in a kitchen corner, puffing his pipe endlessly while the game went on, replacing empty bottles. As is the habit with tobacco pipes, his often went out and he had to relight. This he'd do with wooden matches, scratching each under the bottom shelf of the wall cupboard. A peek underneath revealed a section at least a foot wide, blackened with matches struck over the years. Mike's wife, Adelaid, had the patience of a saint.

At one such gathering, one of Mike's guests had a wee bit too much of The Admiral Himself (Keyes' code name for his favorite whiskey,) and passed out on a living-room couch. There was a radio playing in the living room too, and that couch was made for three upright bodies. So Duke said, "Hell, we can solve that." And together, they slid the passed-out one into the space behind the couch. An hour later, when the game was over and it was time to leave, there was no body there. They panicked, because the man's car was gone, too.

In their collective haze, they figured that he had stumbled out and driven home. They were right. The phone rang, with one very irate wife, in "a fuming, profane rage," quoting Dollar, screaming, "You dumb so and so's, letting that jackass out on the road!"

Mike Keyes retired in 1965, and Leo Dollar was elevated from farm reporter-photographer to farm editor. But he still carried and used that camera for Page 3 feature pictures.

The farmers remained hostile towards The Bee. "It was frustrating to go some place and have the people say, 'The Fresno Bee? What the hell are they doing here," Dollar said. "Even though we were out and among 'em regular as hell. We got refused quite a few times to do a story, because, 'What the hell, it's just going to be in The Fresno Bee, and we don't want that. No sense of you trying to come here and do a story – we don't want that."

As the years went on, the economy changed, things got tight. Prejudice of the farm community against The Bee because of its "attitude" resulted in more hostility. Some ads were pulled. Others were lost, many to special farm publications, some because they were moved to other sections of the newspaper, others because companies got out of the business. Collectively, it all hurt. In-house expenses also went up. Mechanical costs rose. And more workers were required to set the tab up. It cost more in expenses and labor to put out a tab section, as compared with a regular, broadsheet section. So the word went out. California Country Life would become a broadsheet, and would be merged with other news. The familiar tab section would be gone.

The Bee tried to put a good face on the change, claiming it would make the section better. But this didn't fool anyone, least of all the farmers. They were given more reasons to "hate" The Bee. They had lost their baby.

The Bee tackled the negative farm and water stories because, the editors felt, they had to be told. Otherwise, the newspaper would lose all sense of the credibility it had attained through the years. It was a case of a newspaper not being solely concerned with where its bread was being buttered. All aspects of the story had to be covered, printed, whether or not it meant losing ads. So The Bee closely covered activities like the farm-labor situation, the growth of the Cesar Chavez movement to organize farm labor, the problems that industry has with regulatory agencies. In the words of George Gruner, managing editor for the period beginning in 1971:

"We'd try to cover all sides of the situation, and while on the one hand we were being praised for farm-section coverage, on the other hand we would be castigated for the news stories related to the other side."

The biggest problem wasn't the news stories, and wasn't, strangely, the editorials supporting such things as the 160-acre limitation on farm use of federal water, or the Chavez forces in the farm-labor strife. It was, to Gruner's way of thinking, the editorial cartoons. Most of the editorials were written in Sacramento and were expected to be published in all three Bees. The editorial cartoonist was also quartered in Sacramento, and his daily efforts also were to be run in all the Bees. And, of course, they were written or drawn with a Sacramento perspective. Sacramento wouldn't get a complaint when an offending cartoon was published, but those same drawings running in Fresno would set up a firestorm in the San Joaquin Valley. One of the prime "offenders" was Dennis Renault, editorial cartoonist who started working for The Sacramento Bee, and indirectly the Fresno and Modesto Bees, in 1971.

Renault drew a particularly "fire storming" cartoon in 1977, one that was deemed exceedingly offensive by the big operators in the farming community. The valley's Westlands Water District, the largest such district in the nation, was being accused of flaunting the 1902 federal law that put a limit on the amount of land that could be owned by farmers in federal water irrigation projects. The cartoon featured a scarecrow drawn in the likeness of Uncle Sam, bearing the label "Unenforced 160 Acre Limitation," and standing shakily on "Federally Irrigated Farmland." Several defiant crows were flying about or sitting on the scarecrow, and instead of "Cawing," they were "Hawing." As in "Haw, Haw, Haw." Each of the close-up crows bore a different label: Land Corporations, Speculators, Paper Farmers, Lease-Back Deals, Absentee Owners, Foreign Investors.

The cartoon, titled "Birds of a Feather" and published during the Fresno reign of Managing Editor Diz Shelton, hit the nail on the head as far as Bee policy was concerned, but the big farmers predictably were enraged.

"Time after time we would have cartoons that would get no reaction in Sacramento, practically none in Modesto, but in Fresno it would set them off." said Gruner. "A few times, they (the cartoons) were offensive

Robert P. Molander

to the point where I could deal with C.K. (McClatchy). I would object to an editorial or cartoon – I would see them in advance – and I would say, 'I don't want to run this. If this was my paper, I would not run this. I am your editor in Fresno, and I would not run this in my town.' And he would usually say 'OK, don't.' "

The prime agricultural problem in the valley is the lack of water. A desert is defined as an area with fewer than 10 inches of rainfall a year. The annual average in Fresno is about 10 1/2 inches. The Bees, since their inception, were very much in favor of reservoirs and developing water. They thought the federal government had a big reclamation role to play, and believed it was terribly important. It was a direct legacy from the original Sacramento Bee. Developing water, it is generally acknowledged, is good in the overall picture. It's good for the economy, good for the farmers. Without it, the valley wouldn't be the valley.

But Tom Kirwan, chief editorial writer for The Fresno Bee during that period, wondered in later years about the way the policy was developed, questioning whether the Bees erred on the side of not being discriminating enough, that building dams and developing water could be a mixed blessing.

"I think this uncritical policy, which was a pure inheritance from McClatchy, did not cover them with glory," Kirwan said. "They should have seen that with unbridled dam-building there would be a lot of downsides – a lot of environmental downsides, like fish that were being cramped for the sweet sake of building dams and irrigating fields. And I think they had a one-dimensional approach – that by God they certainly backed it! In doing that, they probably contributed enormously to the valley economy. But they did it without much acknowledgment that there were trade offs."

Kirwan points to a paradox there: The original C.K. McClatchy led the battle against placer mining, led the fight to maintain trees, was "very good" environmentally. But in the matter of water development, "They kinda got a mote in their eye. This was a California coming into its own. This dramatic idea of the state water project, moving the water from the north to the south – and the federal development, and the state – all this was a dramatic assertion of California economy, and of the farm economy. It just was that this organization – McClatchy – which was so good on the environment in so many ways, particularly in Sacramento, kind of went lame on the environmental concerns associated with water development."

The struggle for power had gone on for decades. Farmers felt cramped by the 160-acre limitation, and desperately wanted to expand. And powerful outside interests such as railroads – a prime example being Southern Pacific – owned thousands and thousands of acres of land that had been given them by the federal government as the United States encouraged railroads to develop the West. These interests needed water to make this land ownership pay off.

The federal limitation, not to be confused with the state irrigation program, which bore no acreage limitation, provided for recordable contracts. Under them, a farmer could get water for all of his acreage provided that within 10 years of signing the contract and getting the water, he would sell off all his land in excess of 160 acres. It was a limitation ostensibly intended to protect the small farmer. But it didn't work out that way. Large landowners found simple ways around it – deeding 160 acres to a son, another 160 to a daughter, another 160 to a nephew, another 160 to a foreman, ad infinitum.

George Baker, an aggressive young reporter and son of an earlier Fresno Bee reporter with the same name, was hired in 1969 by Shelton. It didn't take him long to dig into the story. Big operations were entering the valley, and buying up land. One of them was Tenneco, which bought the Kern County Land Company and attempted to become an integrated company that would own everything, from the tractors on the land all the way to the final processing of the product.

Even as Baker became seasoned with the intricacies of valley water and politics, he said later, he was highly surprised at how far it had gone. "When I was doing stories about the (state-proposed) Peripheral Canal, the thrust of those stories was that this money (federal subsidies) was all going to benefit oil companies in Kern County. That's who owned all the land down there. Nobody really knew that. That surprised me, because once you got into it, it was pretty amazing, how much of that land (they owned.)"

The Peripheral Canal had been proposed for decades as a means of transporting fresh water from Northern California around the San

Robert P. Molander

Joaquin River Delta and southward for irrigation and municipal use. As such, it would have had no federal acreage limitation.

The Kern County area was familiar to Baker; that's where he dug out the material that resulted in his first stories on the 160-acre limitation and the vagaries of its enforcement. It was 1970, and he did a series of stories on the incorporation of agriculture in the valley, and the way huge companies were trying to accumulate land. In Baker's words, they were "trying to force out some family farmers." It got into federal water policies, pesticides, many side issues.

Gordon Nelson, former city editor of The Fresno Bee, who, in his years as a reporter had written scores of stories on valley water issues and politics, and who later became a lobbyist in Washington D.C. for agricultural interests, points out that the holdings of land barons in the 1800s were huge. He contends that in the 1900s firms such as Tenneco bought up some of these already established holdings, and didn't amass new portions of land.

"What the (1902) law did," says Nelson, "was to put a limit on the amount of land under a single ownership, not the size of a farming operation that could be put together under leases." In addition, the law did not specifically prohibit an individual landowner from owning land in several districts.

One farmer in the Bakersfield area was Ken Frick, a big landowner who farmed with his brothers. Frick was also administrator of the federal Agricultural Stabilization Conservation Service (ASCS), which had offices in most valley counties. The agency oversaw the federal farm subsidies that were being paid out at the time. They were cash subsidies – for cotton, feed grain.

Frick was running the ASCS, as Baker reported, and at the same time his farms were getting subsidies. "There were a lot of questions about the ethics of that, how he was running the program, what kind of money he was getting," Baker said. It got nationwide publicity when Baker's stories were picked up by the Washington, D.C., nationally syndicated muckraker/columnist Jack Anderson. And that didn't make the farmers particularly ecstatic, either.

With that series of stories, the George Baker byline became well known and grudgingly respected in the valley farming community. Readers sensed he wasn't around just to write press releases.

Baker was following in the footsteps of another tough investigative reporter, Ron Taylor, who had started the stories probing the alleged improprieties in the enforcement of the 160-acre limitation law. Taylor did the brunt of his work at The Bee on stories about Cesar Chavez and the rise of his farm workers' union, and its battles with smaller scale farmers on the east side of the San Joaquin Valley. East side growers were not generally related with the Westlands Water District, which wasn't in Chavez's area of focus – he was after grape growers.

Taylor was to move on to the Los Angeles Times reportorial staff, and later authored a book on the valley and its labor problems. The book was made into a TV movie.

Taylor found it hard to keep his hands off the developing stories when he was off the beat. "It was pretty funny," Baker recalled. "After I started covering Chavez, several times Taylor called me up and said, 'You shouldn't be doing this, you should be doing that.' Finally at one point, I said that 'Hey, Ron, this is my beat; I'm going to do it the way I want to do it, and if you don't like it, that's tough.' You sort of had to do that. He was very assertive."

Baker's stories influenced development of McClatchy editorial policy. The Bees became critical of Westlands, and what appeared to be its way of finding routes around the letter of the law, and the spirit of the reclamation law. Baker was the man who essentially got into it, fleshed it out. As a result, the editorial policy was, in part, an echo of his reporting.

Kirwan agrees: "I think they (agricultural interests) were finding ways to organize the structure of farms in a way that got around the 160-acre limitations, which is one aspect of regulations ... It's a complicated thing – the way of organizing ownerships, making – devolving – 'ownerships' to employees, children, children's children, nephews. It was a way of getting around the 160-acre limitation. So The Bee, which had whooped it up for Westlands and the San Luis Project, which is intrinsic to Westlands, was beginning to get critical about the way it was being executed, the way it was carried out. It was right. It was high time to get critical."

Gordon Nelson, the lobbyist, takes his turn at the plate. Initially, he says, The Bee wasn't really interested in the hard news of agriculture – unless it was negative: "The only good farmer is a dead farmer." He points out that the character of The Bee's public policy stands was important. Community leaders knew that once the Bee committed itself to a given course of action, the commitment was firm, that they weren't alone in their battles. The Bee did not shrink from a fight, even in the face of likely failure. That The Bee took on the Westlands farmers is recognized by all sides.

Nelson points to this story involving his coverage of the water beat as a reporter in the early 1950s:

The big west-side farm operators, with Jack O'Neill taking the lead, had mapped and adopted a course of action to create a district under the California Water District Act. This action permitted one vote by members for each dollar of assessed valuation, leaving the farmers in control rather than having all possible voters in the district being involved. (Opponents argued that this gave the largest landowners the power to make their own unimpeded decisions, to the detriment of the small farmers with their fewer votes.)

The Bee assigned Nelson to cover a meeting of the farmer group, which planned to contract for water under the Federal Reclamation Act of 1902. The farmers weren't asking for exemptions, Nelson says, and could live with the proposal that the price at which excess land would be sold was the price the land would have brought before it was enhanced with the federal water.

The results were more than beneficial for the farmers, and for the San Joaquin Valley in general. The San Luis Project was completed and a huge dam was constructed near Los Banos. Through the efforts of Congressman B.F. (Bernie) Sisk, President John F. Kennedy attended the groundbreaking. San Luis was built, and the Westlands landowners put their lands under recordable contracts. Involved, among others, were the Southern Pacific Land Company, the J.B. Boswell Company, and most of the other landowners.

"More excess lands were sold under recordable contracts in Westlands than had previously been sold in the entire history of the Reclamation Act," Nelson says. "The average size of a farming operation in Westlands fell dramatically."

The McClatchy newspapers sided with the farmers on having the federal Bureau of Reclamation construct the San Luis dam, and support began to build. The Bee's backing had much to do with the eventual construction. Its power was never illustrated better. People made commitments based on McClatchy's "laying on of hands," as Nelson delicately put it.

"So (now) comes The Fresno Bee and says the Westlands farmers are a bunch of thieves," he says. "Was The Bee forever committed to the status quo in Westlands? No, it wasn't. It could have presented the facts in the controversy fairly, in an even-handed manner, but it didn't. (Bee reporter) George Baker bought the environmentalist line hook, line and sinker. Baker was replaced by Dick Hall, who understood agriculture and covered the issue much more fairly. His coverage was so fair he was summarily hauled back to Fresno (from Washington D.C.) because his coverage wasn't aggressive (i.e. hostile) enough."

So why did the farmers hate The Bee? There was the monumental disagreement on the 160-acre limitation. Then came a double-whammy – the insidious invasion of the chemical-element selenium, a natural trace element which can become poisonous if concentrated. It made its way into Westlands' drainage water. Brought on through heavy irrigation, the drainage settled at Kesterson, and eventually ravaged wildlife in its ponds.

The irrigation drainage from Westlands, laced with selenium, poisoned thousands of migratory birds in the grasslands of Merced County in the late 1970s. One key spot was the Kesterson Reservoir, in the Kesterson Wildlife Refuge, designated by the government as a holding pond for drainage from the Westlands farms. The accumulation of drainage water in Kesterson, turned salty over five or six years through evaporation and the concentration of impurities such as selenium, resulted in increasing wildlife death and deformity.

Environmentalists were furious, and their protests became more volatile as Fresno Bee science reporter Deborah Blum wrote several stories on the devastation of the wildlife, with accompanying Bee photos showing dead and deformed birds at the reservoir. In Westlands' eyes, it was a no-brainer – the welfare of a few thousand birds vs. keeping hundreds of thousands of acres of valuable farmland in production.

Robert P. Molander

At this point, Westlands manager Jerald Butchert made the politically correct move of hiring Ed (Rusty) Simmons as Westlands' first public information officer. It was a good choice. Simmons was an old hand at KMJ Radio and later at KMJ-TV in Fresno, both owned and operated at the time by McClatchy, and most recently had completed five years as public relations officer for the California Water Resources Association. With that education, he became water-knowledgable, a pro.

He was also a good choice in that his name was well known. He had been hired as KMJ assistant farm editor, although he had no farm or water background. Previously, he played guitar and sang country music, and about a year after being hired he was offered the chance to do a daily KMJ Radio program for children. He accepted, and it led to the formation of Rusty's Rangers. Most young listeners of the radio station became Rangers for Rusty.

Because of this, his name was recognized and trusted by most when he later was hired away from the California Water Resources Association by Westlands. His new assignment was to generate good relations with the press, to advise the public on what the district was doing, to raise public understanding of Westlands' problems. He was taken on in 1977 at a time of severe drought and at the peak of the acreage-limitation controversy. And Kesterson loomed. But at least as important as his public information task, perhaps more so, was his assignment to work on negotiations with the U.S. Bureau of Reclamation on Westland water supply and repayment contracts.

Simmons, who had high praise for The Bee while he was working for KMJ Radio and TV, lost most of his respect during the years with Westlands:

"As I watched what was happening in acreage limitation, I realized that the myth that if you farmed more than 160 acres with federal water (it) was somehow either illegal or unethical was actually being enhanced by The Bee. The Bee always seemed to be on the other side of the acreage-limitation issue. I think most reporters nowadays come out of the school of confrontational, anti-establishment journalism. And although it's hard to believe, I suppose, to some extent, The Bee was a victim of its own reporters."

Simmons estimated that Westlands, which covers some 600,000 acres of farmland, produced about a quarter to a third of all the crops grown in the valley. As he put it, all this agricultural land from Kettleman up to the Delta was in danger of going out of production from the salt build-up, "which is the thing that put Mesopotamia out of business in ancient times. It's always been a problem. It's nothing unique to this area."

Simmons also wanted it known that Westlands farmers were paying heavily for federal water – $7.50 an acre-foot when Westlands "came on line late" in 1963, and $13.50 a foot in later years, when other districts in the nation were paying $3.50."

And he pointed out that Westlands was delivering more than a million acre-feet of water over nearly a thousand square miles through a closed system of underground pipes. "It's as efficient as you can get," he said. "And you talk about saving water? We don't even have an open ditch! We were never able to get over the idea (to The Bee) that in the area of water costs, we have paid most of the capital costs for the Central Valley Project – just our district alone, because of our higher price. Westlands paid more for water than any other contractor in the state of California."

It cost $82 million to clean up Kesterson. Years later, in 1996, Westlands farmers agreed to pay $25.9 million of that tab, plus an additional $4.6 million for further studies of irrigation problems. U.S. taxpayers came up with the rest. Despite the heavy payment, the farmers didn't admit any fault, but went down swinging. Rancher Ed O'Neill, a heavy hitter in the game, charged, "The government was at fault for ordering Kesterson to be used as an evaporation pond. When I'm at fault, I generally pay for my mistake. In this case, the government is being paid for making a mistake."

Still not settled was the matter of the proposed San Luis Drain, which was to carry drainage water into the Pacific Ocean by way of San Francisco Bay and the Delta. Strict environmentalists wanted to close farm operations on land that suffered from the poisonous buildup of selenium-infiltrated drainage water. They also questioned the value of completion of the Drain. The farmers wanted to continue in full production. And as for the Drain, they wanted water held at Kesterson

Robert P. Molander

for short periods, with regulated releases to the Delta, thus solving the problem of accumulated amounts of selenium at Kesterson. The district wasn't specifically trying to sell the idea of the drain, Simmons contended. "It was trying to sell the idea that the problem had to be addressed, and solved."

There was another major thorn in the hide of the farmers – Cesar Chavez. This grand knight of the Hispanic farm workers, some of whom were illegally in this country from Mexico, rode in with demands that these workers be paid commensurate with their labors, and with up-to-date fringes – a minimum wage, unemployment insurance, enfranchisement in the system. Until this time, these things were unheard of – the workers moved up the valley as the crops ripened, and it generally was first-come, first-hired. Few lived permanently on the farms. And even fewer had the guts to ask for higher pay. Enter Cesar Chavez, who dared to tread where no one before him had walked. He rallied farm workers in the valley and sympathizers across the nation with the slogan, "Yes, you can."

Why did the farmers hate The Fresno Bee? Basically, Chavez was the turning point. The seed had been sewn before him, but he was the turning point.

"The farmers hated us (The Bee) long before we started chopping the thing a little finer on Chavez and water," Tom Kirwan said. "These guys (the farmers), they want unyielding, unconditional love and support, or you're not with them. And we were a powerful force that they couldn't control. They're not going to change. You can suck up to them from here until the year 2,000, and it won't change anything."

At the peak of Chavez's power, he claimed nearly 100,000 members in his United Farm Workers Union. He had the backing of many organizations, including The Bee. One of the many obituaries written in newspapers across the nation on his death read: "Chavez's years of struggle brought him worldwide attention and the support of farm workers, politicians, union leaders and clergy – and opposition from other politicians, union leaders and, especially, growers."

His efforts helped define the social and political lives of Hispanics throughout the nation. Marches, strikes and boycotts resulted, primarily concerning non-union table grapes. His backers included Robert F.

Kennedy, and activists such as the folk singer Joan Baez and the Rev. Jesse Jackson.

The Fresno Bee's backing, in the words of Tom Kirwan, "took a hell of a lot of guts." He continued, "Roger Mahony, at the time director of Fresno Catholic Charities and Social Services, took the lead in saying, 'Look, the social gospel instructs us that you must be sympathetic to this man's aspirations.' And, of course, it alienated all kinds of big farmers who were Catholics – a lot of them. It was a very dicey time. The Bee was getting a full ration of crap from them, but so was Roger – and the Diocese. And guys (wealthy Catholic farmers) were pulling away their support." Mahony, later to be elevated to the rank of cardinal in the Roman Catholic Church, took part with Chavez in marches. "Rallies began with the celebration of the Mass," Mahony said at the time of Chavez's death in 1993. "Marches were conducted under the banner of Our Lady of Guadalupe while the Rosary was prayed. And his speeches and writings frequently referred to Gospel values. Cesar Chavez truly understood his Christian vocation to build up the kingdom of God in this world."

Ron Taylor, the Fresno Bee reporter who did most of the initial reporting on Chavez, was an important player in Chavez's rise to power. He understood its importance, and he reported it. But not all Fresno Bee employees backed Chavez. One in opposition was Leo Dollar, editor of The Bee's award-winning weekly Sunday tab, California Country Life.

"The farmers regarded us (the Country Life staff) as the source of impartial coverage," Dollar said. "The antagonism started, not over the water so much (it was) Ron Taylor worshipping this anarchist. And that's all the guy was."

In its editorials, The Bee supported Chavez and his right to organize, and the importance of what he was doing. The farmers awoke late to the fact that Chavez was becoming a powerhouse, and they woefully underestimated him.

The Bee was a powerful newspaper, as the farmers were to learn over the years. Kirwan explains: "It's a powerful force in the community, and you're going to have people resent it – politicians hate that power that they can't control. Other people can't control it. Power centers – it's another power center. You (the newspaper) have to get used to being nobody's favorite boy. But the best you can hope for is to be respected, to do it right, to be as fair as you can be. But you can't try to be litmus paper. You can't try to fit into the woodwork."

Executive Editor George Gruner mused:

"I always said we ought to run an ad – one of my favorite house ads that I wanted to run: 'The Bee Has No Friends.' Meaning, no friends in government, no friends in City Hall, no friends in the power positions in the community. In covering the news, we have no friends. People would say, you're always getting castigated for the fact we run this 'bad news.' Well, if it's news, the people are entitled to know. Whether it's good or bad, it's always been our position to run it.

"That reputation as a strong, fearless news organization was known outside the McClatchy company. It was one of the things that attracted me to come to work for it, one of the things that enabled us to hire good reporters from all over the country. To come to work for McClatchy, because they were recognized as good people to work for, and as reporters' newspapers."

Unfortunately, The Fresno Bee never was to run "Gruner's advertisement."

Chavez instituted a secondary boycott of table grapes, and it was successful in markets in San Francisco and across the nation. It probably was the factor that drew the farmers to the bargaining table. Chavez eventually signed contracts with table grape growers, starting down in the Coachella Valley, and with some of the Reedley- and Fresno-area farmers. He also won contracts with lettuce growers in the Salinas Valley.

His forces fought mostly against farmers in the valley's east side, rather than those in Westlands, who weren't that much into grapes but concentrated more on cotton and other crops. Harry Kubo, president of the Nisei Farmers League, representing mainly the grape farmers in the Reedley area on the east side, where Chavez was opposed bitterly, admitted, "His mere presence lifted the minimum wage."

The Bee wasn't alone in its defense of Caesar Chavez in his battle to help the farm workers. Other supporters included U.S. Senator

Alan Cranston, a powerful California figure; and Jerry Brown, later to become governor of California.

The newspaper stuck by its guns, to answer C.K. McClatchy's 1983 question, and that's what brought on a large measure of the farmers' hatred. To do otherwise would have been to ignore the Cardinal Rules laid down by his grandfather, the original C.K. McClatchy, back there in the 19th century-- that all persons, rich or poor, no matter what their status, must be given equal, fair treatment in the editorial columns of the Bee.

Robert P. Molander

19

Changes

It was deemed time for a change. The Fresno Bee editorial side had been ruled locally (with tight overall supervision from Sacramento) by a series of just four managing editors, from The Fresno Bee's birth in 1922 until the major changes that came about in 1988. Carlos McClatchy held sway as editor from 1922 until his death in 1933. McClatchy brought H.R. "Mac" McLaughlin with him from Sacramento to take over as Fresno's initial managing editor. Mac held the post until retiring in 1949. Then in order came Managing Editors W.E. "Bill" Lockwood. 1949-1959: O.M. "Diz" Shelton, 1959-1971; and George Gruner, 1971-1988. (Gruner's final seven years were as executive editor, a step above managing editor, when that change was ordained by McClatchy Editor C.K. McClatchy in 1982.)

All four were "home grown," each spending many years maturing with McClatchy newspapers before assuming the top editorial post in Fresno. McLaughlin served his first "growing-up" stint in Sacramento, where he was a reporter and city editor of The Sacramento Bee until requisitioned by Carlos McClatchy to serve in Fresno. Lockwood was with the Fresno Republican and "stolen" by The Bee to become its first assistant city editor, later city editor and then assistant managing editor. Shelton was an old-line Fresno City Hall and political reporter who became assistant city editor, then hurdled the city editor's post to become executive editor (which at the time ranked below managing editor) for a year. Gruner came from the Oakland Tribune and the European edition of Stars and Stripes to serve on the Bee's copy desk, then was assistant city editor and city editor. Each of the four had paid his dues. It's the way it was done.

All the top slots were filled by men. But the second C.K. McClatchy, the top editor, was a man for the future. He didn't necessarily believe that the old, traditional way was always the best. Wouldn't it be progressive, he wondered, if the chain had a woman somewhere in command? But where? At the time, there were three possibilities – Sacramento, Modesto and Fresno. Sacramento was quickly ruled out – too close to the chain of command, too many top executives looking over the chosen one's shoulder. It would take a superwoman to survive. Modesto? Almost tiny in comparison, the little sister of the triumvirate, and certainly not ready for local autonomy, a direction toward which C.K. was leaning. Then there was Fresno.

George Gruner, the executive editor in Fresno, had a couple of years to go before possible retirement (there was no longer a mandatory retirement age of 65, a plateau Gruner hadn't reached.) But Gruner was a reasonable man, and he had the highest respect for his boss. The feeling was mutual on McClatchy's part. The plan was to open the top job so as to make easier the transition as various newsroom management positions came open with retirement of the "class of 1990," a group of editors who all would retire at about the same time. Gruner, "well taken care of" by C.K, agreed to step aside. The next issue: Which woman would take his place?

The search went nationwide, eventually centering on Beverly Kees, a woman with a history of successful newspaper positions in Indiana, North Dakota and Minnesota. She would become the first outsider to take the editorial reins of The Fresno Bee. After a couple of surreptitious visits to the Sacramento headquarters and to Fresno, with head-to-head talks with McClatchy, she was quick to accept the offer to become executive editor of The Fresno Bee. That she was to become her own woman became apparent immediately. As he was leaving, Gruner offered any help he might be able to give her: "If you have any questions, please don't hesitate to call." His phone never rang.

Robert P. Molander

C.K. McClatchy wasn't one to give away company secrets, and he kept the word of the Kees hiring largely to himself. But he couldn't resist one "early" announcement (after Gruner had been notified). Desa Belyea, assistant managing editor, had been needling C.K. for years about the lack of women in command posts of any McClatchy newspaper. Soon came the day he sauntered into Belyea's office looking "like a kid with a secret," really pleased with himself. Grinning, he told her that Kees would he on board soon, as executive editor succeeding Gruner.

There had been an unwritten rule among McClatchy newspapers, stemming from Eleanor McClatchy's days in the company president's chair: None of the papers would blow its own horn in print. This included not only favorable mentions of any McClatchy doings in the papers' news columns, but in outreach to the public – visible membership in clubs or organizations was frowned upon. This was relaxed, to a degree, when the top officer on the business side and his counterpart in editorial were offered memberships in private golf clubs, paid for by The Bee. And it was OK to become members in clubs such as the Elks or Rotary. But editors generally stayed at home in the newsroom – until Beverly Kees. She broke the mold. But it was not solely her doing.

McClatchy and his leadership team were anxious to get a female editor on board; it was important to the company. But the brass also wanted it known in the community that The Bee was progressive. Having a female in the editor's chair would have a lot to do with that. So actually, it was C.K. McClatchy who saw the value of Kees being seen in the community.

Where former editors had deemed it necessary to sit in on the daily news conferences, deciding which stories were to be ranked highest on Page 1, which would be on the local page, which to put inside, Kees didn't make it a daily practice to attend those meetings, largely leaving Managing Editor Don Slinkard in command.

Suddenly, The Bee had a presence in the community, something it hadn't had since the days of Carlos McClatchy. It fit her style. But it didn't work out. She adopted a practice of being out nearly every day, becoming the desired presence in the community.

Then, the final blow struck. C. K. McClatchy, the man who had given her the big chance, suffered a fatal heart attack while jogging in Sacramento. Kees had been in the community, as instructed, attempting to fill the dual role – spreading the word in the community, and running the editorial side of The Bee. There were mixed reviews of what kind of a job Kees did and what she did for the paper. Many believe that had C.K. lived, Kees would have survived the cut. But he left the scene, and so did she. One local executive, a woman, said it was a severe disappointment that Kees didn't work out. "It hurts women when one of us fails. And I really wanted her to succeed."

Kees was succeeded as executive editor by Peter Bhadia, who came down from Sacramento. In Fresno, he remained on the job only six weeks before leaving the McClatchy chain for another job. His Fresno accomplishments were threefold. He stayed only long enough to buy a company car, to have his office remodeled and to hire an assistant managing editor/sports.

Next in line was George Baker, an old Fresno hand who had been a reporter and political writer before moving to Sacramento, later becoming city editor there. He was called back to Fresno, where he was a caretaker as executive editor, failing in his bid to make the job permanent. He, like Bhadia, left the company.

In 1994, J. Keith Moyer, a rising star in the Gannett chain, was named The Fresno Bee's executive editor, holding the post until succeeding Robert Weil in 1997 as publisher.

Another major change, one the locals had wanted for years, was the institution of local autonomy. Gary Pruitt, a lawyer, had matriculated in Sacramento as general counsel and then secretary of the company's board of directors. In 1991, at age 34, he was installed as the first publisher of The Fresno Bee since the days of Carlos McClatchy. Fresno would no longer have to check with Sacramento as to which stories should be played where or which candidates should be backed for political office. And it put to an end the bickering that sometimes occurred between the business and editorial sides of The Bee as to which would rule in certain circumstances. The publisher now would decide – without having to contact Sacramento for a decision.

It was followed by a swift succession of local leaders. Pruitt moved to Sacramento, and would become the company's chief executive officer. In Fresno, Robert Weil succeeded Pruitt as publisher, to be followed by J. Keith Moyer in 1997. Moyer later was elevated to Publisher-President.

He hired Charlie Waters as Executive Editor. Waters was elevated to Executive Editor-Vice President.

Moyer realized early on that the McClatchy culture was rare in the newspaper game. Joining organizations, for example. When top brass are joiners, reporters try to recall whether this group or that has ties with their bosses. This can influence the way stories are covered. It's better, it is felt by many, that the bosses stay aloof from those groups. (While Bill Lockwood was managing editor, he was a member of a Rotary Club. It met at noon on Mondays, and every Monday, a reporter was assigned to cover Rotary's guest speaker and write a quick story for Monday's home edition. The stories were dictated via telephone because of the fast-approaching deadline. The reporters were embarrassed by those assignments because of Lockwood's ties to Rotary. Diz Shelton, not a joiner type, ended the practice on assuming the top job.)

Moyer says he was never told McClatchy had a policy regarding publicity for the company. But he quickly added that the lore was passed down, that the family is very modest and doesn't want to be characterized as a power broker. Still, he reasoned, outsiders such as he are necessary so that companies seeking to keep up with the competition can instill more modern ideas and methods, even though it seems unfair to the company veterans who are passed over as the top jobs open up. On that subject, the McClatchy culture, it was clear that the firm can't be bound by tradition. Moyer says, "Frankly, the way Carlos McClatchy in '22 ran the paper was different than when Shelton or Gruner (were in command). The first edition (in 1922) was loaded down with self-promotion. It's never going to be the way it was when the family ran the papers."

Up to Moyer's time, a typical Page 1 of The Fresno Bee carried a local story, maybe two, with the remainder of the page carrying state, national or international news. That, Moyer felt, was a travesty, and he started the practice of leading Page 1 with local news, or at least having that local news prominently displayed on the remainder of the page.

Moyer instituted other changes on the news side, one of which ended the long-standing practice of assigning reporters to individual beats. The change was thought by some to have failed, but in reality it had its merits. The idea wasn't new to the newspaper industry, but it hadn't been tried at The Bee. The reporter pool was divided into teams, each led by an assistant city editor. Each team was responsible for a certain segment of the news, so that all subjects would be covered. And each team had adjoining desks; this included the editor. It seemed like a good idea, and for a time it was. Some fine stories resulted. But dissension arose on the part of the reporters. They complained their privacy was invaded with an editor sitting in their midst. The management argued that if you want private time, don't work at a newspaper. There's nothing private about a newsroom.

The team concept appeared to be working, despite the complaints by the reporters. And if the truth be known, many of them probably came to like it. But when Charlie Waters came on board as executive editor he reverted to the traditional city desk. One result of the experiment apparently wasn't foreseen. Management saw that certain news sources weren't being covered – stories on them were lacking, or nonexistent. As a result group leaders asked to be relieved of duty because it was evident to them, and to management, that they weren't covering the news. The subscribers weren't getting a full dime's worth of news for their 10 cents.

The Fresno Bee saw many major physical changes through the years – a radio station, a TV building across Van Ness Avenue from The Bee, the conversion from hot type to cold type, computers – but the most impressive by far was the construction of the new Bee building across the tracks in West Fresno. The old building, which had served since 1922, couldn't handle the ever-growing newspaper. A new structure was needed, but where? In the mid-1960s, downtown property, such as the Hilton Hotel location, was going at $12 a square foot. The old Bee building area, somewhat away from the city core was worth probably $8 a foot.

The old building could have been remodeled, but at a heavy cost. It needed a great deal of modernization. New fire regulations were strict and had to be followed, once remodeling started. The building wasn't fully sprinkled. Stairways didn't meet safety standards. And there were several tons of metal on the upper floor, where the printers and stereotypers worked. When The Bee moved out, 70 tons of lead were sold from that top floor. Many wondered what had kept the whole thing from collapsing.

The Bee needed elbow room, and there was a nice piece of land on the market, six and a quarter acres at Blackstone and McKinley Avenues, and it already had a railway spur track, essential to The Bee's operation. But that acreage was owned by several individuals and companies and would have to be purchased piecemeal.

It nearly worked. The Bee, through the good auspices of Pearson Realty, bought up most of the whole chunk a piece at a time – all except two corners on McKinley. Those corners were essential to the project. Without them, the only access to the property would be a narrow driveway. Bids were made on those corners, but the whole thing blew up when someone from Sacramento, on a visit to Fresno, let out the word that The Bee wanted to buy the property. Almost overnight, the cost on those two parcels tripled. And down went the plan.

In West Fresno, much of Chinatown had been torn out, and homes on the property that was eventually purchased by the Bee were razed, their cellars filled in as part of a redevelopment project. And the property was available from the Fresno Redevelopment Agency.

The redevelopment folks welcomed The Bee with wide-open arms. The Bee led the way across the tracks, becoming the first purchaser in the area. It was June in 1968, and the newspaper did it up lavishly at the groundbreaking for the new building – flew the redevelopment leaders to the site in a helicopter, served champagne in a circus tent, made laudatory speeches.

The Bee bought eight city blocks, totaling 30 acres, on H Street at 49 cents per square foot. (The present building sits on what was F Street.) Eleanor McClatchy had big dreams for the property. She not only wanted to improve the area, she intended to control its growth. The Post Office had purchased land across H Street from the Bee property. The government then approached McClatchy with the request to buy two blocks at one end of the property for a new Post Office site. A trade resulted, with the Post Office getting the two blocks it wanted and McClatchy getting the land across the street. Bee people had gotten wind of a plan to build a supermarket on that property, and Miss McClatchy would have none of that. Thoroughly modern in her thinking, she envisioned a heliport surrounded by a park. She wanted a sample of scores of things grown in California planted in that park. It never developed, but neither did the supermarket, or any high-rise buildings, another item on her hit list. The McClatchy company eventually sold the land back to the Redevelopment Agency for the same 49 cents a foot that was paid for it. In the planning days for the new building, another major structure was on the drawing board – one envisioned for employee functions – personnel, public relations, a cafeteria, all in one building. Also included would be an editorial library, or morgue, for the combined use of the newspaper, plus the radio and TV stations. The building would have cost an estimated $2.5 million. But the money was deemed needed elsewhere for "more important things," and employee perks such as showers and locker rooms were eliminated.

20

A New Era

Throughout the many years – from the day paperboys tossed the first copies of The Fresno Bee onto the porches of their customers – the newspaper has gone through many changes, each intended to improve the product. In most cases, these changes have been highly successful. Three of them you might label outstanding.

First would be the switch from "hot type" to "cold type." Hot type was aptly named – the metal would be used, remelted and used over and over again. Forms of lead called "pigs" were suspended over, then into, melting pots on linecasting machines. These machines would spit molten lead onto lines of type, The lead would harden, forming slugs of lead type, which could then be locked into place in page forms by printers. A printer could set seven lines of print in a minute (I still remember the Brockton Enterpriser printer who set my name in type. I carried that piece of lead for years).

That change, with photo-based "cold type" replacing lead, came about in 1974. It marked the end for the printers because much of the work they had been doing was now done by machines. The Bee had some 150 printers under contract, and many of them accepted buyouts and were not replaced. Others worked until their contracts expired, and also were not replaced.

Another big change has been the status of women in the editorial department. Where there were none, now there are many. One early result of this "women's movement" came in 1977, when the city editor ordered a hot-weather picture. The photographer went to Lake Millerton and snapped a bathing beauty in a bikini, a picture which ran in the paper the next day. And on that day, a female reporter approached the city desk and demanded the same kind of a photo be run of a man. Rebuffed by the city desk, the reporter complained to the managing editor, who ordered, "Run the photo." So a picture of a man wearing mountains for muscles appeared in the next day's Bee. The women's movement hasn't slowed since.

The third major change was viewed by many as the one most wanted by most employees -- local autonomy. This came about in 2001 when C. Ray Steele Jr., a true Valley newsman, was named publisher and president of The Fresno Bee.

Steele was a local product, raised in nearby Fowler. He was hired by The Bee in 1967 as a reporter, following his graduation from Fresno State University with a degree in journalism. He rose to assistant city editor and metro editor.

Fresno Bee Executive Editor George Gruner recommended to C.K . McClatchy that Steele be taught the business side of newspapers, and Steele moved to Sacramento, starting his climb up the McClatchy corporate ladder. He returned to Fresno in 1986 as business manager of The Fresno Bee,

Appendix A

CARLOS K. McCLATCHY
March 2, 1892 – January 17, 1933

(From The Fresno Bee January 17, 1933)

Carlos Kelly McClatchy, vice president and general manager of the McClatchy Newspapers organization and editor of The Fresno Bee and Republican and son of Carlos K. and Ella K. McClatchy of Sacramento and husband of Phebe McClatchy of Fresno, died today [January 17, 1933] of double influenza pneumonia at the home of friends in San Mateo.

Death came shortly before 10:30 o'clock A.M. while physicians worked vainly to save his life by means of oxygen which kept him alive for several hours. He passed away peacefully shortly after his father and his wife had arrived at his bedside.

The influenza pneumonia that proved fatal had a rapid outset, being of the epidemic form that is prevalent in California. Either it is of the mild form and clears up quickly or is of rapid development with no hope, as attending physicians explained.

Dr. Philip King Brown, chief of the medical staff of the Southern Pacific Hospital, with a corps of physicians, was in attendance.

McClatchy's fever was mild at first but developed rapidly. He had been ill only a few days. Funeral arrangements have not been made.

In the passing of Carlos McClatchy, the West loses one of the most brilliant, progressive and dynamic of its newspaper personalities. Coming from a family of eminent California journalists – his grandfather, James McClatchy, founder of the Sacramento Bee, being a pioneer in the newspaper field – young McClatchy, for he was only in his forty-first year, had a remarkable career.

Born in Sacramento

Carlos Kelly McClatchy was born in Sacramento, March 2nd, 1891, the son of Charles K. McClatchy, owner of the McClatchy newspapers, and Ella K. McClatchy, both of pioneer California stock. He was the brother of Miss Eleanor McClatchy of Sacramento and Mrs. Charlotte Maloney of Seattle.

He attended the public schools of Sacramento and entered Santa Clara University, from which he transferred to Columbia University where he was a member of the Sigma Alpha Epsilon Fraternity. He received a degree of bachelor of science from Columbia in 1911.

Returning to Sacramento, McClatchy began his newspaper career as a reporter on The Sacramento Bee. His rise was rapid and he soon became the capital correspondent for The Bee, playing a prominent role in the progressive movement launched by United States Senator Hiram Johnson and his followers.

Later he became The Bee's Washington correspondent, obtaining a background in national affairs that proved invaluable to him in the editorial work, which was to follow.

When the world war threatened to involve the United States in 1916, McClatchy prepared for service by entering a citizens' military training camp in California, so when war was actually declared he was one of the first Sacramentans to volunteer.

His first assignment was to an officers' training camp at the Presidio, San Francisco, where he enrolled in May, 1917. He was commissioned first lieutenant three months later, and was assigned to Headquarters Company, 362nd Infantry, 91st Division, at Camp Lewis, Washington.

Fought At St. Mihiel

McClatchy's regiment left for France in June, 1918. With two and a half months' training behind the lines he got his baptism of fire in reserve at St. Mihiel in September, 1918.

From this his division was rushed into the Meuse-Argonne offensive, where he went over the top in one of the greatest battles of the war. During the eighteen days of fighting in the Argonne Forest, he distinguished himself not only for personal bravery but as a fearless and efficient officer.

Promoted For Bravery

His service in this engagement won him promotion on the field of battle to the rank of captain at the age of 27. The order from General John J. Pershing bestowing upon him the rank of captain read:

"The commander-in-chief takes pleasure in promoting first Lieutenant Carlos K. McClatchy a captain in the United States Army, in recognition of his gallantry during the attack of Genes."

Genes was one of the most strongly-held German defenses of the Argonne.

The promotion of McClatchy came through the recommendation from the colonel of the 362nd Infantry and the brigadier general of the 181st Brigade who stated that he had shown great bravery and skill at handling troops under terrific shell fire which resulted in saving the lives of hundreds of soldiers.

During this battle McClatchy served as operations officer of the regiment, in charge of the movement of troops, a grave responsibility for a young officer.

Distinguished Record

He continued to serve in this capacity when his regiment was sent to Belgium following the Argonne battle. In Belgium he fought with his regiment in the Lys-Scheldt and Ypres-Lys offensives. Here he again distinguished himself.

Upon his return to Sacramento after the world war McClatchy resumed his newspaper work. He also became active in the organization of Sacramento Post No. 61, American Legion, and was chosen unanimously its first commander.

Due to his initiative in connection with legion activities the veterans' organization acquired the old city library building on I Street between Seventh and Eighth, which is now its headquarters.

While he was at Camp Lewis, prior to entraining for France, McClatchy married Miss Phebe Briggs, daughter of the late Dr. William Ellery Briggs and Mrs. Briggs of Sacramento, January 17th, 1918.

Three children were born of this union, James Briggs, William Ellery and Charles Kenny McClatchy.

Establishes Fresno Bee

McClatchy became associate editor of The Sacramento Bee upon the resumption of his newspaper work following the armistice. Largely on his initiative The Fresno Bee was established in 1922 and he was appointed editor of that paper.

When in 1923 McClatchy assumed the duties of general manager of the McClatchy Newspapers his never-failing enterprise led the way to the purchase by The Fresno Bee of the Fresno Herald, which was merged with the Fresno paper.

Demonstrating his capabilities in the business as well as the editorial end of the newspaper organization, McClatchy was instrumental with his father, Charles K. McClatchy, in promoting the purchase of the Sacramento Star by The Sacramento Bee, into which it was merged.

Under McClatchy's editorship The Fresno Bee grew rapidly until in a comparatively few years its circulation passed that of The Fresno Morning Republican, founded in 1876 by Dr. Chester Rowell.

Acquires Republican

The strenuous battle of a decade between The Fresno Bee, with McCatchy as its directing head, and The Fresno Morning Republican came to an end in March, 1932, when The Republican was sold to The Bee and merged with it.

Robert P. Molander

Anticipating the remarkable development of the radio, McClatchy several years ago recommended to his father the purchase of Station KMJ, Fresno, owned by the San Joaquin Light and Power Corporation.

The station served as the nucleus of the McClatchy radio system that once included, in addition to the Fresno station, stations KFBK, in Sacramento; KWG, Stockton, KOH, Reno, and KERN in Bakersfield.

The Bakersfield station was established through the purchase of station KSMR in Santa Maria.

Due to McClatchy's planning and executive ability in connection with the development of the McClatchy radio system, arrangements were made with the Don Lee and Columbia broadcasting chain to serve all the McClatchy stations.

Appendix B

ELEANOR McCLATCHY
September 27, 1895 – October 17, 1980

Eleanor McClatchy was born to the purple -- a strong woman of a strong family, a bright rising star who dedicated her young adult period to the arts, a choice she intended to fulfill throughout her years. But fate born of necessity changed all that, and in the forthcoming years she was transformed into the editor and chief executive officer of a burgeoning newspaper chain, McClatchy Newspapers -- at the time publisher of The Sacramento Bee, The Fresno Bee and The Modesto Bee.

The change in lifestyle, which came when she was just 32, was unexpected, but swift. Her older brother, Carlos McClatchy, founding publisher and editor of The Fresno Bee, stood in line to succeed their father, C.K. McClatchy, as the chain's chief executive. But Carlos McClatchy died suddenly in 1933 while still in harness in Fresno. C.K. McClatchy soon after made the decision that called for his daughter to take over the chain's operation, to rule from the Sacramento base. Six months before his death in 1936, C.K. wrote her, informing her of that decision. She was to say she knew practically nothing about publishing a newspaper, but "I do know my father's ideals and principles. I will see that these are continued."

Eleanor MClatchy had been happy in New York City, struggling to fulfill her dream of becoming a playwright. Not in the sense of struggling to make a living while also attempting to write or direct plays, because there was always plenty of cash available from a benevolent father, one who ran a taut ship where the newspapers were concerned, but also a man who willingly opened his purse wide to fulfill his daughter's wishes. She was never to wonder where her next meal was coming from. Following a period at Bennett College in Millbrook, N.Y., she had entered Columbia University. There she was laying the groundwork for a career in the legitimate theater. The year was 1936, and life was good -- the Great Depression not withstanding -- for this fascinating woman who was to become, as Time magazine wrote in 1952, "one of the richest and most powerful newspaperwomen in the U.S."

Miss McClatchy, as all employees referred to her (she was granted an annulment after a short-lived marriage), was personally unknown to most, refusing to have her picture taken on most occasions, and refusing to allow her newspapers to acknowledge stories of her considerable largess. About herself, she once said, "I am content to have people think I live in a cave and wear horns."

Regarding news in general, the policy was strict -- few Fresnans, for example, were aware of her support of music, drama and art programs, along with presentations by actors and actresses in familiar stage roles, nearly all to benefit local cultural organizations. She also was a proven supporter of the Fresno area, to the extent that she ordered the second Fresno Bee plant be constructed on the city's poverty-stricken west side in the center of an urban-renewal site. At the time, she was acclaimed for "putting her money where her mouth is."

A telling example of this lack-of-chest-beating policy came in the 1990s, well after her death in 1980. The Valley Children's Hospital was holding a major fund drive, and The Bee donated $250,000. This was announced in a small story on Page 2 of the local-news section. And even that story wasn't instituted by The Bee -- it came in the form of an announcement by the hospital.

Robert P. Molander

About The Author

Robert Molander was born and raised in Brockton, Mass. He graduated from Brockton High School in 1941 and in December of that year joined the Navy following the Japanese attack on Pearl Harbor. He served four years in the Navy. His first ship was the battleship Wyoming, followed by transfer to the Naval Armed Guard, attaining the rank of Signalman Second Class.

The Armed Guard consisted of Navy personnel – gunners, radio operators, signalmen and medics – serving alongside Merchant seamen on Merchant Marine ships. During World War II, 710 of these ships were sunk, and 1,810 Armed Guard sailors were killed in action.

Following his honorable discharge from the Navy, Molander took advantage of the GI Bill and was graduated from Fresno State College with a degree in journalism. He was hired as a reporter on The Fresno Bee staff, and later served as executive sports editor and city editor and ended his career on The Bee as senior editor.

He and his wife, Peggy, have two sons, five grandchildren, and dog named Sing Sing.

www.ingramcontent.com/pod-product-compliance
Lightning Source LLC
Chambersburg PA
CBHW030521100426

42813CB00001B/112